Idolatry

Stephen E. Fowl

BAYLOR UNIVERSITY PRESS

Cover Design by Savanah N. Landerholm
Book Design by Savanah N. Landerholm

The Library of Congress has cataloged this book under ISBN
978-1-4813-1084-0.

Printed in the United States of America on acid-free paper with a minimum of
thirty percent recycled content.

CONTENTS

ACKNOWLEDGMENTS

This volume has had an abnormally long gestation period. I have been thinking about the issues covered in it for a long time. Prior writing obligations as well as some heavy administrative responsibilities kept me from starting any serious writing on this project. A sabbatical at Seattle Pacific University during the 2014–2015 academic year provided me with much-needed space to write a significant part of the book. If I tried to name all of the people at SPU who aided me in this project, I would inevitably leave someone out. Suffice it to say that I am very grateful to Doug Strong, dean of the School of Theology, as well as to the faculty, staff, and students of the School of Theology, for their warm welcome and stimulating conversations. Their invitation to give the Palmer Lecture that year allowed me to present an early version of chapter 2. I was also able to work through the entire argument of this book with a summer class at SPU in 2016.

For thirty years I have been blessed by warm friendships and rigorous discussions with my colleagues in the Theology Department at Loyola. Even when I became dean they continued to welcome me to the lunch table, which is the center of departmental life. I only wish I could get there more often. Jim Buckley and Rebekah Eklund have each read and commented upon several of the chapters of this volume. Their input has improved the book enormously. In addition to their help, one of our graduate students, Lauren Thorp, helped compile the bibliography for this volume.

For the past two years I have been dean of our college of arts and sciences. This was an unexpected interruption in my writing. Nevertheless, the fact that this volume is now completed is in some significant measure due to my associate deans, Cindy Moore, Peggy O'Neil, Jeff Barnett, and Barham Roughani, as well as the support of my provost and long-time friend Amanda Thomas.

My wife, Melinda, has been a companion through many writing projects. At the end of this one, I recognize how much my writing and thinking have been shaped by years of attention from her sharp editorial eye and ear. Thanks. Liam and Brendan, our sons, and Maddie, our daughter-in-law, continue to bring moments of delight into our lives.

Without that sabbatical in Seattle I would not now be completing this book. I want to dedicate it to the faculty, staff, and students of the School of Theology at Seattle Pacific University.

ADVENT, 2018

INTRODUCTION

Although it might not be immediately evident, this book continues work I have been doing for some time. That is, it will seek to engage in theology and theological reflection primarily using scriptural texts. It is neither a theological commentary nor a work of biblical theology. It is not commentary because it does not aim to interpret theologically a specific biblical book from beginning to end. Instead, it ranges widely over a variety of texts that are relevant to the theological tasks and questions I aim to explore.

Using biblical texts to explore theological questions may not be the very antithesis of biblical theology, but it certainly is very different from the aims of standard biblical theologies. At the risk of offering overly broad brushstrokes, biblical theologies typically interpret biblical texts using the standard practices of historical criticism. Such works typically organize, or catalogue, or synthesize biblical material so that one learns what Scripture "says" about a topic. Only after accomplishing this exegetical work might one then venture some theological judgments. As a result, such works of biblical theology tend not to provide a great deal of theological insight. Instead, they often get bogged down in arguments about the unity and diversity of the scriptural material, how it should be organized, and whether one should prioritize one set of themes or ideas or texts above all others. I have made these points before,[1] but it was satisfying to see them reiterated recently in Dale Martin's *Biblical Truths*.[2] After surveying the practice of biblical theology from Gabler down to the recent past, Martin claims, "As long as Christian scholars insist that they are simply 'describing' the theology that is really 'in' the text itself, and then arrive at their conclusions using historical criticism, as long as the 'meaning' they claim to 'find' in the text is supposed to be also what the ancient author 'intended' or the ancient audience would have understood, they cannot produce robust, sufficient, orthodox Christian theology."[3]

Having made this point, I should also add that I will make use of both standard works of historical criticism and several biblical theologies in my discussions of idolatry. These works often contain sharp and perceptive textual and historical observations that can and should be employed in making theological arguments. Most biblical theologies that deal with idolatry in ancient Israel devote a great deal of space to accounting for the rise of monotheism and determining whether or not there is a coherent biblical view about whether there are actually other gods or not; they address the worship practices of ancient peoples; they attempt to organize biblical texts that ostensibly address the topic of idolatry.[4] When and as necessary I will engage and sometimes rely upon insights from these works. Nevertheless, unlike biblical theology's interest in keeping theological considerations at arm's length from the tasks of historical exposition, I seek to have the exposition and the theology mutually inform each other to such a degree that it may be hard to disentangle them. Hence, although I have not addressed a topic quite like this one before, I hope readers will find that the approach here is recognizably continuous with what I have practiced in other works. I do not plan to offer any further argumentation for the validity of this type of theologically interested reading. I believe the case for its legitimacy as one among many forms of scholarly work with the Bible is now well established.

On the one hand, then, this volume continues a type of scriptural interpretation that I have advocated and practiced for many years. On the other hand, idolatry is a new academic topic for me. It has led me to engage texts in which I do not have a great deal of scholarly expertise. This new venture and my interest in it do require some further explanation and introduction.

Many of the more technical examinations of idolatry in the OT treat the subject in the light of the rise of Israelite monotheism. It is only in the light of the rise and development of Israelite convictions about the singularity of God that strictures against the fabrication of images and the worship of other gods make sense.[5]

These are, for the most part, technical works of scholarship that require far more expertise in the history of the ancient Near East than I possess. They also require one to take stands on specific sides of the debates about the history of Israelite religion that I do not wish to take. I have learned from these various studies and I admire their erudition, even though I will not enter directly into the scholarly discussions and debates that animate them. This project has much more pedestrian origins. These lie in the collective puzzlement of several years' worth of students in Introduction to Theology, a class all students at Loyola must take. About 65 to 70 percent of our students identify themselves as Roman Catholic. They manifest various degrees of devotion. As a group, they have very little direct exposure to the Bible. As a result, when they begin to work their way through some of the Pentateuch, they tend to read the stories without many critical filters. They tend to take the Pentateuchal narratives at something close to face value. This attitude disappears when they begin to read the prophets. They do not adopt the righteous anger or penitential self-recognition that one might expect when reading the prophets. Instead, they are angry because they were convinced the prophets were mistaken in their indictments of Israel's idolatry. Sometimes they simply assert that things could not have happened the way the prophets described it. In their eyes, God had performed so many mighty acts for the people of Israel, it was inconceivable to them that the Israelites would turn to idols.

At first this took me by surprise, but it also got me thinking about how and why the people of God become idolaters. Finally, I began to ask them a series of questions that opened up this project to me. First, I would ask how many of them had attended Catholic schools. About 60 percent of them had, for at least some part of their schooling. Then I asked them, "How many of you said the 'Pledge of Allegiance' every day in school?" They all raised their hands. The next question was, "Based on your reading of the OT so far, what does God call it when the people of God pledge their allegiance to something that isn't God?" After some initial squirming and clear discomfort someone would say, "idolatry."

I continued by suggesting that we leave aside for a moment the provocative question of whether saying the "Pledge" is an idolatrous act for Christians. Instead, I asked them, "For how many of you is this the first time in your life that you thought saying the 'Pledge' *might* be idolatrous?" They all raised their hands. I went on to explain that this is how idolatry always happens. No believer in ancient Israel, the early church, or today ever woke up saying, "Today I will worship a false God!" Although idolatry has and continues to occur among the people of God, I am convinced that it is never any believer's immediate intention to engage in idolatry. Rather, idolatry is the result of a number of small incremental moves: a set of seemingly benign or even prudent decisions; a set of habits and dispositions—often acquired through subtle participation in a wider culture; a set of influential friendships. All of these work in complex combinations gradually to direct our attention slowly and almost imperceptibly away from the one true God towards that which is not God.

Further, detecting such deviations is difficult because such turning away from God is rarely total. It appears much more common that our turning away from God still allows us to keep God in view, in our peripheral vision. This is not, however, the straight-on, single-minded love and attention that God seeks from us. For believers, idolatry is much more like divided attention than a sharp change from attention directed solely at God to full-scale devotion to that which is not God.

The bulk of the prophetic writings identify and call the people of Israel away from their idolatrous ways. It must be said, however, that the prophets do not have a great record of success in turning people away from idolatry. Indeed, one thing you can be pretty sure of is that when a prophet comes on the scene to denounce idolatry, things are already in a pretty bad way. Unless we contemporary believers are radically different from our forebears in the faith, when a prophet denounces our idolatrous ways, we are not likely to recognize the charges laid against us; we will be stubbornly unwilling to change our ways, and we will be deaf and blind to the voices and signs God sends our way. In this light, it would seem that rather than have a prophet calling you to repent from things you can barely recognize in yourself, it is much better to locate, identify, unlearn, and repent of the habits and dispositions that lead to idolatry before they do so. It was with that interest in mind that I wrote this book.

The chapters that follow discuss some of the ways in which believers become more likely to move toward idolatry and ways in which they can move in a different, more faithful direction. I would never claim to specify all of the ways in which these movements might occur. Instead, I will examine here a series of dispositions, habits, and practices that, if left unchecked, will tend to lead believers into idolatry. In addition, I will propose alternative dispositions, habits, and practices that, if cultivated within Christian communities, will lead believers away from idolatry. Each chapter is driven by reflection on scriptural texts, though not always the texts that one might expect. Again, I am sure there are other ways of making the case offered here apart from examining Scripture. I have often argued, however, that at its best, Christian theology is a form of scriptural interpretation. This book is one way of trying to show that.

1

THINKING ABOUT IDOLATRY

Why and how do the people of God become idolaters, and what might be done about this?[1] In general terms, these are the questions that animate this book. To advance these questions I want to engage in three distinct tasks in this chapter. First I want to distinguish the idolatry of unbelievers from the idolatry of the people of God. Before going further I should perhaps parse some of the terms that will appear in this book. Throughout this book I will reflect on the idolatry of "believers" or the idolatry of the "people of God" from a Christian perspective. I will engage the relevant texts of both testaments from a Christian perspective. This is so even when many of these texts speak about the Israelites and their life with God and each other. I will thus adopt Paul's view that these texts "were written for our instruction" (1 Cor 10:11). I do not thereby imply any sort of judgment about Jewish claims to belief in the one true God or their claims to be the people of God. Indeed, I suspect that some of these issues may be relevant to my Jewish brothers and sisters, but that is not for me to decide. Rather, I want to be clear that this is a work of Christian theology and not a history of Israelite beliefs and practices.

In that light, I will not be overly concerned with the idolatry of unbelievers. Even so, it will be important at the outset of this volume to draw this distinction clearly. Making this distinction will help explain why certain passages that might seem crucial to a study of idolatry more generally will not receive much attention in this volume. The second task here is to explain why the prophetic writings play less of a role in this study than one might expect. Finally, it would be convenient if there were a single clear account of idolatry

5

recognized by all people at all times. I could then discuss this quickly and move on to the body of the volume. Unfortunately, this is not the case. Yes, for the most part, Scripture thinks of idolatry as the worship of other gods by means of images. While a useful account for conversational purposes, this is not rich enough for the purposes of this volume. Hence, I will conclude this chapter with a denser account of idolatry.

WORSHIPING THE CREATURE RATHER THAN THE CREATOR

Although idolatry should always be avoided, from the perspective of this volume it is worth distinguishing between the idolatry of believers and that of unbelievers. Here at the outset, it may also be useful to clarify some terms. I will speak of believers and the people of God as well as Christians throughout this book. Both OT and NT consistently present unbelievers as idolaters. Whatever else one might say about unbelievers, they fail to worship the one true God. In most, if not all, ancient contexts this was accompanied by the worship of other gods, usually by means of fabricated images. Scripture always condemns the idolatry of unbelievers. I want to argue, however, that the idolatry of unbelievers is a different sort of problem from the movement of believers from faith in the one true God into idolatry.

The bulk of this book will be devoted to this latter phenomenon. First, however, it may be worth reflecting on the idolatry of the nations. There are several reasons for this. First, it will allow me to show that Scripture's general explanation for the idolatry of unbelievers is different from the explanations offered for the idolatry of believers. Distinguishing this will also help me to indicate why certain texts that clearly discuss idolatry do not receive much attention in the rest of this book. They simply are talking about different phenomena. This is true even in cases common to the NT in which idolatrous unbelievers become followers of Christ. As followers of Christ they face a different set of issues and concerns as they confront an idol-soaked world from the perspective of being in Christ.

When it comes to discussing the type of idolatry characteristic of unbelievers and its cause, a key text is Wisdom 12–15. The discussion of pagan idolatry in these chapters seems to be mirrored in Paul's discussion in Romans 1.[2] Wisdom 12 begins by noting that God's spirit is in all things. Through the promptings of that spirit God seeks to move people from error into truth, from unbelief to belief. As yet, idolatry is not the focus of the text. Instead, the focus is on God's mercy. Although God could have justly brought destruction on those like the Canaanites whose sins were great, God sought to call them to repentance (12:10, 18). God's treatment of the Canaanites is illustrative for the Israelites. Moreover, the relatively limited mercy God shows the Canaanites is overshadowed by even greater mercy toward the people of Israel (12:22).

Wisdom 13 builds on the opening assertion of Wisdom 12 that God's spirit is in all things. Chapter 13 begins by establishing that all humans have a basis for belief in God through "the good things that are seen." Ideally, they should have extended their imaginations to probe behind these things to find their creator and Lord (13:1-5). They did not. Too often people treated the beauty and delights of creation as ends, worshiping them as gods.

Wisdom 13:6 initially proposes that at least some of these people are not all that blameworthy. They are searching for God, but they cannot extend their search beyond the very real, but not ultimate, beauty of the world. In fairly short order, however, it becomes clear that such people are, nevertheless, responsible for the failure of their search because the true goal of their search was not that hard to find (13:8-9). Instead, they turned to idols.

By 13:10 the tone shifts much closer to that of Isaiah 44, where idolatry is portrayed as a form of folly. The rest of chapter 13 excoriates the foolishness of worshiping pieces of wood that one might just as well burn to cook one's food; of worshiping and caring for images that clearly cannot take care of themselves; of praying for life to something manifestly lifeless. This continues into chapter 14. Here the author castigates those about to take a sea voyage who trust in an idol more fragile than the ship they are sailing in. In the end, whatever safety they enjoy is due to God's providential care (14:1-5).

The second half of Wisdom 14 seems to indicate that idolatry is not some sort of original failure. That is, idolatry is not directly connected to the first sin narrated in Genesis 1–3. Rather, it arises over time in the course of repeated human error (14:13-14). Moreover, idol worship generates its own corrupting behaviors. By the end of chapter 14, idolatry has accounted for almost all of the vices that Jews traditionally ascribed to pagans. Wisdom 14:27 summarizes this part of the chapter by claiming, "For the worship of idols not to be named is the beginning and cause and end of every evil."[3]

Finally, after a few brief verses on the benefits of worshiping the one true God, Wisdom 15 concludes with a series of condemnations against those who actually fashion idols. Ultimately, the indictment against them is that they too failed to know the one that formed them. That failure led them to form images for others to worship.

In many respects Romans 1:18-32 offers a condensed version of Wisdom's much longer discussion. The rhetorical aim of these early chapters in Romans is to note that God's wrath has justly fallen upon all. The first group in view in this part of Romans 1 is gentiles. They rightly merit God's judgment because of their idolatry. Paul's account of the rise and effects of idolatry follows that of Wisdom 12–15.[4] The created order reveals a sufficient level of God's power and nature that humans should have turned to God and worshiped. Their failure in this regard renders them blameworthy; frustrates their subsequent reasoning about God; manifests itself in idolatry; and results in corrupt behavior. In a manner similar to Wisdom 13, Paul summarizes pagan idolatry and all its attendant evils as worship of the creature rather than the creator (Rom 1:25).

As clear and trenchant as these two accounts are, they are not especially useful for my particular project. First, they address the idolatry characteristic of unbelievers. One can explain such idolatry in fairly straightforward ways. It arises from a failure to move from observation of signs embedded in the beauties of creation that point to God to recognition and worship of the one true God. This initial failure leads humans to misplace their attention and devotion onto the beauties of the created world rather than God. They mistake the sign for the reality. As a result of this failure, pagan life becomes characterized by all types of corruption, crimes, and misdeeds, all of which situate pagans under God's just wrath.

Paul moves from this to note that like pagans, Jews, too, find themselves under God's judgment, but for different reasons. Thus, by the end of Romans 3 all of humanity finds itself in the same place—under God's judgment, but for different reasons. As Romans 5 indicates, this situation is one result of Sin's dominion over God's creation. Idolatry would then be both a sign of Sin's dominion and one of Sin's tools of domination.

Since pagan idolatry is the result of mistaking the sign for the reality and thus worshiping the creature rather than the creator, Paul argues that the only way out of this situation is the radical reorientation to God that comes from being in Christ. In Romans 6 Paul will note that being baptized into Christ transfers believers' citizenship and allegiance from the realm of Sin into the commonwealth of Christ. Indeed, the entire point of the argument in 6:1-14 is that believers have left the realm of Sin behind. Although they may and will transgress from time to time, they and their situation cannot be characterized in the same way Paul characterizes the pagan world in chapter 1. Although it is the case that believers might supplant worship of the creator for worship of the creature, the reasons for this would have to be different from those that characterize pagans outside of Christ. Rather than a failure to know God at all, the idolatry of believers reflects a failure of attention and a failure to embody those things entailed in belief in the God of Jesus Christ.

Thus, mistaking creature for creator, the idolatry of believers reflects their inability to understand properly and to live out the reality of their baptism. Further, in Romans 1 pagan refusal to worship the one true God frustrates their subsequent reasoning about God, leading to further blindness and deeper idolatry and corruption. As Romans moves through its argument, Paul notes that as believers are reoriented toward God their minds are renewed by the Spirit of God so that they are able to "discern what is the will of God—what is good acceptable and perfect" (Rom 12:2). Believers' failures in this regard would again be different from those of unbelievers.

The idolatry of unbelievers should be a cause of concern and compassion for Christians. I am, however, much more interested in the ways and means by which believers, with minds and hearts already under renovation, lapse into idolatry. Such lapses are never to be encouraged, but, likewise, one cannot account for this by referring to the causes and patterns of pagan unbelief. Although one may claim that as they move towards idolatry believers ultimately mistake worship of the creature for worship of the creator, the cause of such a lapse would be different from those that Paul discusses in Romans 1.

We do not, unfortunately, lack for scriptural accounts that narrate, describe, and condemn the idolatry of the people of God. My claim is that these accounts, rather than Wisdom 12–15 or Romans 1, will provide more useful accounts of idolatry for my purposes.

WHERE ARE THE PROPHETS?

The prior paragraphs explain why this volume will not focus on passages that primarily address the idolatry of unbelievers. In this volume I am primarily concerned with the idolatry of believers. In this respect a reader might well expect a focus on the prophets and their writings. After all, the idolatry of the people of God is one of the primary preoccupations of the prophets. Thus, it may seem surprising that I will not make much reference to the prophets in the following scripturally dense, theological account of idolatry. Moreover, the prophetic writings will not play a major role in subsequent chapters either. Given that many discussions of idolatry are primarily devoted to prophetic texts, it may be worthwhile to say a few words about this difference.

First, despite the rich and diverse imagery the prophets use to describe Israel's idolatry, they tend to treat idolatry according to two basic themes. Israel's idolatry is either a form of betrayal akin to adultery or a form of folly. Hence, although the prophets speak repeatedly and at length about Israel's idolatry, they tend to speak of it in the same ways time and time again.

Idolatry as Betrayal

For example, let us look at the beginning chapters of Jeremiah. For long passages in Jeremiah 2 and 3, the LORD relies on images of marital betrayal to describe Judah's idolatry. Judah is persistently portrayed as a wanton woman, eagerly seeking lovers wherever she might find them. In the light of this way of portraying Judah's life with God, several themes emerge. First, Judah does not appear to recognize her behavior in terms of betrayal in the way the LORD does (Jer 2:23). Judah fundamentally misperceives her own behavior. This may strike modern ears as willful self-delusion.[5] It is what lies beneath the student reactions I spoke about in the introduction to this volume. When one recognizes, however, how many aspects of life in this ancient world were tied up with the worship of gods, Judah's disposition may be easier to understand, if not to excuse.

In regard to the prohibition of images of the LORD, M. Daniel Carroll R. writes, "Allegiance to Yahweh was to be fundamental to and inseparable from the web of social, economic, political, and familial relationships, structures, and activities that would be established in the land."[6] This account reflects the fact that all aspects of social life in this time were tied up with what we today would call religion. Think of the world of commerce: significant transactions and contracts at this time required sacrifices. Abandoning these sacrifices would have put the commercial interests of the rich in jeopardy. Think of politics: Judah faced a significant military threat in Babylon to the north. It made political sense to form alliances with Egypt to the south in order to secure Judah's borders (Jer 2:36). These treaties would also have required sacrifices. The alternative seems to have been to leave Judah's political fortunes in the hands of the LORD. Commerce and politics comprise large elements of the life of most elite groups in a population. If the path to success in these areas required some minor sacrifices to other gods, it may have seemed a small price to pay for growth and security. Attitudes such as these lie behind Judah's claim of innocence in the face of the LORD's accusations. The people of Judah did not set out to betray their commitments to the LORD. They were, as they saw it, simply getting by as best they could. This situation is made even worse by the ascendance of officials, priests, and prophets who all proclaim a message of peace. These leaders who should have most clearly seen and perceived Israel's true state before God have misled the people, arguing that God would never let the Temple be destroyed, that at the end of the day it did not serve God's own interests to judge Israel (Jer 4:9-10; 5:12-13).

Idolatry as Folly

The second image for portraying the idolatry of the people of God is to treat it as a form of folly. Here are some examples of this: In Jeremiah 2:26-28, the LORD castigates Judah for calling a piece of wood "my father" and saying to a chunk of stone, "You gave birth to me." These are examples of the foolishness of treating inanimate objects as if they were God, as if they had saving power. The Judeans themselves seem to recognize this. As soon as they are in real trouble and need actual deliverance, they cry out to the LORD, "Save us!" (Jer 2:27). Further, in the first part of Jeremiah 10 one finds one of the great satires of idol worship in the OT. The folly of idol worship is displayed by breaking down the steps involved in producing and worshiping idols. First, an idol begins as something living—a tree cut down, worked by an artisan, covered with silver or gold, and fastened in place. It is now thoroughly dead. It cannot move on its own; it has no living voice; it lacks power to do either good or ill (Jer 10:3-5). In these respects, idols are purely the work of human hands. In contrast, the LORD is the living and true God. Rather than being made, this is the God who makes all things. This God has a voice that causes the earth to tremble. Ultimately, this God will bring judgment on all those who make idols and all those who worship them.

A second aspect of the folly of idolatry appears in Jeremiah 3. Judah's behavior dismays the LORD. The LORD finds Judah's idolatry baffling and disappointing; they gained nothing they did not already have—and better—from the LORD. Instead, their alliances would prove worthless and provoke punishment from the LORD. Judah's idolatry did not simply reflect the folly of ascribing divine worth and capacities to mere human creations; it reflected the folly of abandoning their one true source of life and security, their one true love. Even after witnessing Israel's destruction for the same activities, Judah persists in her folly (Jer 3:6-11).

Most of the prophetic criticism of Israel's idolatry falls under one of these two themes.[7] Hence, extensive examination of the prophets will not yield as much insight for the issues that concern this volume as one might initially expect.

The Track Record of the Prophets

In addition, despite the power of their images and their promise of the LORD's impending judgment, one must admit that the prophets do not have a very good track record of turning the people of God away from their idolatry. There are several reasons for this.

First, prophets such as Jeremiah, Amos, Isaiah, and the rest are not the only ones on the scene claiming to speak words from the LORD. For example, in each of these prophetic books one finds encounters between these prophets and those who argue that God will not ultimately exercise judgment on the people of God. Jeremiah 28–29 and Amos 7–8 provide particular and concrete examples of the conflict between Jeremiah and Amos, on the one hand, and those such as Hananiah and Amaziah, on the other hand, who argue either that God will not send judgment or that it will be relatively short and painless.

This raises the immediate question of how one determines who is a true prophet and who is a false prophet. The OT as a whole has an interest in this general question of how to tell true from false prophecy. Deuteronomy offers the answer: The words of a true prophet come true; the words of a false prophet do not come true (Deut 18:21–22). Of course, this is correct, but it does not really help the people of God at the time they most need it. Waiting to see who turns out to be right is rarely an option.

It would seem that discerning the true prophet from the false prophet largely requires a people whose life with God is faithful, just, and true. This is precisely not the case with the people of God in the contexts in which the prophets speak. Moreover, the prophets are unanimous in noting that the people's idolatry renders them blind and deaf. They are blind to the ways their idolatry has distorted and damaged their relationship with God. They are thus unable to recognize themselves in the critiques of the prophets. Their deafness keeps them from discerning and rightly responding to the word of the LORD delivered by the prophets. Thus, when it is most crucial for the people of God to be able to discern the true prophet from the false prophet, the people's sin has disabled them for just this task. It is really much better never to need a prophet in the first place.

Second, by the time prophets are on the scene, Israel's idolatry has become deep seated. The prophets address a people for whom idolatry has become a habit. Slowly, incrementally, the worship of other gods has become something normal and natural for the people of God. They cannot imagine things otherwise. Habit shapes imagination; imagination focuses one's hearing and seeing. An imagination shaped by the habit of idolatry can no longer listen to or hear a prophetic call to repent.

For example, Jeremiah 17 begins with God's observation of the ways in which Judah's idolatry is deeply ingrained. It is inscribed on their hearts in the way words might be chiseled into stone. One of the key points here is that idolatry and righteousness do not just happen. They are the result of patterns of life, habits of thought, learned actions and responses. In short, believers are formed into both righteousness and idolatry. The fact that few, if any, Israelites ever sought to be formed into idolaters should remind us that some of the most long-lasting formation in our lives happens without us really recognizing it. The fact that one is not actively seeking to be formed in one way or another does not mean that formation is not occurring. Our desires, habits, and actions are always being formed and shaped. Moreover, as this passage notes, our formation has a direct impact on the formation of subsequent generations of believers. Attentive, watchful, prayerful reflection is a crucial practice to develop if one is to resist being formed toward idolatry and the punishment that follows in its wake.

The arguments of this volume are founded on just this observation from Jeremiah, and this is why the prophets do not play much of a role. The prophets recognize and point out idolatry once it has happened. Given that the prophets also make it painfully clear that it is very hard to recognize and repent of our idolatry, it is much better to avoid developing the habit of idolatry in the first place. This means that believers must attend to matters of formation, of the cultivation of habits and dispositions that will help them resist idolatry, and of recognizing which habits and dispositions will incline them toward idolatry.

THE IDOLATRY OF BELIEVERS

Since this volume will focus on believers and the ways in which they move into and away from idolatry, it will be important to try to provide some sort of account of idolatry. Even if one distinguishes the ways in which unbelievers and believers each become embroiled in idolatry, one still needs some account of what constitutes idol worship, especially for believers.

In Exodus 20 (and Deut 5) God introduces what we have come to know as the Ten Commandments by reminding Moses and Israel that "I am the LORD your God who brought you up out of the land of Egypt, out of the house of slavery" (20:2). This recapitulates the story of the previous nineteen chapters and establishes clearly the identity of the one who gives the commandments. This is the one who, against the odds, freed a band of slaves from what was at the time one of the most powerful empires on earth. Throughout those earlier chapters in Exodus we are told that events happen in the way they do, "so that you might know that I am the LORD" (e.g., Exod 6:7, 27; 7:5, 12, 17; 8:22, 64; 10:2; 14:4, 18). All of that is presumed in the introduction to the commandments in Exodus 20:2.[8]

The people of God are then told they shall not have any other gods before the LORD. As part of that commandment the Israelites are prohibited from making any image for the purpose of worshiping it—no idols (20:3-5).[9] The Reformed churches and the Orthodox churches treat the prohibition about having other gods before the LORD (20:3) as the first commandment and the prohibition on creating idols (20:4-5) as the second commandment. Roman Catholics and Lutherans take these verses together as one commandment. (They get to ten by splitting up coveting things and people.) I am not that interested in resolving the issue of how to number the commandments. Moreover, by the time we get to the latter portions of Isaiah it is clear that the folly of idol worship is used as a way of ridiculing the worship of other gods. That is, by that time in Israel's life, the idea of having other gods before the LORD is taken to be inextricably tied to worshiping idols.

It would be nice simply to say that idolatry is the worship of other gods, particularly by means of fabricated images of those gods. That definition would seem to cover the issues raised in Exodus 20:1-6 regardless of whether one takes these verses to present two separate commandments or one complex commandment. Although worshiping other gods by means of images certainly counts as idolatry, there are several reasons why it is not a rich enough account of idolatry. The following pages will offer ways of adding depth and richness to a notion of idolatry.

The Golden Calf

First, although worshiping other gods by means of images is idolatry, worshiping the one true God by means of images also can be idolatrous. The prototypical example of this is found in the episode of the golden calf in Exodus 32. This account is filled with narrative quirks and rough edges; it is complex in terms of its compositional history; there are numerous exegetical puzzles.[10] Despite these, the passage offers several relatively clear points about idolatry. First, there is no sense that the calf represents another god. It is meant to represent the LORD (32:4-6). That is, the Israelites' idolatry in this instance is not so much a turning away from the LORD as the fabrication of an illegitimate image of the LORD.[11] It will be important to my discussion, then, to attempt to figure out the nature of this illegitimacy.[12]

When we turn to the passage directly, it appears that two interrelated concerns impel the people and Aaron to conspire to make the calves. First, Moses, "the man who brought us up from the land of Egypt" (32:2), has been gone for an extended period of time. Moses has mediated the LORD's presence, will, and words to the Israelites from the beginning of their journey out of Egypt. Without Moses, it is unclear how the Israelites will engage and be engaged by the LORD. At the very least, the calf signifies a rejection of the pattern initiated by God through which the LORD interacts with the people. It is an attempt to supplant one way in which God's presence, will, and words are mediated to the people with another that is more clearly under human control.

A second and related point is that in the absence of Moses, it is unclear how the people will know that the LORD is still committed to being present among them. Indeed, in the aftermath of the making of the calf, in Exodus 33, the LORD was not willing to "go up among you." Instead, Moses met with the LORD in the "tent of meeting" outside the camp (33:7-11). As Nathan MacDonald notes, "Exodus 33 confirms what is implicit in Exodus 32 that the calf is an illegitimate attempt to make YHWH present, and even after its destruction the continued presence of YHWH with his people stands in jeopardy."[13] The completion of the tabernacle resolves this threat.

In addition, one cannot rule out the possibility that the production of the calf reflects the desire for a God who is much more open to manipulation, whose oracles and instructions will be under the control of priests. This is in sharp contrast to the LORD who promises to make Israel a great nation, to give them a prosperous land, and who will be God to them forever (Gen 17:7). These promises invite the Israelites to follow a God who acts in powerful, terrifying ways; whose actions cannot always be predicted and anticipated, whose timing does not always match up with the hopes of the people, yet whose love is always steadfast. The making of the calf is a way of domesticating a rather untamed LORD.

It is important to note, however, that the calf is not primarily a problem because it uses the material in relation to an immaterial God. Given that Exodus 35–40 offer a painstaking account of the building of the tabernacle and all that goes with it, it is clear that these material elements are suitable to provide a place for God's presence to dwell among the people. The tabernacle instructions reflect God's commitment to sanctify the material. If the calf represents the Israelites' attempt to ensure, define, and regulate God's presence among them, then the tabernacle represents God's commitment to abide with the Israelites on God's own terms. The calf as idol is not a turning away from the one true God to worship other gods; it is the people's illegitimate attempt to shape, control, and limit the one true God; to make, in effect, a new, more manageable and domesticated version of the LORD.[14]

THE BRONZE SERPENT

Indeed, this undomesticated LORD can even command something that comes very close to idolatry when the LORD commands Moses to fashion a fiery serpent of bronze in Numbers 21:4-9. Impatient with their long journey from Egypt to the promised land, the Israelites complain against the LORD and Moses. The complaints are familiar: there is not enough water; the food is terrible; we wish we had never left Egypt (21:5). Without any consultation between God and Moses, we read that God sends poisonous serpents into the Israelite camp. Many Israelites die. The people repent and ask Moses to pray to the LORD on their behalf. In response to Moses' prayer, the LORD instructs him to fashion an image of a "fiery" serpent and attach it to a pole. If those who are bitten by the serpents will look at the bronze serpent, they will be healed.

God would seem to be advocating actions that come very close to idolatry. Unlike the golden calf, this serpent is not directly identified as the LORD. Nevertheless, the creation of the serpent at God's command, and the healing or salvation that it brings, would seem to tie the image to the LORD, albeit less directly than the people tie the image of the calf to the LORD. Indeed, by the time Hezekiah attempts to purge Israel of her idolatries in 2 Kings 18:4, this serpent was functioning as an idol and he destroyed it.

It would appear that later interpreters also saw the implicit difficulties in this text and have tried to address them. Wisdom 16:5-7 retells the account in such a way as to stress that the suffering of the Israelites was quite limited and designed only to produce obedience to the commandments. Moreover, it was not the serpent who saved the people, but God. The creation of the image was simply a type of test. In Philo's account, the details of this incident are largely glossed. As a result, the story becomes a lesson for the virtuous on the importance of obedience and patient endurance.[15] Finally, in John's Gospel this story becomes an image through which Jesus will be able to bring salvation to the world (John 3:14; 8:28; 12:32-34; 19:37).[16]

Regardless of whether God's own commandment here leads Moses to produce an idol, it seems clear that long after the event the image became an idol and needed to be destroyed. The ways in which subsequent interpreters of this text such as Philo and the author of Wisdom approach the story further supports the view that this is a very ambiguous episode that seems to come close to idolatry.

INTENTIONS MATTER

The example of the bronze serpent notwithstanding, in light of the ways that Nehemiah 9:18-20, Psalm 106:19-23, and Acts 7:39-43 all speak of the Golden Calf incident, it is clear that making images of the one true god generally constitutes idolatry. I say "generally" because of such passages as Judges 17. There one learns about a man named Micah[17] who lives in the hill country of Ephraim at a time when "there was no king in Israel and people did what was right in their own eyes" (17:6). The first two verses of the chapter are obscure, but it appears that a sum of money was stolen from Micah's mother.[18] She cursed the money (perhaps also the person stealing it) in Micah's hearing. It is not clear how much time elapses, but we learn that Micah was the one who actually stole the money, and he returns it. The question hanging over the text at this point is whether the curse will come to pass. Given the earlier episode with Jephtha and his oath (12:29-40), one might readily expect this curse to fall on Micah.

Perhaps hoping to defuse this situation, Micah's mother says, "May my son be blessed by the LORD." She also consecrates the money to the LORD. As part of this act, Micah's mother took some of the money and had an image[19] made, which was placed in a shrine in Micah's house. In addition to this, Micah has an ephod and a teraphim made and makes one of his sons a priest. Every indication is that this is a shrine of the LORD and that Micah intends his son to be a priest of the LORD. Micah seems to be aware that this is a highly irregular situation. Hence, when he comes across a Levite from Bethlehem looking for a place to live, he promptly installs this person as his priest. Indeed, he sees the appearance of the Levite as a sign of the LORD's favor (17:12), thus defusing the possibility of his mother's curse falling on him. Nowhere in the text is Micah judged to be an idolater. Although we learn nothing directly of the motives of any of these characters, their actions all seem to indicate a desire to repent and to act justly before the LORD. It would seem that what we might infer about their good intentions in difficult times might change how one evaluates an action that one would, under different circumstances, condemn as idolatry.

I recognize that this text is difficult to interpret. There are alternative ways of reading it. I have certainly drawn inferences from rather limited textual evidence. Further, one could note that there are numerous episodes in Judges where we do not learn God's views, such as the death of Jephtha's daughter in 11:34-40. Hence, this incident with Micah is simply one of those episodes that recount the unraveling of Israelite society during this unsettled time, and we have no basis for thinking that God approves of Micah's actions.

In response, I would note the following: First, Jephtha's daughter is ritually mourned every year (11:40). The text leaves a reader in no doubt that this was an awful incident and should not be emulated. Second, and more importantly, in Judges 8 Gideon does something very similar to Micah. After defeating the Midianites, Gideon refuses the people's request to rule over them. Instead, he asks each of them to donate a gold earring that they had taken in despoiling the Midianites. Just like Micah, Gideon then casts that gold into an ephod and sets it up in his hometown. Although the text does not directly call this an act of idolatry, it comes pretty close in 8:27-28. Again, as with Jephtha's daughter, the text makes it clear that this was an unworthy act, not to be repeated.

If Judges 17 presents us with a situation in which the aims and intentions of the participants render an otherwise idolatrous act acceptable, Ezekiel 14 presents an episode in which the intentions of people's hearts, independent of any images they create, allow the prophet to reject their otherwise acceptable request. In Ezekiel 14, some elders from among the Israelites in exile come to Ezekiel. One must assume these elders want the prophet to bring some matter before the LORD. Before the elders can even utter a word, however, the LORD rejects them because they have "taken their idols into their hearts" (הֶעֱלוּ גִלּוּלֵיהֶם עַל־לִבָּם [see 14:3, 4, 7]).[20] In addition, in 14:5 we read that the LORD desires to grab hold of the hearts of those who are estranged from the LORD "through their idols." The LXX clearly seems to think that this represents an internal activity because throughout Ezekiel 14, when the Hebrew uses the term גִלּוּל to speak of idols that are taken into the heart, the Greek uses a set of nouns to speak of internal thoughts and dispositions (τὰ διανοήματα, τὰ ἐνθυμήματατῶν, ἐπιτηδευμάτων). In contrast to this, the LXX uses εἰδώλων in Ezekiel 6:13 to speak about idolatrous practice. All of this is to say that even in the OT, when the fabrication of idols was common, one could commit idolatry in the absence of such images.

My point in examining these two texts is not to relativize the LORD's views on the Israelites' fabrication of images, regardless of whether they are images of the LORD or of other gods. On the whole and for the most part, such acts constitute idolatry. Rather, my point is that these two examples indicate that the LORD does not account for the practices of the people of God apart from their intentions and the contexts in which they are living. This becomes important both when Israel is in exile and as the early Christian movement advances beyond the confines of Jerusalem into the cities of the Roman Empire. One way to see the role of such contexts relative to matters of idolatry is to look at space and who controls various spaces.

CONTROL OF SPACE

When the Israelites are in their own land and able to regulate their own spaces and practices, matters of idolatry become starker. The lines of responsibility and judgment are clearer. The necessary forms of repentance are more straightforward. In those cases when various kings allow the worship of idols to flourish, prophets denounce such practices with clarity and vigor. In such circumstances, it becomes much easier to account for idolatry as a form of betrayal or folly.

When they control spaces, the Israelites are called to purge their land from idols. This is a persistent message of the prophets. Alternatively, when the Israelites are in exile, or when the first Christians move into the Greco-Roman world, they do not regulate the spaces and there are few spaces that have not been touched by an idol in some way. These worlds are saturated with deities. Home, profession, city, empire, all of these aspects of life and others as well are connected in various ways to idols and deities. When they are not in control, believers are expected to negotiate their way through idol-soaked spaces without becoming stained by idolatry. Of course, what such negotiation means and requires is rarely clear and straightforward. On the one hand, when avoiding idolatry's stain seems impossible, then resistance is called for, as in the cases of Daniel or in 1 and 2 Maccabees or in the stories of early Christian martyrs. On the other hand, these are exceptional cases, not the norm. There were many other exiles in Babylon besides Daniel and his friends. Indeed, Jeremiah tells such exiles to build, plant, and marry. They are to seek the *shalom* of the city to which God has sent them. They are to pray for that city. Indeed, the LORD tells the exiles that "in its *shalom* you will find your *shalom*" (Jer 29:5-7).

Moving to the NT, one of the most fundamental ways it speaks about the conversion of gentiles is that they have "turned to God from idols" (1 Thess 1:9 cf. 2 Cor 6:16). Indeed, although gentiles turning to Christ did not need to be circumcised and all that entailed, they did need to make a clean break with their pagan past. The demands of turning from idols to God require thoughtful negotiation in a world filled with idols.

In addition, Christians are admonished to "guard yourselves from idols" (1 John 5:21) or to "flee from idolatry" (1 Cor 10:14), with the full recognition that this cannot mean moving to some space untouched by idols.[21] Indeed, in the very context in which Paul admonishes the Corinthians to flee from idols, he is also giving them fairly sophisticated instructions about eating meat sacrificed to an idol. This would indicate that contexts matter when it comes to thinking about idolatry and that we may learn something from examining Paul's comments to the Corinthians on these matters.

CONTEXTS MATTER

At the beginning of 1 Corinthians 8, Paul turns his attention to food sacrificed to an idol (Περὶ δὲ τῶν εἰδωλοθύτων).[22] Some of the primary interpretive difficulties of 1 Corinthians 8–10 reside in the fact that Paul appears to say in theory that a Christian can eat idol-food in 1 Corinthians 8 and the end of 1 Corinthians 10. Alternatively, the beginning of 1 Corinthians 10 is filled with admonishments against idolatry. Further, 1 Corinthians 9 seems to have no direct connection to what precedes it in chapter 8 or follows it in chapter 10. By looking at this passage in some detail here, I want to argue that the entirety of 1 Corinthians 8–10 represents Paul's concrete attempts to present the Corinthians with a faithful path that displays how they might make a break with idolatry even as they continue to live in an idol-soaked world.

Derek Newton's significant work on sacrificial food in Corinth allows readers of Paul's letter to understand a set of distinctions that are important for understanding the argument of these chapters. First, Newton displays the wide diversity of views regarding the status of images and their veneration in cities like Corinth. It is not as if members of the Corinthian congregation would have shared a single coherent view about the status of idols. From this, it becomes plausible to claim that although Paul may have had a clear and distinct sense of what constitutes idolatry (εἰδωλολατρία), it may not have been at all clear to the Corinthians what practices constituted idolatry.[23] In fact, rather than two relatively identifiable groups, one "weak" and the other "strong," it is much more likely that there was a wide range of views among the believers in Corinth about what sort of engagements might constitute idolatry. Further, the fact that in 5:9-13 Paul recognizes that it would be impossible for the Corinthians to break off all contact with idolaters (εἰδωλολάτραι) and that in 10:7 he commands them not to become idolaters seems to set up a situation in which misunderstandings could abound.[24]

In chapters 8–10 Paul appears to make several fundamental distinctions. First, there is a difference between idol-food (εἰδωλόθυτα) and idolatry (εἰδωλολατρία). Secondly, although we may not have a clear picture of how pervasive idol-food may have been in the markets, there appear to have been a large number of contexts in Corinth in which one might consume idol-food. Even when such eating might have occurred in a pagan temple (ἐν εἰδωλείῳ κατακείμενον [8:10]), those activities might have been relatively far removed from the actual sacrificial act.[25] This would account for why some Corinthian believers would not have readily seen that eating εἰδωλόθυτα was connected with idolatry and others might disagree.[26]

Paul asserts that in reality idols are nothing, that there is one true God (8:4), and that anything sold in the meat market can be consumed as long as one recognizes that it belongs to the Lord (10:25-26; cf. 1 Tim 4:4). Nevertheless, particularly with regard to eating idol-food in various temple contexts, Paul's comments in 8:7-13 are pervasively negative. It is not something Paul could ever imagine doing himself; he disapproves of Corinthian believers doing so.[27] Nevertheless, Paul does grant that those with "knowledge" that an idol is nothing have "a right" (ἡ ἐξουσία) to eat idol-food in temples (assuming they are not implicated in the sacrificial cult). This right, however, must be abandoned in favor of the higher demands of love, which manifest themselves in concern for other members of the body of Christ.

The idea that free people would willingly give up a right would have seemed preposterous to most people in Corinth. It would have been seen as a servile act, a repulsive thing to do. In that light, before further discussion of idol-food and idolatry, Paul addresses this issue in 1 Corinthians 9. In this chapter Paul points to his own example as a free apostle who gives up his rights (ἡ ἐξουσία [9:4, 5, 6, 12, 18]), becoming a slave to advance the gospel.[28]

In chapter 10 Paul returns to the issue of idolatry. Making reference to Israel in the wilderness and alluding to Exodus 32, Paul notes that even the people of God can turn to idols. The Corinthians must not become idolaters as some of the Israelites did (μηδὲ εἰδωλολάτραι γίνεσθε καθώς τινες αὐτῶν [10:7]). This admonition is reasserted in 10:14, "flee from idolatry" (φεύγετε ἀπὸ τῆς εἰδωλολατρίας). Given that Paul has already addressed idol-food (εἰδωλόθυτα) eaten in pagan temples (εἰδώλια) and the conditions under which one might participate in this activity, he must mean something different here in chapter 10 when he speaks about idolatry (εἰδωλολατρία).[29] He clarifies his views in 10:14-22.

Here Paul reminds the Corinthians that when they partake of the cup and break the bread in the Eucharist they are drawn into a participation, a sharing, or communion in the body and blood of Christ himself. This participation is fundamentally incompatible with participation in any other sort of sacrifice to another being. Having already indicated the idols (εἴδωλα) are not gods, Paul now asserts that nevertheless εἴδωλα are beings of a certain sort. They are demons (δαιμόνια). There can be no mutual participation in the Lord and in demons (10:21). According to Newton, "the difference between 1 Corinthians 8 and 10:14-22 is not the difference between 'social' temple meals and 'religious' temple meals, but rather the difference between degrees of involvement. Paul was uneasy about believers' relatively passive eating of [εἰδωλόθυτα] in 1 Corinthians 8, but he was positively outraged by the possibility of a believer actively and actually sacrificing and then eating *thusia* in 1 Cor 10:20-22."[30]

Finally, in 10:23–11:1, Paul addresses sacrificial food consumed outside of any temple context. Although we cannot really know the proportion of meat in the market that would have been offered in sacrifice, it seems reasonable to assume that at least some if not all the meat at any given dinner party in a home would have been offered in sacrifice. On the one hand, Paul recognizes that believers are free to eat all of this meat as long as it is done with thanksgiving. On the other hand, they are not free to ignore how their behavior affects both their pagan hosts and the body of believers. As in chapter 8, the overriding concern here is to seek the benefit of others rather than oneself (10:24).[31] In this respect, Paul is merely imitating Christ (11:1; cf. Phil 1:27– 2:11). Throughout this final section, the assumption must be that the Corinthians will need to make a host of judgments as a community about specific cases regarding idol-food. The edification of the body will be the overriding consideration in these judgments. At the same time, they are in no case to become complicit in any actual sacrifice. They cannot participate in Christ's sacrificial meal and sacrifices to demons.

The world of the first Christians was filled with idols and spaces touched by idols. Paul's admonitions in 1 Corinthians 10:7 and 14 to avoid "becoming idolaters" and to "flee the worship of idols" reflect positions consistent with the OT and the practice of Jesus and his early followers. At the same time, there appears to have been a great degree of diversity and complexity of views within congregations regarding the extent to which various activities and material artifacts were implicated in the worship of idols.[32] This was even the case for activities in pagan temples.

Such situations of complex and competing evaluations of activities and contexts called the early Christians to engage in patterns of judgment that would enable them to negotiate faithfully their paths through their day-to-day engagements with the world. If we take 1 Corinthians 8–10 to be the NT's most systematic account of how to make these judgments, several rules of thumb emerge. First, there are no occasions when Christians can be complicit in acts of sacrifice to pagan gods. Moreover, they need to be vigilant to ensure that their participation in the one bread and one cup of Christ's death does not become diluted by participation in any similar sacrificial acts. At the other end of things, all the food sold in the market can be consumed under the recognition that it belongs to the Lord and can be eaten with thanksgiving without obviously becoming implicated in idolatry. Further, all patterns of judgment must be governed by love for one's brothers and sisters in Christ. No matter how near or distant an activity or artifact may be to an idol, any believer's freedom with regard to these activities or artifacts is circumscribed by the requirement to seek, according to the example of Christ, the benefits and interests of others rather than oneself.

Of course, as Christianity becomes an entrenched presence in the Roman Empire, more and more distinctly idol-free places, activities, and artifacts emerge. The more Christians come to control the spaces in which they live and move, the easier it becomes to demarcate ways in which Christians can flee from or guard themselves from idolatry.

Further Issues

I am aware that the preceding discussion has not yet rendered an account of idolatry. Rather, it has tried to touch on some of the diverse ways Scripture addresses idols and the ways Scripture addresses believers and their relationship to idols. Before I offer an account of idolatry that will take these scriptural concerns into account and will serve the purposes of this book, I want to address some issues that move beyond the bounds covered by Scripture.

Moving beyond Scripture's specific concerns with idolatry, two particular issues emerge as potentially relevant to my discussion. The first concerns the role of images in Christian formation and worship. I address many of these issues in subsequent chapters of this volume, so I will say relatively little here. The second issue addresses particular approaches to Scripture's rich discussion of idolatry in light of the fact that the great majority of Christians in the West live in contexts where people do not purposely fabricate idols.

Images

Both Judaism and Islam have been much more rigorous than Christianity in proscribing any images of God. There are a number of reasons for this.

For Christians, the conviction that God became incarnate in Jesus Christ makes the issue of images of God more complex, ambiguous, and contentious. Christians are followers of an invisible God who nonetheless took on human flesh. They are also heirs of the OT's prohibition on the fabrication of images of God. In this light Christians have faced philosophical and theological issues concerning how God's creation can manifest the invisible God. Can the created world mediate God truthfully to humans? If so, how? Can the created world be instrumental in the worship of the one God without that worship being idolatrous?

On matters of representing God, Christians, chiefly because of convictions arising out of the doctrine of the incarnation, have been more open to the possibility of using representations of God in worship and of the possibilities of God's presence being mediated through the created world, especially in the elements of the Eucharist. Even here, however, Christians are divided. Orthodox, Catholic, and many Lutheran and Anglican Christians tend to be much more open to the idea that the material world can have sacramental importance, mediating God's presence to believers. Nevertheless, even these Christians would recognize the possibility that their representations of God and their worship could become idolatrous. Negotiating the tensions involved in this has been one of Christianity's ongoing challenges. I will address some of these matters in chapter 2, which is about forgetting and remembering.

In addition, Christianity's evangelistic impulses encourage Christians to translate their sacred texts and their faith into idioms that unbelievers can understand.[33] One sees this already in the NT, but it certainly has continued down to the present. In contrast, Islam and Judaism have been much less eager to translate their sacred texts.

Once they moved down this road of translation, Christians realized that in certain times and places, images have proved to be much more significant than written words for instructing the faithful, directing their worship truthfully, and deepening their love for God.[34] This confluence of convictions, scriptural prohibitions, and evangelistic impulses can help account for the fact that Christians have often struggled to come to grips with the use of material (and even mental) images in Christian formation and worship.

Although I would argue that this should always be a matter of ongoing concern for Christians, there are specific occasions when this struggle has come to the fore quite dramatically. Think of the iconoclastic controversies of the eighth and ninth centuries. Icons are painted pictures depicting Christ or the Virgin Mary or other saints. There was a long history in the Eastern churches of using and/or venerating icons in worship. This practice persisted for an extended period without generating much controversy. A combination of the rise of forms of Monophysitism (a movement that diminished the importance of Christ's human body and, therefore, the usefulness of images of that body) along with pressure from Judaism and Islam, which saw icons as proscribed images, led Emperor Leo III to declare all icons to be idols in 725.

As these theological issues became entangled in ecclesiastical and temporal politics, the controversy lasted through much of the ninth century, with icons still retaining an important place in Christian worship, particularly in the East. Now even in the West many Christians devoutly engage icons as part of their prayer, contemplation, and worship.

The Protestant reformation also generated forms of iconoclasm. Given the strong preference for the image over the word in late medieval piety, it is not that surprising that various reformers would oppose the use of images in worship. John Calvin, in particular, was suspicious of the capacity of creaturely artifacts made by sinful humans to mediate the divine truthfully in liturgical contexts.[35]

In our current time, one can see that these issues are sometimes tied into larger philosophical questions around representation and signification. These more abstract philosophical and theological questions have their own long histories, distinct from questions of idolatry proper. There are, however, ways in which they can be drawn together. For example, the French philosopher/theologian Jean-Luc Marion, in his phenomenological account of God and of theological language, offers an account of the difference between an idol and an icon.[36]

For Marion, the essence of idolatry is not in the fabrication of the idol but in the act of making the idol the focus of one's "gaze" or attention.[37] "Gaze" as a philosophical term has roots going back to Sartre. It also plays a significant role in Lacan's psychoanalytic theories and in Michel Foucault's discussions of power distribution. The gaze is not simply the act of seeing. It reflects a desire on the part of the subject to know, acquire, comprehend, or control the object of one's gazing. The gaze is as much about establishing a particular sort of relationship between subject and object as it is about the practicalities of vision. As Marion describes it, in the case of idols or icons, the desire expressed or implicit in the gaze is to see, to know, or comprehend the divine.

An idol will then be that which stops one's gaze and, unbeknownst to the seer, simply reflects it back.[38] In this regard, almost anything, including signs and concepts, can be idols, foreshortening or truncating one's vision so that one mistakes a reflection of oneself or another human projection for God. In this respect Marion is following in the tradition of Romans 1:23-25, where idolatry is characterized as mistaking the creature for the creator.

The icon, by contrast, focuses and properly directs one's gaze towards the true God. The icon becomes one way of directing human desire for God in the right direction. In doing so, the icon also helps to render the invisible God more visible.[39] The icon must do so, however, by undermining or challenging one's gaze, reminding us that God is not an object to be controlled or comprehended. We humans do not even generate our desire for God. Rather, it is responsive, dependent upon God's prior desire for us.

Although Marion's phenomenological, postmodern approach may seem quite distant from the concerns of the Bible, they share a common recognition that idolatry often stems from failing to distinguish creator and creature properly. In addition, they agree that idolatry often arises from a failure of attentiveness, an inability or unwillingness to focus one's attention and desire upon God in the face of myriad distractions. Moreover, because Marion's idol masks its capacity to reflect one's gaze back to oneself as if it were revealing God, it is basically a form of distraction. This distractedness and its associated lapse into idolatry are not significantly different from the criticisms of Israel's idolatrous practices outlined in the OT. Finally, because Marion's idol hides rather than reveals, it becomes easy to see idolatry as a habit that, once it begins, is ever more difficult to recognize, let alone break. Although I do not address Marion's work further, subsequent chapters reflect many of these same concerns.

In addition to these more general issues about images, any account of idolatry that will be relevant to contemporary believers in the developed countries must deal with the fact that, for the most part, people no longer fabricate idols.

Idolatry without Idols?

Over time, the establishment of Christianity within the Roman Empire eventually pushed out the worship of other gods and eliminated the widespread presence of purpose-made idols. In the light of the demise of the idol-saturated world that Paul and the early church knew, Christians found themselves in an unusual position, even if they did not narrate that position in the way I am about to. On the one hand, Christians were heirs to a rich and diverse scriptural language related to idols and idolatry, particularly the idolatry of the people of God. On the other hand, they were increasingly living in worlds where people had stopped fabricating images that they worshiped.[40]

Christians within these worlds tended to develop two particular ways in which to think about idolatry. First, there is a tendency for idolatry to become either a catch-all term for a wide variety of sins or the source of all sin. Even before the ascendancy of Christendom, Tertullian treated idolatry as humanity's principal sin. Others subsequently followed.[41] Hence, in the genealogy of sin, all sins are tied in some way to idolatry.[42] This strategy would enable much of the rich scriptural criticism of idolatry to continue to have life even as the fabrication of images of gods and the worship of such gods became less common in Christendom. Scriptural language about idols now applies to sin generally since all sin has its genesis in idolatry. Theological analysis that adopts this approach focuses on analyzing sin in such a way as to establish its true lineage in idolatry. In this way, idolatry simply becomes another word for sin.

Such an approach may or may not yield a true hierarchy or a genealogy of human sin.[43] Before even beginning to figure out how to evaluate such claims, it may be wise to consider whether it would be useful to have such a hierarchy or genealogy of sin even if one could convincingly establish it. In my life and, I assume, in the lives of many other believers, my various sins and vices are interconnected, hard to recognize, and difficult to repent of. It is not clear to me that my prayers regarding my sin, my work—under the guidance and grace of the Spirit—to identify, confess, and disentangle myself from my sin, or my hopes and prayers for avoiding sin in the future are in any way enhanced by being able to trace the lineage of all my sin to idolatry. Indeed, Scripture has a rich vocabulary for accounting for human sin, and idolatry is simply one sin. Even if it is the most serious sin, it need not be the source of all sin. For the purposes of this volume, I will not seek to tie all sins to idolatry.[44]

Instead, I hope to display and examine some the dispositions, habits, and practices that incline believers toward idolatry, as well as those dispositions, habits, and practices that might dispose believers toward greater faithfulness. Offering such analysis will not require me to offer a genealogy of sin that ties all sin to idolatry. It will oblige me to offer a fuller account of idolatry in the present.

The second strategy that Christians have adopted in a world without purposely fabricated idols will seem more familiar. The central aspect of this strategy is to treat almost any aspect of the created world as a potential idol. This strategy operates from the conviction that the real problem with idolatry is that it misdirects love and attention that should solely be focused on God and focuses it on something or someone else. Thus, any thing (or any activity) that receives a disproportionate amount of, or an inappropriate degree of, human attention and longing can become an idol. Such things as devotion to a particular nation-state or a particular sports team come to mind as good candidates for this. In fact, there is a stream of theological reflection that seeks to identify specific aspects of our world as contemporary idols. One finds this tendency in much modern Christian reflection on idolatry, both scholarly and popular. Again, the strength of such an approach is that it enables scriptural language critical of idolatry to continue to live and be active in a world that does not have purpose-built pagan temples or purposefully fabricated idols.

One result of this strategy is that the focus of theological analysis related to idolatry shifts to identifying what counts as an idol and why.[45] Idols now are things or activities that were not created for the purpose of worshiping specific gods. Rather, one now identifies idols because they are things that occupy so much of our time and attention that one might claim that these activities or things function as gods for us. They rule and order our lives in the way that the one true God seeks to rule and order our lives.

This approach has generated some very probing and insightful theological analysis, such as one finds in the work of Jacques Ellul.[46] Of course, once someone identifies some thing or some activity as an idol, it also tends to generate a counterargument that it is not this thing or activity, but something else that is really an idol.[47] Debates arise between those trying to distinguish the disease from the symptoms. Such activity is, of course, important if the patient is to be healed. Unlike diagnostic procedures in medicine, however, there do not seem to be many widely accepted tests that one can perform to aid in formulating precise diagnoses in the realm of idolatry. Without question, work such as Ellul's can point out genuine distortions in the lives and practices of believers in particular times and places. It can also remind believers that material habits and practices reflect and shape one's life with God for good and ill. In many respects, such work functions much as prophetic criticisms of Israel's idolatry do.

I want, however, to offer two interrelated cautionary remarks at this stage. First, as noted above, prophets do not have a great record of success in turning people away from idolatry. We should not expect the voices of contemporary prophets to have more success in penetrating our blindness and deafness than the voices of biblical prophets. Secondly, identifying idols and idolatry in this way depends on people already treating some object of activity in such an all-consuming way that it becomes an idol. That is, according to this approach, idols tend to be identifiable only once idolatry is already taking place. Believers can really only begin to discern whether one thing or activity might constitute an idol once that thing or activity is perilously close to or already functioning as an idol. To continue with the medical metaphors, since diagnoses depend on the manifestation of disease, such a process does not allow for a great deal of preventative care to happen.

Despite these drawbacks, I do find that this approach offers some positive ways forward for the account of idolatry I need to offer here in this volume. First, its account of idolatry is either implicitly or explicitly driven by views such as one reads in Deuteronomy 6:4-6. God seeks our wholehearted, single-minded love and attention. Anything that diverts one's love and attention from God is, at least in principle, threatening to become an idol or to function as an idol. This resonates with several elements of Scripture's account of idolatry. For example, it allows one to note that although the people of God often turned to worship other gods, they rarely abandoned the worship of the LORD in a wholesale way. Rather, they tended to split their attentions between the LORD and numerous other gods. Although this was a generally accepted practice in most of the surrounding pagan cultures, the LORD exercised an exclusive call on the love and attention of the people of God. This suggests that an account of idolatry that will serve my purposes should begin by focusing on the positive notion that the LORD seeks and requires our wholehearted, single-minded love and attention.

If one begins there, then idolatry should seem more like a process of slowly turning and directing our love and attention away from the one true God toward things that are not God.[48] I recognize that such a claim suggests that there may be some point in this process before which one is not an idol-ater and after which one is. For example, in the case of 1 Corinthians 8–10, discussed above, participation in the sacrifice was clearly on the idolatry side of that division. Eating idol-food in a temple, under the right conditions, may be on the other side. This is one of the primary drawbacks of treating idolatry more like a process than a single clearly demarcated act or set of acts. In the case of 1 Corinthians the clear line Paul draws regarding idol worship does not account for many of the other options facing the Corinthians. With regard to these situations, Paul offers a set of considerations that will help the Corinthians make good judgments.

Wherever the line between idolatry and something near to but not idol-atry gets drawn, it is obvious that it is best for believers to avoid getting close to such a line in the first place. In addition, it would seem that Scripture indicates that the closer one gets to this line, the less likely one is to be able to discern the line and to avoid crossing over into idolatry.

Further, this notion of idolatry as a process of directing our love and attention away from God toward something that is not God helps make sense of what I take to be a truism for which I do not plan to offer any further argument. That is, I take it as self-evident that no believer in ancient Israel, the early church, or twenty-first-century Baltimore decides at a single point in time to begin to worship a false god. Nevertheless, the witness of history, the testimony of our own eyes, and, if we are honest with ourselves, the examination of our own hearts makes it clear that believers are quite capable of turning away from the one true God and following something that is not God.

Given this premise, it would seem more likely that believers end up in idolatrous situations through a series of small, incremental moves: a decision that seems prudent here, a wise compromise there, the acquisition of a set of seemingly benign dispositions and practices along the way. These are the ways by which, little by little, largely without us noticing, our attention is gradually directed away from God toward something else. I would also suggest that just as with our biblical forebears, our turning away from God is rarely total. It appears much more common that such turning often still allows us to keep God in view, in our peripheral vision. This is not, however, the straight-on, single-minded attention that God seeks from us.

If these assumptions and suggestions are correct, then a couple of things follow. First, in a world that does not purposely fabricate idols anymore, it will not always be clear when this incremental process of turning away from God formally results in idolatry. Alternatively, given that God seeks our wholehearted, single-minded devotion, it may not be all that important to demarcate some point beyond which our turning away from God formally constitutes idolatry.

Secondly, and more importantly, it would seem that rather than have a prophet calling you to repent from things you can barely recognize in yourself, it is much better to locate, identify, unlearn, and repent of the habits and dispositions that lead to idolatry before they do so. This is what I plan to focus on in this volume. That is, I am hoping to contribute to those conditions and situations that might enable believers to avoid the need for a prophet. With this aim in mind, the next chapter will begin with an examination of Deuteronomy 6:4-14.

2

FORGETTING AND ATTENDING

INTRODUCTION

As I indicated in the previous chapter, the account of idolatry I proposed there is driven more by the constructive claims of Deuteronomy 6:4-6 than by strictures against the worship of other gods by means of images. This results in a notion of idolatry (at least the idolatry of believers) that is more like a process than one specific action. Idolatry is a process that slowly, incrementally misdirects believers' attention and love away from the one true God toward other things or people. If this is the case, then the best way to understand the move to idolatry is primarily in terms of the acquisition of habits, practices, and dispositions that ease and even accelerate this process of directing love and attention away from God. Avoiding or counteracting these habits, practices, and dispositions requires the cultivation of alternative habits, practices, and dispositions. The remainder of this book will concentrate on displaying and exploring these various habits, practices, and dispositions.

Thus, I want to begin by focusing on Deuteronomy 6:4-5 and the ways in which the commands of these verses are developed in vv. 6-14. This will allow me to examine some of the dispositions and practices assumed in this passage and the relationship between those dispositions and practices and idolatry.

Both in Exodus 20:1-17 and Deuteronomy 5:6-21, the giving of the commandments is embedded in the story of God delivering the Israelites out of slavery and leading them toward the promised land. The admonition to have no other gods before the LORD and the prohibition of making and worshiping images are not abstract, arbitrary demands. Rather, they derive their initial force from that fact that they recall the LORD's powerful mastery of Pharaoh and the Egyptians, freeing the Israelites from slavery. As a result, within the context of Deuteronomy, the call to have no other gods before the LORD is often connected to acts of remembering, remembering the story of God's deliverance. Not surprisingly, then, we will find that the call to avoid following other gods is connected to acts of forgetting. Remembering and attending to the story of God's redemption and the commandments that flow from that story will lead the Israelites to follow the LORD alone. Forgetting the LORD and all the LORD has done will lead to following other gods and worshiping idols (Deut 6:11; 8:10-20; 11:13-17; 31:20 and 32:15-18). Immediately it would appear that forgetfulness is a disposition that leads to idolatry. Active, attentive remembering disposes one toward faithfulness.

In this chapter I would like to explore these dispositions through an examination of Deuteronomy and Deuteronomy 6 in particular. I hope to show that the single-minded, wholehearted love of God called for in 6:4-5 is connected to practices of remembering that lead to faithfulness and seeks to avoid practices of forgetting that will lead to idolatry. It is also important to recognize that despite the proscription of material images and idols, the task of worshiping the LORD first and foremost is intimately, though complexly, tied to our presence in and relationship to the material world. I thus hope to make clear that forgetting and remembering God is not simply, or even primarily, a mental exercise. Rather, it requires close attention to the material world and our place in it as well as our connections to one another in the body of Christ. In the worlds of the OT and the NT, there are very few, if any, cases of gods of any type being worshiped in the absence of some material image. Even the aniconic LORD still requires the Israelites to use material elements both to remember and to display their commitments to the LORD.

SHEMA

To make this point and to develop some of its implications for those who wish to avoid lapsing into idolatry, we can begin at no better place than that passage known as the Shema in Deuteronomy 6.

Deuteronomy 6:4-5 contain a number of interpretive complexities. For example, Deut 6:4 begins with a great confession or assertion. It is not, however, immediately clear what is being confessed. The phrase is composed of just four Hebrew words. Further, as in many Hebrew phrases, the verb "to be" is left out. Thus, simply rendering an English translation will require some significant interpretive work. The NRSV inserts a verb in the first clause to produce this translation: "The LORD is our God, the LORD alone." If one inserts the verb in the second clause, the verse reads like this: "The LORD our God, The LORD is one." This seems to be the way the LXX takes it.[1]

Each of these ways of translating the verse emphasizes different things. The central point of saying the LORD is our God, the LORD alone, is to emphasize the exclusive relationship between Israel and the LORD rather than emphasizing something about God's nature.[2] That is, rather than an assertion about monotheism, this text affirms Israel's exclusive relationship with the LORD. Whatever gods other peoples might worship, Israel's God is the LORD.[3]

To render the phrase as "The LORD our God, The LORD is one" makes an assertion about the LORD's singular nature. This would seem more like an assertion of monotheism, though it is probably the case that a philosophical account of monotheism does not really align well with the concerns of Deuteronomy or the OT more generally.[4]

In addition, a key interpretive puzzle lies in how to interpret the assertion that the LORD is אֶחָד. In Hebrew this word is commonly used to designate "one." In this context, one could argue that it should carry the sense of "alone." Of course, with regard to a passage such as this, what "this context" is might be difficult to determine. For example, this text has a prehistory about which we know some, but not many, things. That would seem to be one context within which to examine this passage. Further, Deuteronomy as a whole provides a context for this passage that is not the same context as the one provided by the prehistory of these verses. In addition, this text plays a significant role in both Judaism and Christianity.[5] That, too, is a context or contexts within which one might set this passage. I am neither interested in nor able to engage in debates about this text's prehistory. Further, although nothing in what follows is designed to undermine or negate the interpretations that arise out of later Jewish or Christian contexts, I am not concerned with those matters at present. Instead, I want to focus on Deuteronomy 6:4-5 in the context of Deuteronomy 6 and the rest of Deuteronomy more generally.

To aid in this, I will rely closely on Walter Moberly's work on Deuteronomy 6:4-5. Christian reflection on Deuteronomy 6 has focused narrowly on 6:5. This is probably an inadvertent result of Matthew's having Jesus quote Deuteronomy 6:5 as the greatest commandment in 22:37-38. In light of that, Moberly encourages Christian interpreters to also attend to Deuteronomy 6:6-9, arguing that 6:4-9 form an interconnected web of belief, confession, and practice. I find this argument compelling and will add that 6:10-14 should also be considered part of this context. Hence, what follows should be seen as supplemental to the very important interpretive work Moberly has already done on 6:4-5.

Moberly begins by stressing that on both grammatical and logical grounds one should read v. 5 as an inference that follows from v. 4. Thus, whatever it means to say that the LORD is "one" implies that the LORD should be loved wholeheartedly and without reserve.[6]

Working backwards, then, "If unreserved love is the appropriate response to, and consequence of, the declaration that YHWH is אֶחָד then אֶחָד should have the sense that is commensurate with this."[7] Moberly finds that the most obvious parallel use of אֶחָד is Song of Songs 6:8-10. In this passage the lover makes clear that although he has, in theory, a large choice of women to pursue, there is really only one for him, only one that is worth his attention. Given that, it really does not matter how many other alternatives he has; there might be five others or five thousand. It does not matter, since he has found the one for him. In this context אֶחָד has the sense of "the one and only," the one for whose sake the lover would gladly forsake all others.[8]

"On this reading," Moberly observes, "the argument that 6:4 is *either* about an exclusive relationship between YHWH and Israel (with other gods recognized) *or* about the nature of YHWH as 'one' (with other gods denied) is misleading and offers a false alternative. If YHWH is 'one' in the sense of 'the one and only,' then it means that He is such that the people of Israel must be exclusive in their faithfulness and allegiance to Him."[9] In this light, Moberly offers the following translation of 6:4-5: "Hear, of Israel: YHWH our God, YHWH is the one and only. So you should love YHWH your God with all your thinking, with all your longing, and with all your striving."[10]

This offers some much-needed clarity to the debates about how to understand 6:4. The clarity we gain here, however, simply pushes us to much harder questions. Two questions in particular are, What does it really mean to love God in this way?[11] And, can such love be commanded in this way and still be love? Beginning with the latter question, one should note there are other OT texts that seem to command emotions, feelings, or attitudes (at least of individuals). For example, Leviticus 19:17-18 reads, "You shall not hate your kinsfolk in your heart. . . . You shall not bear a grudge against your country-men."[12] Nevertheless, it does seem difficult to demand that another person have a particular feeling or emotion. To the extent that we focus on love as an emotion or feeling, the answer is likely to be that one cannot command love. This is made even more unlikely if one recalls that this command is addressed to Israel as a community, a people. If commanding an emotion of an individual is hard to imagine, it is much more difficult to imagine God commanding an emotion of an entire people. All this indicates that such love is not going to reside primarily in the emotions.[13]

Another way forward lies in Tigay's observation that Hebrew verbs for feelings often refer as well to the actions that are conventionally tied to such feelings.[14] Thus, the command to love in Deuteronomy 6:5 is a command that at the very least requires one to do the things that stem from or are entailed by the feeling of love. Although it is much more conceivable that God commands the actions entailed in a single-minded, wholehearted love of God, it still leaves a gap between feeling and doing that might merit further consideration.

Perhaps one way of comprehending the relationships between emotions and the actions that lie beneath the surface of this commandment is to think of love as a virtue. If one thinks of love as a virtue, a settled disposition to act in a particular way, then it seems just as likely that doing the actions of love will help to cultivate the feelings and emotions of love as that the loving emotions will generate loving actions. Further, it is important, from a Christian perspective at least, that we not think of love of God in static terms, as a one-time achievement. As one advances in the faith, one's love grows and is ultimately brought to completion at the day of Christ. Even then, however, perfected love continues to generate the desire to love more in much the same way that exercising a muscle increases its capacities for further exercise.[15]

Thinking of the love that God commands as a virtue that combines action and emotion in some complex relation may help to refine and address the question of whether love of God can be commanded. It nevertheless raises the question of what are the actions appropriate for a people who are commanded to love the LORD with all their thinking, longing, and striving. From the perspective of Deuteronomy 6:4-5, it would appear that the primary action that would appropriately display this comprehensive love of God is a single-minded fidelity to the LORD, worshiping, following, and attending to the LORD and the LORD alone.[16] This would lead to the following questions: How and in what manner does one display fidelity? What are the practices that both support and display such fidelity?

How to Practice Remembering

This is precisely what Deuteronomy 6 is interested in. That is, as the chapter moves beyond 6:5, it becomes more interested in helping the Israelites remain faithful to their one and only love. Deuteronomy 6:6 indicates that the key to doing this is sustained and systematic attention to "these words." The referent of the phrase "these words" is not exactly clear. The phrase could cover a rather large scope, such as all of Deuteronomy, or all of the commandments. No doubt, God does want the Israelites to give sustained attention to these. Nevertheless, given that the subsequent instructions imply that "these words" can be written and read in relatively small spaces, it is likely that the phrase "these words" refers to 6:4, "the LORD our God is the one and only."[17] "These words" are to be kept in the heart; recited regularly, particularly to the next generation; and discussed at all times and places. They are to appear on one's person and on private and public structures such as houses and gates (6:6-9; see also Deut 11:18-21).

It would appear, then, that maintaining the single-minded fidelity required by wholehearted love of the LORD requires some very public actions. These concrete practices are manifestations of Israel's love of and allegiance to the LORD. As importantly, these practices serve to enhance and develop the capacities of the people of God to remember, to focus and sustain their attention on "these words." Remembering and keeping "these words" constitute some, but not the only, ways of loving God in the comprehensive manner commanded in 6:5. "The display of allegiance to YHWH on one's person, in a way that will remind both self and others, means that in a world of contested allegiances Israel is required to be up front and courageous about its allegiance (v. 8). The marking of places where one lives, both domestic and civic, with this allegiance (so that one becomes aware of it at the point of transition into those places), likewise means that Israel's allegiance is never privatized but rather is integral to all the space that Israel inhabits (v. 9)."[18] Concrete practices displaying Israel's single-minded allegiance to the LORD reinforce the notion that love of God is not simply or even primarily a set of interior exchanges between the mind or heart of the believer and God. These practices involve the material world. Without producing images of the LORD, it is clear that houses, gates, and things one wears on one's body all serve to remind the people of Israel where their love and allegiance must always lie. Using the material world in these ways aids and supports Israel as they seek to remember and attend to "these words."

The manner in which 6:6-9 develop the call of 6:4-5 makes it clear that one of the dangers God anticipates is that the Israelites will forget the LORD their God. Subsequent verses will speak more directly about the challenge of forgetting the LORD. Prior to that, however, this danger is countered by the types of attentiveness prescribed in 6:6-9.

The Jewish interpretive tradition is filled with vigorous reflection on how and in what ways faithful Jews should observe and embody these verses.

On the whole, however, Christians have paid little attention to these verses, especially the more concrete prescriptions regarding "these words."[19] In this light, Moberly notes that Christian reflection on this passage traditionally moves in two particular ways. One is focused on the singularity of God as asserted in 6:4. When Christians retained the OT and this text in particular as part of their Scripture, it provided a theological pressure point against which assertions about Jesus' identity with God pressed rather forcefully. The other main point on which Christians have focused in interpreting this text is inevitably and correctly governed by Jesus' hanging all of the law and the prophets on the wholehearted, single-minded love of God and of loving one's neighbor as oneself (Matt 22:34-40//Mark 12:28-31//Luke 10:25-28). In the light of Jesus' proclamation, this double love commandment becomes a catalyst for all types of Christian reflection and practice. Hence, it is not surprising that Augustine makes the double love command the hermeneutical key to all scriptural interpretation.[20]

Given these interpretive trajectories, it is not surprising that Christian attention to these verses shifted away from the prescriptions for remembering found in 6:6-9 and the concrete practices these verses advocate to help maintain a wholehearted, single-minded love of God over time. Without negating the interpretive paths Christians have followed with regard to these verses, it is also important for Christians to recognize that these verses describe practices that offer crucial resources for remembering God and loving God well.

Moberly is particularly concerned with developing Christian ways of understanding the concrete practices of 6:6-9. Jews have felt themselves obligated to observe these practices and have devoted a great deal of scholarly and theological effort to figuring out concretely how and when to do so. Although Christians have not focused much effort on observing these practices, Moberly argues that Christians have developed "*alternative,* and in certain ways *equivalent,* practices to those envisaged in Deut 6:6-9."[21] He points to regular recitation of the Lord's Prayer in worship. In addition, the wearing of crosses, the making the sign of the cross, and the use of crosses on buildings offer a symbolic shorthand, signaling allegiance to Christ.[22] Even in the light of these cases, there is still room for Christians to reflect further about how they might appropriately display their identity and allegiance on their bodies and on relevant buildings in the present.[23]

Moberly's essay primarily focuses on 6:6-9 in the light of 6:4-5 in order to suggest particular ways that the people of God can display their identity and allegiance to God. I would like to extend Moberly's concerns in two ways. The first continues to reflect on the practices of 6:6-9 and their applicability to Christianity. The second is to continue reading Deuteronomy 6 to look at vv. 10-14. These verses warn about forgetting the LORD and following other gods. In this light it will also become clear that the practices displayed in 6:6-9 reflect habits and patterns of life that will enhance believers' capacities to remember God in the face of opportunities to forget God.

Attending to Deuteronomy 6:6-9

Judaism has tended to take the commands to keep "these words" (6:7) in your heart, to recite them to your children, and to talk about them regularly in the direction of liturgical practice and daily devotion. It also seems that these commands point in a catechetical direction, too. The telling and remembering of "these words" in a variety of times and places and across generations are catechetical moments, as crucial for attending to "these words" as any material practice. Following most commentators, I have already noted that "these words" must at least cover the confession that God is our one and only and the resulting command that believers should have a single-minded, wholehearted love of God. For Christians, catechetical attention to "these words" would mean at least two things.

First, they would need to understand "these words" in ways that are shaped and regulated by the NT. In saying this I am not simply referring to the fact that Jesus makes the command to love God with a wholehearted, single-minded love one of the hooks on which the whole law hangs. Christian attention to these words would also have to factor in the NT's strong claims that place Jesus within the identity of the one God of Israel. That is, Christians would need to acknowledge both God's singularity as "these words" do, and include God's son within their understanding of that singularity. This need not and must not lead to a rejection or superseding of the OT. Nevertheless, "these words" will inevitably appear to be somewhat different words when Christians come to keep, recite, and talk about them. Further, Christians should anticipate, without becoming overly defensive, that it will probably not be evident to Jews that Trinitarian doctrine is a form of keeping the words of Deuteronomy 6:4-5.

Secondly, understanding Deuteronomy 6:4-5 in Trinitarian terms implies that Christian catechetical practice is not limited to understanding these words in the light of the NT, but also in the light of Christian doctrine. This is because the NT's strong claims about Jesus' identity relative to the one God of Israel are necessary, but not sufficient elements for Trinitarian reflection. Until the scriptural assertions about God's singularity, on the one hand, and the inclusion of Jesus within the identity of the one God of Israel, on the other hand, are regulated by Nicene doctrine, these dual assertions can appear to be in a competitive, if not contradictory, relationship. The credal formulations of Nicaea provide Christians with a scripturally derived way of organizing and relating the diverse theological and christological claims of Scripture.[24] Without this regulative framework, Christians can recite "these words" as often as they wish. They simply will not understand them properly, and these words will not provide a resource of remembering, attending to, and ultimately loving God. If Christians are to keep, recite, and talk about these words over the course of generations, their catechetical practices will need to include an understanding of these words in the light of the long history of Christian thinking, praying, and acting.

Biblical scholars are notorious for lamenting the state of biblical literacy among Christians. As bad as this may be, the state of Christian learning about doctrine and church history is far worse. Further, there is ample evidence that the catechetical practices of many churches are in serious disrepair. Nevertheless, Christians need to understand "these words" in the light of the NT, Christian doctrine, and history. If these words and their history are not well understood, then they can hardly act as a deterrent to "forgetting God" (cf. 6:10-14).

In response, one might point to numerous examples and accounts of poorly performed catechetical practice that limited, frustrated, or suppressed the theological imaginations of the faithful. Those are not the inherent results of catechesis; they are the results of catechesis done poorly. Further, believers should not expect that their catechesis will say all that can be said about God. Christians can and should keep, recite, and teach these words without assuming that they have thereby captured all that one might say, hope, or pray about God. Nevertheless, catechesis can set up some parameters within which Christians can go on to say an inexhaustible number of things to and about God. At its best, catechesis forms, enlivens, and expands Christians' imaginations rather than foreshortening them. Rather than short-circuiting Christian reflection on God, it seems much more likely that inattention to catechesis and the resulting ignorance in these matters can result in distorted versions of "these words," leading people to forget God by inviting them to remember a misunderstood God. If Christians' catechetical practices are not in good working order, then it becomes ever more likely that their symbolic practices will not signify properly. Indeed, should the symbolic role of these practices become detached from their catechetical moorings, they risk becoming free-floating images that lose their precise symbolic force.

They will not appropriately symbolize one's allegiance to those outside the faith and will not help the faithful remember God and avoid following other gods. Catechesis is one way of maintaining symbolic actions so that they continue to do their work.[25]

We can see how this might happen in several important ways. First, consider the following scenario proposed by Nicholas Lash:

> If, in thirteenth-century Italy, you wandered around in a coarse brown gown, with a cord around your middle, your "social location" was clear: your dress said that you were one of the poor. If, in twentieth-century Cambridge, you wander around in a coarse brown gown, with a cord around your middle, your social location is curious: your dress now says, not that you are one of the poor, but that you are some kind of oddity in the business of "religion." Your dress now declares, not your solidarity with the poor, but your amiable eccentricity.[26]

Lash's point is not to criticize the Franciscans. Rather, his point is that even if believers perform exactly the same actions they have done for centuries, the changing contexts in which those actions are performed mean that the actions, in this case an intentional manner of dress, symbolize something different. Whether or not the Franciscans should change their dress, they would have to do a significant amount of teaching or catechesis to allow their actions to be perceived in the ways in which they would wish them to be perceived.

Secondly, when symbols become detached from their catechetical moorings, they are much more likely to be preyed upon by others and used to serve others' purposes. For example, consider the ways in which crosses and crucifixes have now become simply one more piece of jewelry for many people. The wearing of crosses may no longer signify one's allegiance to Christ. Rather, it may signify one's attachment to a certain lifestyle, fashion sense, or social status.

In post-Fordist[27] capitalist economies such catechetically detached symbols can then be used to market other things, including Christianity. For example, in 1998 my own diocese sought to open some new mission churches in the fast-growing suburbs and exurbs of Frederick County. They were aiming in particular to attract young people in their mid-twenties and early thirties. To aid in getting the word about these churches out to the wider community, the diocese hired an advertising agency. They put together several very provocative television commercials. This caused quite a stir. In response, the local public television station invited the priest in charge of this mission as well as a marketing professor and me onto one of their public affairs programs to discuss this issue. The segment began by airing one of the TV commercials. For about ten to fifteen seconds the camera panned an ornate crucifix while baroque music played in the background. At the very end of the spot we were shown the tagline "Of course people with pierced body parts are welcome in our church!"[28]

The piece was very well produced and snappy. After watching it I asked the priest what he would tell people when, after several months of attending church, they come to him and say, "The piercing you Christians are talking about is not an assertion of personal identity; it is not a statement about fashion or lifestyle choices; it is about giving up your life and dying with Christ." I suggested that, to the extent that this ad played on distinctly different notions of piercing without further explanation, it is a classic example of the bait and switch.

These are simply two ways in which concrete signs and symbols may become detached from their catechetical roots and lose their capacities to signify in the ways they might have at an earlier time. My point is that all of the concrete symbolic actions Christians undertake in order to display their wholehearted love and allegiance to God require such catechetical roots if the actions are to be rightly aligned with God. Further, if these actions are to aid in remembering rather than forgetting God, they must also retain their connections with the stories, doctrines, and prayers on which they are based. Moreover, both examples noted above should serve as reminders that this catechetical rootedness is not a one-time achievement. It has to be regularly maintained, as Deuteronomy 6:6-7 implies. Otherwise, when our children ask, "What do these things mean?" we will either misinform, or mislead, or simply fall silent.

Here is one further example. I recently covered Deuteronomy 6 within an Introduction to Theology class for first-year students. They were particularly taken by the material practices advocated in 6:6-9. When I explained phylacteries to them, they found that very strange. I went on to mention that Loyola does similar sorts of things to help students and faculty remember our identity as a Jesuit university. I noted that virtually all classrooms have some sort of cross or crucifix in them. Another student remembered that there is statue of Saint Ignatius in our quad.

I then asked them to remind me which dorms they lived in. The answers were "Hopkins," "Campion," and "Flannery." I noted that those were all people's names. "Who were these people?" They did not know. Most of them did remember that there was a plaque at the entrance to "Hopkins" explaining who Hopkins was. Their assignment for the next class was to learn something about the people their dorms were named after.[29] Unfortunately, the weekend intervened and only two of them completed the assignment. One student learned a fair bit about Edmund Campion, S.J. The other learned that "Flannery" was not the last name of the person her dorm was named after. Rather, it was named for Flannery O'Connor, though she knew nothing about O'Connor. Several students guessed that "Hopkins" was named for Johns Hopkins. I reminded them there was already an entire university named for Johns Hopkins and assured them that it was unlikely that we would name a dormitory after our local lacrosse rival. I sent someone to read the plaque at the front of the building. She reported that the dormitory was named for Gerard Manley Hopkins, S.J. They had never heard of Hopkins, though one student was familiar with the phrase "The world is charged with the grandeur of God."

We reflected on this situation in the light of Deuteronomy 6. In some respects, although the students might be charged with a lack of curiosity, it was also clear that no one had taken responsibility for telling them about the Jesuit and leading Roman Catholic thinkers whose names graced so many of our buildings. No one told them these things in the repetitive intentional ways described in Deuteronomy 6. This seems to be one of the particular ways in which we may fail to attend properly to these words. Someone has to take responsibility for explaining these matters to new members of the community. Otherwise we end up repeating a pattern of neglect that allows these words to be set adrift, signifying little other than, in our case, a particular location.[30]

Forgetting God

Immediately after the commandments in 6:6-9 to "keep," "recite," "bind," and "write"—commandments that invoke the use of the material world to help Israel maintain its single-minded fidelity to the LORD—the passage shifts to anticipate threats to that fidelity. As the passage develops further in 6:10-14, we read of warnings about ways in which Israel may be tempted to "forget the LORD and follow other gods." One implication of these warnings is that to abandon or deviate from these practices in 6:6-9 is one way to begin that movement away from God, which at some point manifests itself in idolatry.

As 6:10-14 indicate, when Israel enters the land, an inheritance granted and enabled solely through the LORD, they will reap the benefits of houses they neither built nor furnished and fields they neither plowed nor tended, as well as a stable water supply. When the covenantal promise of land has been fulfilled and fulfilled abundantly, the Israelites will be tempted to forget the one who made and fulfilled the promise. In forgetting this, they will increase the likelihood of abandoning their single-minded fidelity to the LORD and of following the gods of the surrounding people. Oddly, faithfulness on God's part threatens to beget forgetfulness on Israel's part.

One can easily see that Deuteronomy 6:10-14 seems to assume that material prosperity threatens fidelity to the LORD. In the light of this, Christians in the United States may be inclined toward two fairly straightforward moves. The first is to recognize, with Deuteronomy and Jesus, that wealth is a threat to one's ability to follow God with the single-minded fidelity that whole-hearted love of God requires. The second is either to disdain or to disparage the material world as the seedbed of idolatry.

The first consideration about the threat of wealth requires more development in subsequent chapters. I want to address and develop the second claim more directly here. The contrast between the practices and behaviors presented in 6:4-9 and those in vv. 10-14 is not between the spiritual confession and love of God, on the one hand, and the material threat to that love that prosperity poses, on the other hand. Rather, the contrast is between attentiveness and forgetfulness (cf. Deut 4:9). Deuteronomy 6:4-9 presents the call to wholehearted, single-minded love of God and things Israel can do to attend to that call. Deuteronomy 6:10-14 presents occasions for and the dangers of forgetting the LORD. Both the requirements of attention and the possibility or threat of forgetfulness make use in various ways of the material world. The same furnished houses that will lead the Israelites to forget are the ones where "these words" are written in order to help them remember. To gather the harvest of grain, grape, and olive promised in 6:11, the Israelites will have to pass through the gates where "these words" are written. My point is that the material goods that Israel is to inherit in the land are not simply opportunities for forgetting the LORD. They are also embedded amidst the very material symbols and actions that serve to aid remembering and attending to the LORD as their "one and only."[31] The single-minded love of God called for in 6:5 is displayed through concrete practices of recitation and remembering. There is, therefore, no sense of spiritualizing the love of God in ways that disdain the material world.[32]

This would indicate that in addition to attending to a single-minded fidelity to and whole-hearted love of the LORD, the people of God will need to attend to the ways in which the material world can both aid this cause and threaten it. Given that the concrete practices and the material world in and of themselves can be helpful in loving the LORD above all others, what is it about the bounty that God promises Israel in 6:10-11 that also calls forth the admonition to "take care, that you do not forget the LORD who brought you up out of the house of slavery" in 6:12?

The text is silent on the matter. One can note with Telford Work that "the regression in tribal focus and solidarity from Joshua to Judges illustrates the temptation to drift and fragment in settled times (32:15-18)."[33] Many other commentators offer similar observations: "Deuteronomy and other books frequently point out that prosperity causes people to forget that they are dependent on God for all that they have."[34] This is true, but it simply points to a tendency without really explaining how it might lead to the worship of other gods.

In this regard, Deuteronomy as a whole may have a bit more to offer us. For example, Deuteronomy 6:11; 8:10-20; 11:13-17; 31:20; and 32:15-18 all link eating one's fill in the bountiful promised land with forgetting the LORD and turning to other gods.[35] Most of these passages simply assert the link between eating one's fill and forgetting God as if it were a naturally occurring phenomenon. Only Deuteronomy 8:10-20 spells out a more direct connection between eating one's fill and forgetting the LORD. Both 8:14 and 8:17 provide the keys. In 8:14 there is a warning that after partaking of the bounty of the land the Israelites might "exalt" themselves, thus "forgetting the LORD." Deuteronomy 8:17 is even more explicit. After being reminded of all that God had done for the Israelites and the bounty that God had provided, the people are warned, "Do not say to yourself, 'My power and the might of my own hand have gotten me this wealth.'"

It would appear that after one has eaten one's fill, the temptation to forget the LORD lies in forgetting one's dependence on God. This is a failure to remember that even the prosperity that results from Israel's own work in the land is still ultimately dependent upon the LORD's provision. From the perspective of Deuteronomy 8:11-20, eating one's fill invites a form of self-absorption and self-aggrandizement that leads to forgetting the LORD.

Deuteronomy links eating one's fill with forgetting God. Both Deuteronomy 8:11-20 and 6:10-14 go further than this. They note that eating one's fill leads to forgetting the LORD, with the result that the Israelites will begin to follow the gods of the surrounding people.

This last step is harder to follow. As Deuteronomy 8:14, 17 indicate, eating one's fill can initiate a dynamic between self-exaltation, self-absorption, and self-aggrandizement that results in forgetting the LORD. One can imagine that self-exaltation and forgetting get bound together and feed off of each other in ways that make it difficult to discern which predicament precedes the other. Regardless of whether self-exaltation leads to forgetting the LORD or forgetting the LORD is the first act of self-exaltation, it is not clear how this dynamic leads one to follow other gods. It would seem that the dynamic of self-exaltation that leads one to forget the LORD would also short-circuit the following of any god.

It may simply be the case that, as Augustine noted, "the punishment of every disordered mind is its own disorder."[36] Hence, the initial displacement of the LORD from the center of one's love and attention simply opens one up to further disorder, such as, but not limited to, following other gods. The initial self-deceptive move opens the door to further deceptions and seductions, of which following other gods is simply one of the most grievous. There may be little else to say to help explain how the type of self-exaltation that leads to the forgetting of the LORD would also lead to the following of other gods. Following other gods would simply become the unintelligible action of a disordered heart.

We should, however, be slow to ascribe unintelligibility to anyone's actions. As Alasdair MacIntyre points out, intelligible actions are primary to unintelligible ones.[37] Hence, before making that move, it may be useful to examine one of the other passages that links eating one's fill and following other gods. In 11:15-16 one also finds the theme of eating one's fill. Israel's wholehearted love of God results in the LORD's provision of adequate and timely rain yielding abundant harvests, harvests that allow the Israelites to eat their fill (11:13-15). In that situation, the Israelites are to "take care, or you will be seduced into turning away, serving other gods and worshiping them" (11:16). Both the MT and LXX speak of the Israelites' hearts being "lured" into following other gods (cf. Job 31:9, 27).[38] It may be the case, then, that when one has eaten one's fill, there is a greater likelihood of being seduced or lured into following other gods. In Deuteronomy 12:29-32 and 13:6 similar vocabulary is used to speak about the seductive capacities of doing what is widely done by pagans, yet prohibited by God. Idle curiosity and the thrill of doing what is prohibited all may contribute to the seductive power of following other gods.[39] What this does not yet explain, however, is how the self-exaltation that leads believers to forget their dependence upon God and mistakenly to trust in their own resources may also open their hearts to being seduced into following other gods. How might self-absorbed, self-aggrandizing people who no longer remember or need the LORD be seduced to following another god? Why would such self-absorbed people worship any god once they have forgotten the LORD? Here Deuteronomy seems to offer very little direct guidance. What follows are possible suggestions. They are by no means definitive.

First, self-absorbed people who have forgotten the LORD and deceived themselves into thinking that they are the source of their own prosperity and good fortune may find the lure of other gods unthreatening. Such believers may feel themselves in many respects superior to these other gods, capable of controlling, or at least managing, the demands and influence of such gods since those gods do not demand the wholehearted love and single-minded attention that the LORD commands.

We may find some evidence of this view at the beginning of Zephaniah. Just when they are on the verge of coming under God's judgment, Zephaniah characterizes certain citizens of Jerusalem as complacent, "resting on their dregs" (1:12). They have built houses and planted vineyards. They have certainly eaten their fill. At the root of their complacency, however, is this claim in 1:12: "The LORD will not do good, nor will he do harm." This is a very particular form of forgetting God. Their forgetfulness has led them to think that God is irrelevant and uninterested in them. If we can extrapolate from this disposition, then perhaps we can understand the seductive power of following other gods.

The seductive power of following other gods does not lie so much in their claims to power and their promise of using that power on behalf of their followers. Rather, such gods appear attractive to self-absorbed, complacent believers because they require so little from them. Such believers can "follow" these gods while still presuming to be in control of their lives and surroundings. Sacrifices to such gods may work like a weak form of insurance. Active participation in the worship of these gods may bring a sort of status. Perhaps such people can even presume to "follow" those gods in addition to following the LORD. In this light, following other gods becomes an activity that confirms someone's self-made status. Ultimately, such gods are not "followed" so much as used as one piece in a self-constructed edifice of self-sufficiency. The capacity of such gods to seduce or lure believers' hearts is connected to their ability to appear controllable, usable, and a suitable accompaniment to those who think that they eat their fill through their own cleverness, industry, and self-infused virtue. One might even say that the cascade of error resulting from eating one's fill in a way that leads to self-exaltation, the forgetting of God, and the following of other gods is ultimately a form of self-worship.

To the extent that these other gods have a reality beyond oneself, however, it may turn out that such gods are more demanding, less capable of manipulation than one first thinks. Their capacities to control believers may far outstrip believers' capacities to control them. Although believers may think that their engagements with such gods are limited, fully subject to the self-absorbed believer's powers of self-control and self-making, this may turn out not to be the case.[40]

Again, I want to be clear that I am offering some speculative reasons in the absence of any direct explanation in Deuteronomy. Even if one cannot fully explain how eating one's fill and forgetting the LORD lead to the worship of other gods, one must recognize an almost invariable pattern that ties eating one's fill in the promised land to forgetting the LORD. It is repeated so often in Deuteronomy that one could almost treat it as an inevitability. Before taking that step, however, it is important to look at Nehemiah 9:25-26. This passage seems to gloss Deuteronomy 6:10-12, noting that the Israelites captured cities, took possession of a rich land, and ate their fill. Nehemiah goes on to add that having eaten their fill and become fat, the Israelites "delighted themselves in your [the LORD's] great goodness." Indeed, in Nehemiah's account, the Israelites seem to have followed the command of Deuteronomy 8:10 that upon experiencing the bounty of the promised land, they should eat their fill and bless the LORD.

An attentive reader of Nehemiah will note, however, that after the Israelites have eaten their fill and delighted in God's goodness, Nehemiah 9:26 begins then with the surprising "Nevertheless, they were disobedient." This would seem to support further the claim that eating one's fill leads to forgetting God. The conjunction here between eating one's fill and disobeying God, however, is not causal. There is no normal or necessary connection between eating one's fill and forgetting God. One should also note that in Nehemiah the focus is on a disobedience that resulted in killing the prophets and not in forgetting God. Delighting oneself in God's great goodness should not have led the Israelites to abandon the LORD as their one and only, yet it did. What seems clear is that "eating one's fill" is a two-edged sword. In Nehemiah it can lead to delighting in the goodness of God. In Deuteronomy it leads to forgetting God.

Throughout Deuteronomy the image of eating one's fill in the promised land is tied to forgetting God. As Nehemiah's gloss on this theme indicates, however, the connection between eating one's fill and self-exaltation is not necessary. Rather, it seems that forgetting the LORD, self-exaltation, and following other gods are all dangers that arise from eating one's fill in a way that does not lead to delight in God's goodness. Despite our best hopes, Deuteronomy does not fully explain the process that leads from self-exaltation to forgetting God and following other gods. Doubtless this is a complex process rather than the result of any single decision that believers either communally or individually make at one definable point in time. Moreover, this disposition of forgetfulness is not simply about a failure of memory. Forgetting the LORD involves more than a failure of memory. It also tied to a failure to practice the right forms of attentiveness and to keep those practices of attentiveness rooted in catechesis.

The one point that is consistently repeated throughout Deuteronomy is that the dynamic of self-exaltation, forgetting God, and following other gods all begins when the Israelites have eaten their fill in the promised land. Deuteronomy does not explicate all that happens between eating one's fill, exalting oneself, forgetting God, and following other gods. In the same way, Nehemiah 9 does not relate how eating their fill led the Israelites to bless the LORD. Nevertheless, the clear way in which Deuteronomy places all of these steps together means that if believers are to counter our dispositions toward idolatry, we should attend to this matter of eating our fill. More particularly, it would appear, then, that one of the first steps toward remembering God, properly situating ourselves relative to God, and avoiding idolatry has to do with learning how to eat our fill in a way that leads to delighting in God's goodness.

How to Eat One's Fill

Perhaps the first thing to say is that some believers will rightly feel uneasy about the idea of reflecting on eating one's fill when there are many who live daily with severe levels of food insecurity as well as other forms of poverty. Nothing in the following reflections should deter believers from working to alleviate hunger and poverty on local, national, and global levels. Those are large tasks for which believers should be prepared to offer themselves, their time, and their money. Moreover, nothing in the following reflections should undermine the serious Christian practice of fasting for specified periods of time. Both before and after such periods believers can eat their fill. Indeed, the comments below about hospitality and generosity will invite believers to welcome those whose needs are more significant than their own. All of these points of unease, however, make it clear that one of the first things to do is to sharpen the notion of eating one's fill for those of us who have enough, and then some.

As I was in the midst of preparing an early draft of this chapter, I often passed by a billboard as I walked home. It was an advertisement for the Washington State Fair. There was a picture of man attempting to eat a cheeseburger that was roughly the size of his head. The tag line read, "Washington won't take full for an answer."[41] I have no doubt that the Washington State Fair is a wholesome enterprise for families from around the state. I simply raise this example not because it displays some new deformation in our economic life, but because it so nicely illustrates what has been the central doctrine for the cultures of post-Fordist capitalism for quite some time. As Michael Budde notes, "Reversing St. Paul's dictum ('anyone unwilling to work should not eat,' 2 Thess 3:10), the postfordist economy dictates that if people will not eat (and drink and buy compact discs and travel abroad and purchase the latest fashions, home appliances, and the like) in sufficient volume, then no one will work."[42] Budde continues by noting that however capitalism after its Fordist phase is to be understood and regulated, "it will doubtless include as major aspects those institutions, norms, and practices that related to the construction of consumption (in appropriate degree and kind)."[43]

Before eating our fill leads to delighting in or forgetting God, believers today need first to establish the conditions under which we might eat our fill. Believers today need to think about consumption in ways that our predecessors in the faith could not have imagined. Unless believers can achieve some measure of success here, they do not need to worry about eating their fill and forgetting God. Their unreflective participation in a culture that "won't take full for an answer" will already threaten to render them into subverters of the common good, destroyers of the environment, enemies of the poor, and indifferent or hostile to the claims of the gospel.

This indicates that before contemporary believers eat their fill in ways that lead them to delight in God's goodness, they first need to learn how to live within and resist a culture that won't take full for an answer. They need to develop capacities and skills to discern when enough is enough and to struggle to live in that light. One of the first steps in beginning to think about what is enough is to begin to figure out what questions to ask at the outset.

For example, if the questions we ask are simply focused on identifying the bare minimums that we need to survive, we are pushed to think we could get by with a little food and water, limited if any clothing and shoes, diminished and spartan shelter. Indeed, there are far too many in our world who lack even this much. Divesting oneself of one's possessions to this extent would still enable survival. No one, however, would mistake people in such circumstances for flourishing humans. To the extent that this volume focuses on believers in the United States, one would have to say that such people would have lost the capacity to function in most of the contexts in which they lived and worked. That is, their material needs might be covered, but their social needs would not.[44]

Instead of focusing the questions on identifying what is the bare minimum needed to survive, Christians with more than enough might begin by asking, "What do I need to occupy the place where God has put me with a sufficient level of dignity?" Obviously, this type of question is very different from questions about the bare minimum needed to survive. For example, it suggests that answers to questions about what is enough will differ for people based on their location and state in life.[45] In addition, once this question is asked, it may lead to questions about how one has landed in a particular place and station in life, whether one has really been placed there by God, and whether that place has been secured through or results in the oppression of others or whether it is possible to live faithfully in such a position. For example, I find it hard to believe that one could faithfully argue that God has called one to engineer guidance systems for first-strike nuclear weapons or that one has a divine vocation to be a lobbyist for the tobacco industry. I find it equally unlikely that God has called someone to be a victim of domestic violence, to be trafficked, or to be racially profiled.[46] Clearly, pursuing this line of questions faithfully may invite large-scale change and repentance.

Further, this initial question of what one needs to live with dignity in the place where God has called one and those questions that may follow on from it focus on individuals. These questions cannot, however, be answered well by individuals for themselves. There are two reasons for this. The first is that most of us have well-honed capacities for self-deception. If we try to struggle with these extremely demanding questions by ourselves, we are likely to misrepresent ourselves to ourselves. If we try to answer questions about our status and place in the world and what we need to occupy those places with dignity on our own, we are less likely to generate answers that will lead to faithful living.

The second reason for not trying to answer these questions by ourselves lies in the fact that Deuteronomy's concerns about eating one's fill and ultimately following other gods are not concerns addressed to individuals, but to the whole people of God. Of course, as I have already noted, Scripture has numerous examples of idolatry committed by individuals. Nevertheless, Scripture's accounts of the dispositions and practices that lead toward or away from idolatry most often focus on communities, not individuals. Hence, if the questions about what we need in order to occupy with dignity those places where God has put us are ultimately to move a community to eating its fill in a way that leads them to delight in God's goodness, they need to be argued, discussed, answered, and embodied by a community. Moreover, they will from time to time need to be reexamined by a community. Further, what counts as a sufficient level of dignity will need to be argued out by a community over time and may need to be revised in the light of changing circumstances.

In addition to probing what it means to have enough to live with dignity in the places where God has called us, Christians are called to love their neighbors. Indeed, along with loving God wholeheartedly, Jesus claims that love of neighbor is the other hook on which all the law hangs. Hence, our accounting of what is enough might also include sufficient means to love our neighbors through acts of hospitality and generosity and even activism.[47]

In a culture that won't take full for an answer, I suggest that believers who want to delight in God's goodness in the course of eating their fill will need to think of their lives in these terms: modesty with regard to possessions; deep riches in terms of their relationships forged in acts of hospitality in which they give and receive generously; and temperance in terms of how they gain, use, and dispense their wealth. These three terms would seem to comprise a minimum standard within which believers can usefully imagine and participate in "eating their fill" in ways that might invite delight in God's goodness.

I have taken these three elements from David McCarthy's book *The Good Life: Genuine Christianity for the Middle Class.* In discussing precisely these matters, McCarthy points out that "modest living is not good in itself, but is measured by our openness to giving and receiving a gift. . . . Modest living is good insofar as it makes us dependent upon gifts."[48] Modesty with regard to possessions, then, will not simply be about the amount of things we have. It will be about an amount that will leave us dependent upon gifts. We should never seek possessions as a way of rendering us independent of others. This resonates with Deuteronomy's concern that the abundance of the promised land will lead the Israelites to forget their dependence on God. It would seem much harder to forget one's dependence upon God if one is regularly dependent on one's neighbors and even upon strangers.

Given my comments above about self-deception, I recognize that it would be hard for me to make an adequate judgment about the amount of possessions I have. I have enough self-knowledge to know that if it turns out that I have relatively few possessions for someone who occupies my position, it is not because of modesty. Rather, it reflects the fact that I hate to shop and I have become increasingly impatient with what I take to be clutter in my life. Moreover, I know that I fail in terms of modesty because I am very uncomfortable with having to rely on others to meet my needs. Too often my things are a way of keeping me from being dependent on the gifts of others. In this respect, true modesty with regard to possessions enables the deep riches in terms of their relationships forged in acts of hospitality and giving and receiving generously. The latter requires the former.

Our oldest son brought this home to me one very snowy day. Our first house in Baltimore did not have a driveway. We were surrounded by a sidewalk on two sides, and people parked in the street. All of that meant that when it snowed, nobody could move around until we had cleared a lot of the snow. There was one snowblower in the neighborhood. It was temperamental and difficult to start. The unofficial rule in the neighborhood was that if you could get it started, then you could use it first. Once it was started, however, we aimed to keep it going for anyone else to use. A corollary to this rule was that once it was started, people needed to make sure the sidewalks for the older folks in the neighborhood were clear. We were all dependent on the generosity of the fellow who owned the snowblower, on the mechanical skill of others who seemed best placed to get the thing started, and on everyone's willingness to make sure we cleared the sidewalks and steps of the elderly in the neighborhood. Clearing snow was one of those unplanned occasions that ended up bringing the whole neighborhood together.

We later moved to a more rural/exurban house. We had a driveway and no sidewalks. Everyone else in the neighborhood had a snowblower. As we were shoveling out from the first large snowstorm, my oldest shouted above the roar of all the snowblowers that in our old neighborhood there was only one snowblower, but we did not have to do much shoveling. In this neighborhood he could see five snowblowers, but we had been working hard for a couple of hours shoveling and had not talked to anybody.

In addition to modesty with regard to possessions and the richness of relationships that follows from offering and receiving gifts, McCarthy seeks to rehabilitate the notion of temperance. He argues that temperance should not be confused with abstinence. Rather, temperance is closer to self-control. Thus, it is not strictly a form of self-denial. Rather, temperance enhances rather than limits our engagements and enjoyment of things because the self, not the thing, is in control. In this way, our engagement with things does not create disorder in our lives. Instead, it allows for a fuller, richer life. "Temperance is the virtue of putting human good at the center of our relation to things."[49]

At this point it is worth remembering the earlier discussion of Deuteronomy 6:6-9. The concrete practices believers adopt in order to help them keep "these words" and remember God must remain catechetically rooted, tied to the narratives, doctrines, and prayers that gave them their particular shape and rationale. This would be equally true for practices of modesty, temperance, hospitality, and generosity. Otherwise it would be relatively simple for these practices, once detached from the shape and intelligibility they gain from their role in Christian faith and worship, to become elements in processes of self-improvement that have little, if anything, to do with Christianity. Temperance can easily become an exercise in willpower for selves that no longer find their identity to be embedded in the ongoing story of God's redemption of the world in Christ. Under such circumstances, questions around eating one's fill can shift from the dynamic of forgetting God or delighting in God's goodness. Instead, believers' approaches to food can become driven by the desire to produce a certain type of body and attain a certain vision of health, most of which are damaging despite sometimes being clothed in scriptural language. These habits that McCarthy discusses will enable believers to make some progress in resisting a culture that won't take full for an answer. This should then enable believers to eat their fill and delight in God's goodness to the extent that we recognize God as the source of all the good gifts we have. Recognizing this certainly will help us avoid the self-exaltation and forgetfulness of God that Deuteronomy warns against. It will help us to partake with thanks. I, however, think there is more to say here about eating our fill.

One danger that afflicts us in ways that would have been unknown to our biblical forebears is that we are separated and perhaps even alienated from our food and most of our other possessions. Many of us have no contact with anyone who grows or produces the things we eat, drink, wear, or otherwise use. Many of us have never fixed or repaired any of our possessions, let alone understand how they were made and how they work. Indeed, several of our most expensive possessions are designed to keep us from working on them.[50]

I would like to suggest that this situation may also shape our capacities to eat our fill and delight in God's goodness in several ways. My overall suggestion is this: The more we separate and isolate our things from people (those who grow, produce, and service those things and those with whom we enjoy them) and places (where and how things are grown, produced, and serviced, and where we enjoy them), the harder it will be to partake of things in a way that leads us to delight in God's goodness. In that case, we become much more likely to enter into the dynamic of self-exaltation and forgetting God and, ultimately, following other gods. The more abstracted and alienated we become from the production of our food, drink, clothes, and other possessions, the more likely we are to fall prey to forms of self-exaltation tied to forgetting God. The less connected our things are from the people who grow, produce, build, and service them, the more likely we may be to take them simply to be the fruits of our own purchasing power. A culture that won't take full for an answer cannot survive if sufficient numbers of people refuse to separate themselves from places and things in these ways.

Further, a culture that won't accept full for an answer requires extremely high levels of disposability to thrive. Even as believers make progress in determining how much is enough, the habits of disposability may remain. To the extent that believers see their goods as immanently disposable and replaceable, it seems hard to imagine that this will not shape the quality of our delight in God's goodness.

Finally, as I noted above, biblical accounts of eating one's fill and either delighting in God's goodness or forgetting God are accounts about a community's activity, not simply the work of individuals. Believers would have to attend to both the outcomes and results of their own eating and to those of their neighbors. The greater the level of disconnection there is between individuals and their things, the harder it would seem to be to exercise the type of accountability imagined in the biblical accounts.

Such accountability may seem unimaginable for many congregations in the United States today. A culture that won't take full for an answer cannot be sustained unless our consumption of and participation in goods and services remain matters of private choice.[51] Moving matters of consumption from the private into the ecclesial realm will require and invite some rather difficult discussions. Recently, several large denominational bodies have discussed and altered their patterns of investment. They have made decisions that aim to improve the alignment between their investments and their convictions about the gospel. This is good. Nevertheless, those funds are understood to be communally owned and subject to community monitoring. It is not quite the same with individuals' wealth, property, and consumption. Much like questions about how we have come to occupy our present state, these are questions that would need to be discussed, argued, and negotiated over time by communities of wise believers.

As important as it is for communities of believers to discuss, argue, and negotiate these matters, it is equally important that they recognize that being able to entertain these potentially divisive and sensitive discussions faithfully and successfully is a high-level achievement. These discussions represent the deep end of the pool of ecclesial common life, and as such it may not be the best place to learn how to swim.

It may be a wiser course of action for Christians to begin to develop their capacities for thinking about, discussing, debating, and arguing about matters of wealth and consumption by beginning to practice concrete acts of hospitality and generosity in which our homes and our lives begin to be opened to disruptive friendships with those whom God puts in our way. I suspect that Christian communities that can discuss matters of their members' place and state in life and their consumption of goods and services in ways that enable them to eat their fill and delight in God's goodness will have already established patterns of hospitality and generosity.

The paragraphs above are some, but by no means all, of the considerations that help to sharpen the notion of eating one's fill in a culture that won't take full for an answer. They do not guarantee any level of success; they do not represent the only ways to make progress in these matters. Indeed, local Christian communities can and should offer the wider church their own accounts of how they learned and developed their capacities to eat their fill.

To conclude this chapter, it is crucial to recognize that one of the first contexts for Christians to hone our capacity to eat our fill in ways that will lead us to delight in God's goodness is through attentive participation in the Eucharist.[52] Where else can we best learn to eat and delight in God's goodness than in this meal where we participate so completely in the story of God's redeeming love for the world? For Christians, this meal is the first place for remembering God. In parallel to the concrete practices of Deuteronomy 6:6-9, the Eucharist is the foundational concrete action by which believers identify God as their "one and only" and commit themselves to finding their freedom in service to this God.

In this meal, gifts are offered to God; those gifts are transformed and received back from God. In this exchange, our capacities to offer thanks and to receive with gratitude are deepened. As our capacities to eat our fill and delight in God's goodness are sharpened through participation in the Eucharist, we may find that such worship may be exactly the preparation we need to open our homes to eat with others.[53]

For Christians in the United States, eating one's fill is both more complicated and more difficult than it may have appeared to our biblical forebears in Deuteronomy. Like them, however, Christians today are still faced with the challenge of eating one's fill in ways that lead to delight in God's goodness rather than to forgetting God.

Throughout Deuteronomy the trope of eating one's fill in the bounteous promised land appears tied to forgetting the LORD and worshiping other gods. I have tried to articulate how this forgetting may lead to idolatry, as Deuteronomy is not very clear about these connections. Further, I have raised issues about Christians in the United States who already have more than their fill can resist a culture that won't take full for an answer. To follow on from this, in the next chapter I will address the claim in both Ephesians and Colossians that greed is idolatry.

3

BOUNDED AND UNBOUNDED DESIRE

In the previous chapter I developed the notion, first broached in chapter 1, that idolatry represents a decisive point in that process in which our love and attention are incrementally directed away from God toward that which is not God. This idea that we might understand idolatry as a process led to an examination of Deuteronomy 6:4-14. In that passage the people of God are called to a single-minded, wholehearted love of God. Living into this calling requires both the cultivation of habits and practices of remembering and the avoidance of those things that would lead to forgetting God and following other gods. The practice that Deuteronomy regularly (though not clearly) ties to forgetting God is "eating one's fill" in the promised land. The previous chapter concluded with a discussion of how believers in the present might address the challenges of eating one's fill without forgetting the LORD.

As I suggested in chapter 1, by the time of the NT the challenges facing the churches addressed in Paul's letters are somewhat different from those faced by the Israelites on the verge of entering the promised land. Where Deuteronomy focuses on keeping the love and attention of the people of God focused on the one LORD, Paul is, for example, more concerned with addressing believers who until relatively recently were immersed in the idol-saturated world of the Roman Empire. Paul devotes significant portions of his letters to helping these believers faithfully to negotiate their paths through such a world. In chapter 1 I also examined how Paul executes such a strategy in 1 Corinthians 8–10 regarding meat offered to idols.

In contrast to this detailed and subtle discussion in 1 Corinthians 8–10, Paul directly, but perhaps less clearly, confronts idolatry in Ephesians and Colossians.[1] In Ephesians 5:3-5 and Colossians 3:5, Paul identifies greed with idolatry. In this chapter, through an examination of these two texts, I hope to show how one ought to understand greed in order to account for how Paul might identify greed as idolatry. In addition, I will argue that Ephesians and, to a greater degree, Colossians both suggest that the habits and practices of thanksgiving and gratitude will help believers avoid the greed that is idolatry.

Ephesians 5:3 indicates that a greedy person (πλεονέκτης) is an idolater. Similarly, Colossians 3:5 indicates that greed itself (πλεονεξία) is idolatry. It would seem, then, that these two verses place greed squarely on the agenda of a study such as this one. Both the last chapter and a general familiarity with the Gospels would also indicate that wealth and possessions have a clear connection to idolatry. Although wealth and greed are intimately connected, I will treat them separately. This is because I want to argue that their connections to idolatry are different and therefore they should be engaged in different ways.

Several questions and issues emerge from Paul's straightforward identification of greed with idolatry. First, although there are a number of texts in the OT and from the second temple period that indicate that greed is often a precursor or leads to idolatry, this is not what Paul says in Ephesians and Colossians. He identifies greed (or the greedy person) with idolatry. This needs some explanation.[2] In order to offer one explanation, I will look at the wider context of Ephesians 5 and Colossians 3 as a way of trying to be clear about the nature of greed and the connections that join greed to idolatry. It will become evident that although Paul seems to use the vocabulary of greed in fairly conventional ways, it is not at all clear how such conventional notions of greed can be identified with idolatry.[3]

To make this identification clearer, I will explore greed in relation to a doctrine of creation out of nothing. In this light, I will argue two points. First, understanding greed in the light of a doctrine of creation makes better sense of Paul's identification of greed with idolatry than a more conventional notion of greed as grasping for more than one is due. Indeed, unless one offers a robustly theological account of greed, such as a doctrine of creation can provide, Christians will have some difficulty in understanding Paul's comments. That is, it will be difficult to discern how greed can be identified as idolatry in the ways Paul does. If one does not offer such a theologically grounded notion of greed, one will have to make recourse to more conven-tional notions of greed as desiring or pursuing more than one is due. If one pursues this conventional, first-century notion of greed, one encounters two problems. First, one has the difficulty noted above of how to identify greed with idolatry as Paul does. Secondly, in a world such as ours that (for very good reasons) is not as comfortable with making clear judgments about what specific people deserve as first-century people were, we may be faced with a troubling conclusion. We may be led to claim that greed is not—as Gordon Gecko asserts—good. Rather, without agreed-upon standards for desert, greed is no longer possible. Such a recognition should not lead us to rejoice that this pathway to idolatry is no longer open to us. Instead, it is a sign of how much countercultural work Christians may need to do if we are to speak robustly to such contemporary matters as the growth in income inequality. All of that is in addition to the long process of forming, shaping, and bounding our desires so that we are not led into idolatry.

Further, clarifying Paul's claims about greed will also clarify the disposi-tions and practices Christians might cultivate in order to avoid the greed that is idolatry. I will focus on gratitude and thanksgiving as the dispositions and practices best able to counter greed. These dispositions and practices are ways in which God, through the Spirit, helps to order and focus our desires properly. It may not come as a surprise, then, that it is in the contexts of Colossians 3 and Ephesians 5 that Paul displays in some detail the role of thanksgiving in the Christian life. To begin I will turn to Ephesians 5:3-5 and Colossians 3:5, where Paul identifies greed and idolatry.

THE CONTEXT OF PAUL'S CLAIMS IN EPHESIANS AND COLOSSIANS

At the conclusion of a list of characteristics that are not fitting for those called to holiness, characteristics that Paul is eager for the Ephesians to avoid, he claims that no one who is greedy—that is, an idolater—will have a share in the kingdom of Christ and God. In the context of Colossians 3, greed is one of a list of vices that mark an "earthly" habit of life that Paul admonishes the Colossians to put away. Now that they are in Christ, their habit of life should lead them to focus on things "above." Colossians uses the more intense and even violent image of putting these "earthly" habits of life to death, in order to stress the need for believers to make a comprehensive and decisive break with their pagan past. Although the context of Colossians is relatively clear—listing "greed" as one of several vices to be avoided and then asserting that "greed is idolatry"—we are not told enough. In this respect the context of Ephesians 5 is richer and certainly comprehends everything one would want to say about Colossians. Hence, I will focus on Ephesians 5:5 at this point and then return to Colossians 3 later.

Ephesians 5:3-5 is part of a longer discussion about the common life of the Ephesian congregation that runs from the beginning of chapter 4 through the end of the epistle. This overall section is guided by Paul's admonition to the Ephesians in 4:1 to "walk in a manner worthy of your calling." This admonition reflects two discrete actions: God's calling and the Ephesians' walking. Whatever else Paul wants to claim about the Ephesians' walking, all of those claims depend on God's prior calling. Ephesians 1-3 focuses on this calling.

With regard to the Ephesians' walking, one should note that Paul also invokes the image of walking worthily in Philippians 1:27 and 1 Thessalonians 2:12. This idea always entails acts of judgment on the part of each congregation. Although Paul will give direct and concrete prescriptions to the Ephesians throughout chapters 4-6, the ongoing task of walking worthily always requires believers to discern the fit between their actions or possible actions, on the one hand, and some set standard, on the other hand. Thus, to succeed in this task, the Ephesians and all other believers need to develop a set of habits and dispositions that will enable them to recognize that certain actions and not others will result in a common life that conforms to the standard to which they aspire—that is, their calling in Christ.

Specifically, in 4:1-16 Paul discusses a number of habits, practices, and dispositions essential for the Ephesians if they are to walk in a manner worthy of their calling. These habits, practices, and dispositions are all directed toward maintaining the "unity of the Spirit in the bond of peace" (4:2). As Ephesians 4 develops, Paul shifts to addressing a number of things the Ephesians should avoid (4:17-24). These are practices, habits, and dispositions that would have been characteristic of the Ephesians prior to their incorporation into the body of Christ. In this respect Paul indicates that walking worthily requires the Ephesians to make a clean break with their pagan past and to live in a manner that clearly distinguishes them from the surrounding culture. To illustrate this Paul uses the image of taking off an old set of clothes and putting on a new set tailored by Christ.

Being clothed with these new Christ-tailored garments entails a transformation in the common life of the Ephesian church. This will involve adopting some new practices and avoiding others. Paul describes these in 4:24–5:2. Although scholars have long recognized that the vocabulary here is fairly conventional, the christological and ecclesiological context in which Paul deploys this vocabulary gives it a distinctively Christian tone.

Paul's identification of greed with idolatry appears in the following section, 5:3-14. Here Paul again uses fairly conventional vocabulary to articulate a number of vices the Ephesians should avoid. The vocabulary here describes practices that Jews and Christians would have typically used to castigate pagan culture.

As with Colossians, Ephesians 5:3-14 begins with a set of admonitions to the Ephesians to steer clear of a variety of activities. Paul initially names three of these activities: sexual misconduct (πορνεία), uncleanness (ἀκαθαρσία), and greed (πλεονεξία). The first of these terms is closely associated with a wide range of sexual misconduct. This may also be true of the second term, which is often translated as "uncleanness." At the same time, Paul understands that sex is never really a separate category of activity. Then as now, sex is bound up with issues of purity, identity, power, and desire, issues that implicate most aspects of life. Many English versions translate the third term in the list, πλεονεξία, as "covetousness." This is not an inaccurate translation, but it does obscure the fact that in 5:5 the greedy person (πλεονέκτης) is further identified as an idolater.[4] To retain this connection it might be better to translate this vice in 5:3 as greed also.

GREED 1.0

In Hellenistic Jewish texts ranging from the LXX, the Pseudepigrapha, Josephus, Philo, as well as the rest of the NT, πλεονεξία usually refers to that disposition of wanting, seeking, and holding onto more than one is due or more than one should have.[5] This overweening desire can be focused on money, but it need not be limited to money.[6] Sometimes the notion of what one is due or should have is presumed to have been set by nature or natural circumstances.[7] Other times it seems to depend on God.[8] In addition, Philo and Josephus both seem to assume that those with power are almost always greedy.[9] This combination of greed and power generally issues in violence and is thought to be the cause of most wars.[10] Even the poor, however, could be greedy. They would simply lack the power and means to act on that desire. On the face of things, and at this point in the discussion, we have little reason to think that Paul is using this term in any other than a completely conventional way to refer to the desire for more than one is due.

As I already noted, Paul aims to get the Ephesians, like the Colossians and his other primarily gentile congregations, decisively to separate themselves from their pagan past. In addition to this, Paul urges in 5:3 that none of these vices should be "noted" among the Ephesians. Most contemporary commentators take this as an admonition for the Ephesians to avoid even talking about such practices.[11] This is a strange interpretation on several counts. First, it seems hard to imagine any sort of moral reasoning going on among the Ephesians if they cannot even talk about particular practices to avoid. Further, Paul mentions such practices himself in 1 Corinthians 5, for example. In addition, it is hard to understand how mentioning a practice is, in itself, problematic. Most importantly, this is not the way the Greek verb ὀνομάζειν is used the two other times it appears in the epistle. In both 1:21 and 3:15 it refers much more precisely to naming something, to recognizing something and identifying it.

It therefore seems much better to take this verse as admonishing the Ephesians not only to stay away from these practices, but also to make sure that no one outside the congregation can note the presence of these practices among them. Paul's concern here would not be about what the Ephesians mention among themselves, but how they are perceived by those outside the congregation. In this way Paul is reflecting not only a concern for the integrity of the Ephesians' witness to their neighbors, but also a concern that the lives of the Ephesian Christians might bring God, Christ, and/or the gospel into disrepute needlessly.[12] This is consistent with Paul's concern throughout 5:3-14 with the ways in which the Ephesian church interacts with and is perceived by the wider culture. This concern will become relevant later.

The immediate reason Paul gives for avoiding all sorts of sexual misconduct, uncleanness, and greed is that such things are not "fitting" for those called to holiness. Paul has already established that God has called the Christians in Ephesus to holiness (1:4; 2:19-22). Moreover, he has just reminded the believers in Ephesus that they have been "sealed" by the Holy Spirit (1:13). Holiness is simply a constitutive part of Christian identity. Given Christian identity, particularly as narrated by Paul in chapters 2 and 3, certain practices are ruled out as fundamentally incompatible with that identity. This, then, is the context in which Paul identifies greed with idolatry in 5:3.

Paul adds to this list of vices in v. 4 by noting that indecency, foolish talk, and coarse jesting are also inappropriate.[13] The vices of v. 3 then reappear in v. 5. We read that no sexually immoral person, no impure person, and no greedy person will have a share in the "kingdom of Christ and God." In v. 5, however, the nouns are altered so that they refer to people who engage in these vices rather than the vices themselves.

Although there are a few parallel texts that note that love of money or avarice leads to the abandonment of God and the worship of idols,[14] here in Ephesians 5:5 and in Colossians 3:5 greed, πλεονεξία/πλεονέκτης, is directly identified as idolatry. It is striking that Paul focuses on greed, πλεονεξία, not love of money, φιλαργυρία (e.g., 1 Tim 6:10) as idolatry. Further, he does not make the point that greed is a precursor to idolatry; it *is* idolatry, or, in the case of Ephesians, the greedy person *is* an idolater.[15] Given that Paul appears to use πλεονεξία/πλεονέκτης in very conventional ways, the difficult question concerns how this might constitute idolatry.

By identifying greed as idolatry without explaining how this is so, Paul may be assuming that this identification was self-evident to his audience. If this is the case, however, we do not have much evidence for it. For example, much of the history of this verse's interpretation tends to treat greed as if it were the same as wealth and to treat wealth or abundance as a condition that disposes one toward idolatry much in the way Deuteronomy treats these matters (see Deut 6:11; 8:10-20; 11:13-17; 31:20; 32:15-18). In this light, Ephesians 5:5 is also often read alongside Matthew 6:24, where Jesus points out the impossibility of serving both God and Mammon.[16] In the case of Matthew, Jesus seems to be describing incompatible objects of desire. In this light, is it clear that serving Mammon rather than God would constitute idolatry. Greed, however, is not the object of desire. Instead, it describes the character or nature of our desire. Thus, it would not seem to fit easily within the same scope as Matthew 6:24. That is, one might say that interpreting Ephesians 5:5 in the light of Deuteronomy or Matthew 6:24 makes the interpretation of Ephesians 5:5 conform to other scriptural patterns of thought. Nevertheless, reading Ephesians 5:5 in the light of either Matthew 6:24 or Deuteronomy does not take as full an account of what Ephesians 5:5 actually claims—that is, that greed *is* idolatry.

Greed 2.0

If we are to make better sense of Paul's claim that greed is idolatry, I suggest that it may be fruitful to begin by returning to look at the doctrine of creation, in particular, creation out of nothing. As several scholars have noted, this doctrine is not directly articulated in Scripture.[17] I have no stake in claiming that the biblical authors thought in terms of this doctrine. In Romans 4:17 Paul identifies God as "the one who brings to life those who were dead and calls into being that which was not." This claim, however, is hardly a full-blown account of creation *ex nihilo*. It does give us some reason to expect that later Christian reflection on the God who calls into being that which was not might be acceptable to Paul's way of thinking even if he did not articulate things this way himself.

Doctrinally, Christians want to assert that before God's creation there was nothing. This is because "there could be no reality independent of, and potentially resistant to, the divine will, nor could it be supposed that the world as we know it is a lower, inferior part of the divine being."[18] Such a recognition establishes that divine being and human being are fundamentally distinct. "The divine is life, truth, goodness, beauty; created being *receives* life, truth, goodness, beauty from the divine, but is in itself, nothing."[19]

In the light of this relationship between creator and creature, we read in Genesis that immediately upon creating humans in the image of God, God blesses the humans. In the course of blessing the humans God addresses one of their most basic needs and desires—hunger. God's first words to the humans are "See, I have given you every plant yielding seed that is upon the face of the earth, and every tree with seed in its fruit; you shall have them for food" (Gen 1:29). This indicates two things. First, it shows that humans are created with desire (or hunger), for which God graciously provides fulfillment. Our hungers or desires are not the result of a deficiency in our creation, nor the result of our sin. Rather, desire is built into being a creature, and humans share the desires particular to all creatures. Moreover, humans have a distinct desire for God that is tied to being created in the image of God.[20] Secondly, this offering of the material world typifies the relationship between God and humans in the garden. As Alexander Schmemann notes, "All that exists is God's gift to man and it exists to make God known to man, to make man's life communion with God."[21]

In the garden God's gift and human desire are in right relation to each other. This then enables communion with God. There is, in the conventional sense of πλεονεξία, no greed. It is important to note, however, that is not because human desiring is proportioned to what is due to each. Rather, it is that human desiring is properly ordered in relation to God's gracious provision to best enhance the prospects of communion with God. Strictly speaking, humans are due nothing from God. Nevertheless, they are graciously offered a share in fellowship with God (1 Pet 1:4). Moreover, this fellowship with God also enables and sustains one's proper relationships to others and to the rest of creation.

In the light of Schmemann's initial reflection on God's provision for human hunger, one can then see that the fall is precipitated by humans eating what was not offered. They have grasped at something beyond the gifts God has given; their desire has outstripped God's gracious provision. It certainly seems reasonable to characterize this grasping at something beyond God's gifts as greed. Rather than desiring more than one is due, greed would be desiring something more or other than what God has offered or provided— that is, communion. Indeed, in the Greek text of the Life of Adam and Eve we read that Eve's πλεονεξία results in the fall.[22]

In this light, greed rejects and thus breaks the communion between God and humans (as well as the communion between God, humans, and the rest of creation). If one thinks of the refusal of God's gift of fellowship as the most fundamental way in which humans turn from God or forget God, then we have a basis for understanding how greed can be idolatry in a way that might be distinct from the other vices Paul admonishes the Ephesians to avoid.

If there is some plausibility to this, it can help make better sense of Paul's claims about πλεονεξία and idolatry in Ephesians and Colossians. Recall that according to the conventional uses of this term in the Greek of Paul's day, πλεονεξία referred to desiring or grasping for more than one is due. In a world highly structured by social status and location, it was relatively straightforward to discern what was due to whom given their relative position in society. In this light, it is certainly possible to offer a coherent account of greed, but it remains difficult to account for how greed can be idolatry.

In the light of a doctrine of creation out of nothing, humans are, strictly speaking, due nothing. They are, nevertheless, created with desires for which God offers abundant provision. Moreover, they are both created with a desire for God and graciously offered communion with God. The God who wills communion with them graciously addresses their desires. In doing so, God renders humans capable of remaining rightly and peaceably related to God, others, and the rest of creation. In this context, greed is not primarily about wanting more than one is due. Rather, greed is the reflection of desire that is unbounded and unconcerned to live within and maintain God's gift of communion.[23]

Greed does not transgress a social standard of what is appropriate; it distorts and damages a relationship of communion by desiring something other than God or by subverting that desire for God. In effect, it is the rejection of that communion and a turning away from God to attend to that which is not God—hence, idolatry.

This specification should remind believers that idolatry at its root is a misdirection of love and attention away from God and toward something else that is not God. It is crucial to understand, however, that this is not a judgment that the created world is itself the problem. The material world as such, including such things as food, commodities, and works of art, or even sex, need not draw our attention and love away from God. Such things would appear to be given by God to address our hungers. When well-ordered and properly related to God, these desires can in many cases further sharpen our vision of God and enhance our devotion. Our desiring and engagements with the material world threaten to become idolatrous when and if they truncate or misdirect our attentions from God.[24] It is important to note here that desire does not need to be extinguished, but rightly directed.[25]

Further, when the misdirection of our desires becomes idolatrous, it not only damages our communion with God, it also damages our communion with each other. This recognition is deeply embedded in Scripture in a variety of ways. Narratively, it is striking that after the communion between God and humans is damaged in Genesis 3, what follows is the first murder in Genesis 4 and a subsequent spiral of violence such that by Genesis 6:11 God calls creation "corrupt and filled with violence." In the prophetic literature, it is quite common to recognize that Israel's idolatry is inextricably tied up in the corruption of their economic, legal, and social life. Nowhere is this clearer than in Amos 5. Finally, there is the stirring admonition from 1 John 4:20-21, "Those who say, 'I love God,' and hate their brothers or sisters, are liars; for those who do not love a brother or sister whom they have seen, cannot love God whom they have not seen. The commandment we have from him is this: those who love God must love their brothers and sisters also." These examples should suffice to note that the greed that idolatrously abandons communion with God for that which is not God cannot but distort our relations with others.

Some significant points follow from this. First, we now inhabit a world in which the ordering, binding, or limiting of desire poses a severe economic threat since it would dramatically disrupt our patterns of consumption. Given this and the fact that we have largely (and perhaps wisely) abandoned regimented accounts of what specific people are due, it may actually be ever more difficult, if not impossible, to specify what counts as greed. This may account for why the unprecedented levels of income inequality we experience today can generate so little political traction. If, as was noted in the previous chapter, we live in a culture that "won't take full for an answer," then how can one sustain the judgment that some have too much? The extent to which discussions about income inequality gain any traction at all is testimony to the fact that the gap between the top earners and the rest of the population has become so great that it offends even when there is no widely held standard against which to base that judgment. Even so, most of the arguments in favor of narrowing this gap are based on data indicating that such levels of inequality are in nobody's long-term financial interest rather than on the transgression of some agreed-upon limits to our desires. There are numerous powerful arguments that may lead believers and others to work toward the reduction of current levels of income inequality because of the disproportionate impact of such inequality on the poor both locally and globally.[26] In the absence of widely accepted ways for thinking about limits on our desires, it would be hard to argue against it on the grounds that it constitutes greed—at least as traditionally understood.

Instead, Christians may want to focus on contemporary manifestations of greed by noting the impact of such widespread discrepancies in wealth in terms of our communion with God and one another.[27] In his homily on the rich man who decides to pull down his barns and build new ones to hold his abundant harvest, Basil the Great says, "Though his barns were filled to bursting with the abundance of his goods, his miserly heart was still not satisfied. By constantly adding more to what he already possessed, augmenting the existing surplus with annual increases, he fell into this intractable dilemma. He refused to be satisfied with what he already had on account of his greed, yet neither could he store the new harvest on account of its abundance." Ironically, "What would cause others to rejoice causes the greedy person to waste away."[28] Basil's solution to this quandary is to share generously with those in need.[29] For Basil, this sort of greed is a sign both that the greedy fail to recognize their dependence upon God and that their greed also breaks the bonds that hold us together with one another.[30]

Secondly, if greed is idolatry in the sense of unbounded desire that breaks the bonds of God's gift of communion, how might Christians avoid Paul's admonitions and judgments against πλεονεξία and the πλεονέκτης? At a general level this must require a shaping or directing of our desires so that they are more properly proportioned and directed to God's gift of communion, so that we more fully desire that communion. Until that time when we will know just as fully as we have been known, when our communion with God is transformed by the reconciliation of all things in Christ, it would seem that to avoid the idolatry that is greed, our desires need to be shaped, directed, and healed by the work of the Spirit.

Unlike those religious and philosophical traditions that seek to extinguish desire, Christianity has focused on the formation and training of desire. There is a rich tradition within Christian theology devoted to training desires. Rather than unpack that tradition, I plan to focus on a more narrowly Pauline line of inquiry, returning to Colossians 3 and Ephesians 5. In these passages,

I will suggest, Paul offers a brief but particular course in the training of desire so that we can avoid the idolatry that is greed.

THANKSGIVING

Recall that in 5:3 Paul rehearses a set of activities the Ephesians are to avoid. Among these is greed (πλεονεξία). By 5:5 these activities are touched on again. This time Paul uses πλεονέκτης to speak of greedy people and identifies such people as idolaters. In between these series of vices, which are inappropriate to those called to holiness, Paul says, "Let there be thanksgiving" (εὐχαριστία [5:4]). Against all of these, the single term "thanksgiving" stands as the sole counterweight to the six vices mentioned.

The introduction of thanksgiving injects an interesting twist into the discussion.[31] So far, the vices to be avoided in this passage are all related to interactions with others. The antidote to all of these destructive patterns of behavior and speech is not renewed focus on improving interpersonal relations but thanksgiving to God. There seem to be several respects in which this might be so.

Recall that I have argued that greed's identity with idolatry is tied to desire that is unbounded and unconcerned with what God has offered, that is, communion. The desires of the greedy become incorrectly or inappropriately focused on other people or on aspects of the material world. For Paul, and believers more generally, desires for others and for the material world are not wrong in and of themselves. Rather, such desires need to be ordered in relation to our ultimate desire for God. Thanksgiving is a way of educating, reforming, and refocusing our desires toward God. Cultivating the habit of thanksgiving enables believers to love God properly and to love others and the rest of creation in ways that enhance rather than frustrate their communion with God.

We can begin to see this by looking at the ways in which Paul uses the verb εὐχαριστέω and the noun εὐχαριστία. Typically, Paul's letters begin with expressions of thanks to God for the communities to which he is writing (see Rom 1:8; 1 Cor 1:4; 2 Cor 1:11; Eph 1:16; Phil 1:3; Col 1:3; 1 Thess 1:2; 2 Thess 1:3; Phlm 1:4). Paul's thanks is always directed to God and takes into account the work that God is doing in these congregations. In 1 and 2 Thessalonians this general theme of Paul's greeting is extended into the body of the epistle as Paul repeatedly offers thanks for the community, its reception of the gospel, and the joy it has brought to Paul (1 Thess 2:13; 3:9; 2 Thess 2:13; see also 1 Cor 4:15). He even offers thanks for his coworkers Priscilla and Aquila (Rom 16:4). Those of us who read Paul's epistles regularly and have become familiar with his epistolary conventions can often treat these thanksgivings in a cursory way. These thanksgivings reflect a deep love and desire for the people in these communities, and such desire leads him to thank God. Even when he is frustrated by and with these communities, this does not seem to diminish his longing for them or his gratitude to God.[32]

Further, when it comes to the material world, and food in particular, Paul holds the view that "all of God's creation is good and nothing is to be rejected if it is received with thanksgiving" (1 Tim 4:4). Paul expresses similar views in Romans 14:6 and, tellingly, with regard to being served meat that may have been sacrificed to an idol in 1 Corinthians 10:30.

Thanksgiving plays a central role in Paul's collection for famine relief in Jerusalem, too. In 2 Corinthians 9 Paul urges the Corinthians to be generous in giving money for this collection. Perhaps surprisingly, their generosity does not result in Paul's gratitude to them, but in offerings of thanks to God. Although he does not use the term εὐχαριστία in Philippians 4:10-20, the same theme appears. The Philippians' generous gift to Paul results in thanks to God, who will then repay the Philippians. Moreover, earlier in Philippians 4:6, Paul has proposed that thanksgiving is the alternative to being anxious about one's needs.

Throughout his letters Paul extends thanks to God for his coworkers and his congregations. Further, he indicates that thanksgiving can properly sanctify believers' engagements with the material world, both the things they consume and the things they give away. These verses in themselves suggest that thanksgiving is a fundamental disposition and practice that will help believers rightly situate their desires for God, others, and the rest of creation in a way that will short-circuit the greed that is idolatry.

In Ephesians and Colossians Paul offers an even fuller display of the role thanksgiving may play in educating, forming, and reforming the desires of believers. Indeed, one can argue that in these letters Paul suggests that thanksgiving may be the summative act of the Christian life. Although the identification of greed with idolatry in Colossians 3:5 is not juxtaposed with thanksgiving as directly as it is in Ephesians 5, Colossians 3 does say a bit more about the role of thanksgiving in the Christian life. Hence, I will focus on Colossians, recognizing that what is said more directly in Colossians about thanksgiving could be inferred in Ephesians as well.

Colossians begins with Paul thanking God for the Colossians' reception and growth in the gospel. As Colossians 1 continues Paul displays the focus of his prayers for the community. In particular he prays that God will strengthen the community to endure whatever may befall them. He further prays that such endurance will be a cause of joy for them, leading them to offer thanks to God for granting them a "share in the inheritance of the saints in the light" (1:12).[33] As Paul continues it becomes clear that this inheritance has been established through Christ's reconciling work on the cross. In 1:15-20 Paul describes this work as the restoration of communion with God, noting that Christ's role in creation makes him the fitting vehicle through which the Father restores communion with "all things."

The key passage for my purposes is Colossians 3:12-17. Here Paul continues the images of death and renewal that stood behind his admonition to put to death a range of earthly practices, of which greed, which is idolatry, is one.[34] What follows is a series of imperative verbs that build on each other and that are intimately bound up with thanksgiving.[35]

The first imperative enjoins the Colossians to clothe themselves with particular habits and practices. Having stripped off this old earthly self, the Colossians are urged to clothe themselves with a range of dispositions and practices (compassionate hearts, kindness, humility, meekness, and patience and forbearance) so that they may properly forgive each other and live reconciled lives (3:12-13). Paul then goes on to say, "Above all, [clothe yourselves][36] in love, which binds everything together in perfect harmony" (3:14).

In addition to this, or in the light of having done this, the Colossians are to let the peace of Christ be the ultimate arbiter over their hearts. Most immediately, Paul addressed the peace of Christ in 1:20, where the blood of the cross is the catalyst in reconciling all things to God, particularly in restoring communion with alienated humans.[37] Many English translations render this imperative in 3:15 as "Let the peace of Christ rule in your hearts" (NRSV, ESV, NIV, KJV). This is not strictly incorrect, but it does not quite bring out the idea that the Greek imperative βραβευέτω refers to acting as an arbiter or umpire in a contest.[38] The imperative here seems designed to impress on the Colossians and all believers that the desires of the heart need to be subjected to Christ's arbitration. This seems very similar to Paul's admonition in 2 Corinthians 10:5 to bring every thought captive to Christ. The idea in each case is not to obliterate thoughts or desires but to subject them to Christ's healing gaze.

In that light, there is little reason to think that allowing the peace of Christ to arbitrate the desires of one's heart will be peaceful. Rather, subjecting the desires of one's heart to the peace of Christ is part of the hard work of spiritual transformation; this will not be quick, simple, or painless. Nevertheless, Paul indicates that the practice of allowing Christ to arbitrate the desires of the Colossians' hearts is directed toward two particular ends. First, as 3:15 continues, it enables the unity to which God has called the body of Christ, (cf. Eph 2:14-16). Secondly, Paul goes further. He indicates that allowing the peace of Christ to arbitrate in their hearts will enable them to fulfill the imperative to "become thankful people" (εὐχάριστοι γίνεσθε [3:15]). The construction of this series of imperative verbs could indicate that when, or to the extent that, the peace of Christ arbitrates the desires of the Colossians' hearts, then they can and will become thankful people.

Thus far, I have suggested that Christians may avoid the greed that is idolatry to the extent that their desires regarding all things are properly ordered toward communion with God. Cultivating the habits of thankfulness appears to be one of the ways that Paul imagines Christians can maintain the proper ordering of their desires. Becoming thankful people, however, depends on the extent to which the peace of Christ arbitrates the desires of believers' hearts.

Before moving further in Colossians, it is important (but not surprising) to point out that, although Colossians is rarely invoked in most liturgies, this pattern is deeply woven into the movements of the Eucharist. In my own tradition we enter the service asking that the thoughts of our hearts might be cleansed by the Spirit so that we might worthily magnify God's holy name. In more traditional forms of the initial penitential rite we confess that "we have too much followed the devices and desires of our own hearts."[39] Only in the light of confessing these and other sins, receiving forgiveness and absolution, and sharing the peace of Christ are we then able to offer our sacrifice of thanks and praise. Participation in the Eucharist regularly places us in that position where we learn how to let the peace of Christ arbitrate the desires of our hearts so that we can become properly thankful people.

Such a scenario reminds us that becoming thankful people is not a one-time achievement but an ongoing work of a lifetime devoted to allowing the Spirit, the Spirit of Christ, to arbitrate the desires of our hearts. This will no doubt involve rooting out and transforming distorted habits and affections and cultivating others as the Spirit invites us ever more fully to desire that which God desires for us. Further, although Paul uses imperative verbs here, they are in the third person. Neither the Colossians nor contemporary believers are the initiators of these activities.[40] The peace of Christ can arbitrate the desires of our hearts because God has called us back to God through Christ. God has moved to restore the communion that God desires with us.

Returning to Colossians, Paul concludes this passage by commanding them to let the word of Christ dwell (ἐνοικείτω) in them richly. This will enable them to help each other cultivate wisdom and to sing thankfully in their hearts to God.[41] If, as I have suggested, these imperative verbs build on each other, then, to the extent that the peace of Christ arbitrates the desires of believers' hearts, the word of Christ can dwell in them richly.[42] The upshot of this indwelling is that the Colossians will be able to grow in wisdom and in their capacity for gratitude. This would seem to be an important supplement to the notion that cultivating the habit of thanksgiving is the way to avoid the greed that is idolatry. This is because even though our desiring may be disordered, unbounded, and unconcerned by God's desire for communion with us, people desire what is attractive to them. That is, we desire the good. As fallen humans, however, we are often mistaken about what the good is. The vices listed earlier in Colossians or in Ephesians always confront people through their attractiveness, through their ability to appear to be virtuous, or to play upon some aspect of virtue or beauty without actually resulting in beauty or virtue. Thus, they are able to distract believers' attentions and hearts away from God. The wisdom that results from the indwelling of the word of Christ is crucial for discerning the difference between those things worthy of our desire and those things that only appear so, between desires ordered to enhance communion with God and those that will frustrate such communion.[43]

The culmination of all these imperative verbs is action. "Whatever you do in word or deed, do all of these things in the name of Jesus, thanking God the father through him" (3:17). Action in word or deed should be done in the name of Christ and in thankfulness to God. The verb "to do" in 3:17 is not in the imperative voice. Nevertheless, it seems to carry the force of a strong admonition since it covers "all things." One might argue that the forcefulness of an imperative verb is assumed. Alternatively, it is not crucial that it be so. The preceding series of imperatives has presumed a scenario that, if realized, will in the normal course of things result in all things being done in the name of Christ with thankfulness to God. It need not be commanded; it will be the unforced result of all the other imperatives.

CONCLUSION

In both Ephesians 5:3-5 and Colossians 3:5 Paul identifies greed with idolatry. Without question, Paul is casting a new metaphor by identifying greed with idolatry.[44] Nevertheless, it is not self-evident how this identification is supposed to work. One possible way of doing this is through attention to the doctrine of creation. Through this one can see that God implants desire, including a desire for God, within humans. God meets that desire through offering humans communion with God. As long as their desire was rightly aligned with God's offer of communion, humans enjoyed fellowship with God. In Genesis 3 we read that humans desired something beyond what God had offered and, in effect, turned their back on God's offer of communion. This desire, which is unbounded and unconcerned with communion with God, is greed. That such greed rejects God's offer of communion and pursues other things that are not God sustains the claim that greed is idolatry. This, then, becomes one way of making sense of idolatry. In addition, this leads to several ways of rethinking conventional notions of greed and their applicability to the contemporary world. I should be clear at this point. I am not claiming that my reasoning that ties greed to idolatry through a doctrine of creation replicates Paul's reasoning or the reasoning of any member of the Ephesian or Colossian congregation. Given the cryptic nature of Paul's comments on this matter in both Ephesians and Colossians, I am not sure we could reconstruct his reasoning with any degree of confidence. Nevertheless, I will claim that this does make sense of Paul's claims in ways that are consistent with a whole network of Christian convictions and practices.

More importantly than reconstructing Paul's reasoning in tying greed to idolatry, by returning to Ephesians 5 and Colossians 3 I have suggested that Paul seems to offer "thanksgiving" as that disposition and practice which works to counter the greed that is idolatry. Colossians 3 in particular offers a dense account of the ways in which growth in Christ both sustains and is sustained by habits of thanksgiving.

In the next chapter I will explore fear and insecurity as dispositions and practices that inevitably move the people of God into idolatry and the ways in which the practice of love may help us to cast out fear.

4

INSECURITY, LOVE, AND MISSION

INTRODUCTION

In the previous chapter I examined Paul's claim in Ephesians 5:3, 5 and Colossians 3:5 that greed is idolatry. Rather than taking greed in its conventional sense of desiring or grabbing for more than one is due, I argued that the best way to understand how greed could be idolatry is in terms of a doctrine of creation. Understanding that God's gift to humans of communion with God suggests that one way of understanding greed is in terms of grasping at something other than God's gracious offering of communion. Rejecting communion with God in favor of something that is not God becomes idolatry. Further, in the light of Ephesians 5 and Colossians 3, Paul seems to suggest that habits of thanksgiving are the appropriate habits to cultivate in order to avoid the idolatry that is greed.

In this chapter I want to explore the notion that habits of disordered fear and insecurity often direct the people of god toward idolatry. The first texts I will examine come from books of Kings. This will lead to an exploration of Isaiah 30–31 and Luke, where further manifestations of fear and insecurity are connected to lapses toward idolatry.

Fear is a disposition that threatens to lead the people of God into idolatry. Part of this threat lies in fear's close connection to love. Indeed, I will go on to explore the claim in 1 John 4 that love, when it is perfected, casts out fear. Thus, one might claim that love, particularly the love of other believers, is the habit that might keep at bay the fear that leads to idolatry. At the same time, I want to suggest that this love, as understood by the writer of 1 John, has the potential to be dangerously parochial and inward looking if it is not also combined with an account of Christian mission that addresses this. The chapter closes with such an account.

FEAR—THE GOOD AND THE BAD

As a way of directing the scriptural explorations at the heart of this chapter, I want to begin with some brief observations about fear. On the one hand, fear is an emotion or an emotional response to certain stimuli. We think it perfectly normal to be afraid and to flee from the oncoming car about to hit us. A loud and unexpected noise causes us to jump in fright. The sound of the dentist's drill causes us to break out in a cold sweat. We treat the person who is utterly incapable of fear as someone with a disorder. On the other hand, we also consider someone who cannot and does not feel joy in moments of great success, or revulsion in acts of senseless violence, or compassion in the face of someone's genuine pain as also deficient in important respects.[1] Fear is not always a bad thing. In some cases, lack of fear reflects a serious problem.

Although there may be some respects in which fear is simply a deeply inbred instinct or emotion that is beyond our control and beyond moral examination, this is not always so. There may well be respects in which what we fear and how much we fear and when we fear are open to examination, judgment, and change in the light of reflection. That is, there are some respects in which fear is largely amoral and some respects in which fear should be subject to moral reflection.

In his examination of fear and the moral life, Scott Bader-Saye rightly reminds us that although fear is a crucial element in our moral lives, in and of itself, fear is neither evil nor a vice.[2] Nevertheless, "excessive or disordered fear can tempt us to vices such as cowardice, sloth, rage, and violence. It can also inhibit virtuous actions such as hospitality, peace-making, and generosity."[3] In this respect, fear shapes the type of people we become, coloring our perceptions of what is going on around us and guiding judgments about the proper course of action.

This type of fear is deeply connected to love. Indeed, one can say that fear comes from love.[4] This is due to the fact that love creates and recognizes the possibility of painful loss or limitation. Fear arises out of the recognition of the potential of loss of those we love. At the same time, fear of loss or limitation can sharpen and enhance our love. Thus, "Fear exists at the nexus of love and limitation."[5]

Augustine poignantly displays this connection between love and fear at the point of loss. In book 4 of his *Confessions* Augustine reflects on the death his close friend. Their friendship was "sweet to me beyond all the sweetnesses of life that I had experienced."[6] When that friend suddenly dies, Augustine is overcome with grief, a grief that exhausts him. "I found myself heavily weighed down by a sense of being tired of living and scared of dying. I suppose the more I loved him, the more hatred and fear I felt for the death that had taken him from me."[7]

In response to such love and loss, one might adopt a stoic approach, an attempt to overcome or eliminate fear and the pain of loss through reducing or eradicating one's loves and attachments. One sees this approach in many of the standard romantic comedies. The story begins with a central character who, when faced with the loss or rejection of a loved one, vows never to love again. The hero reasons that fear of suffering the pain of another lost love is more powerful than the joys that love might provide. Nevertheless, over time and in the presence of the right lover, the hero overcomes fear of loss and loves again.[8] The message here seems to be that this sort of stoicism cannot sustain a flourishing human life for very long. Moreover, it would seem to point out that regardless of the pain our loves might inflict on us, we should not attempt to obliterate our desires and capacities for love. This would, as Augustine recognizes, put us in a very difficult position. "What madness not to understand how to love human beings with awareness of the human condition? How stupid man is to be unable to restrain feelings in suffering the human lot!"[9]

What Augustine and the Christian tradition more generally come to see is that in order to avoid this "madness" humans cannot and should not seek to obliterate their desires out of a fear of the suffering that comes with loss. Rather, our love has to be rightly ordered in God. Love rightly ordered in God is able to love the right things in the right ways at the right times. Properly ordered love will not eliminate fear. It certainly will not eliminate the pain of lost loves. It will, however, keep our fear properly ordered, too. I will have more to say here when it comes time to think of how to avoid the fear that disposes us to idolatry. For now, this is sufficient to provide some basics about fear. In some respects fear is natural to us; it is tied to love and the possibility of loss; as our love and our capacities for love find their proper order and shape in God, our fears will likewise be ordered and shaped.

At the same time, Bader-Saye has already indicated that fear can lead us into vice (and idolatry) when it is disordered, when we come to seek safety and security above all else. "Disordered and excessive fear has significant moral consequences. It fosters a set of shadow virtues, including suspicion, preemption, and accumulation, which threaten traditional Christian virtues such as hospitality, peacemaking, and generosity."[10] As I now move on to discuss specific biblical passages, I want to show that it is precisely these fear-driven shadow virtues such as suspicion, preemption, and accumulation that dispose believers towards idolatry.[11] Again, strikingly, this idolatry rarely is the result of knowingly pursuing evil. Rather, it is much more likely to be the result of seeking an apparent good or a real good in the wrong way.

Fear, Suspicion, Idolatry

Despite its auspicious beginnings, Solomon's reign does not end well. His entanglements with foreign wives lead to idolatry and bring God's judgment. God tells him that the bulk of his kingdom will not pass to his son, but to another. Moreover, in 1 Kings 9:15-25 we learn that in order to rebuild parts of Jerusalem and other cities, Solomon introduces policies of forced labor among the Israelites.[12] If this were not enough to cast him as a new Pharaoh, we also learn in this chapter that he marries a daughter of the Egyptian king. In 1 Kings 11:26 we are introduced to Jeroboam, the one who will subsequently become king over the ten Northern tribes. Because he is industrious, Solomon puts Jeroboam in charge of all the forced labor required of the tribe of Joseph. The prophet Ahijah, through a very public symbolic act, informs Jeroboam that God will give him control over ten of the twelve tribes of Israel because of Solomon's idolatry (11:31-33). In a scene that further invokes themes from Exodus, when Solomon hears of this he tries to kill Jeroboam, who flees to Egypt (1 Kgs 11:26-40).

After Solomon's death his son Rehoboam assumes the throne. Jeroboam returns from Egypt and the two meet at a great national gathering in Shechem designed to confirm Rehoboam as king. Instead of lodging a counterclaim to the throne, Jeroboam asks on behalf of the nation that Rehoboam lift the "heavy yoke" of forced labor that Solomon had imposed (1 Kgs 12:1-4). Rehoboam decides to take a few days to consider this request.

His father's counselors urge Rehoboam to accede to this request. Instead he follows the rather bawdy advice of his buddies and declares that he will make things even harder on the people (cf. Exod 5:6-9). Without the capacity to invoke any plagues to gain redress from their oppressor, the people reject Rehoboam and his policies and turn to Jeroboam as their king. Rehoboam flees back to Jerusalem, where he will reign over Judah and Benjamin. Thus, in a manner that achingly recalls Moses leading the people out of slavery in

Egypt, Israel is divided. Indeed, in contrast to Exodus, the establishment of the Northern kingdom requires very little struggle or violence. The division of the monarchy happens with remarkable ease.

Jeroboam sees his first tasks as securing the integrity of his kingdom and the loyalty of his people. Despite the fact that the LORD has promised to sustain Jeroboam's kingdom as long as he keeps God's commandments and walks in the way of the LORD, Jeroboam suspects that the Israelites are not fully loyal to him. He recognizes that walking in the ways of the LORD will require the Israelites to go up to Jerusalem, to Rehoboam's kingdom, to offer sacrifices and to worship the LORD. Jeroboam not only fears for his own safety, but he fears that if the people regularly worship in Jerusalem, their allegiance will shift to Judah (1 Kgs 12:25-27).

In Exodus 32, the people's fear that Moses had left them led to the casting of the golden calf. Here, in 1 Kings 12, the Moses-like Jeroboam fears that the people will leave him. This leads him to make two sets of golden calves. He tells the Israelites, "You have gone up to Jerusalem long enough. Here are your gods, O Israel, who brought you up from the land of Egypt" (1 Kgs 12:28, cf. Exod 32:4). Of course, one cannot simply produce new gods. These new gods need a new priesthood and new places of worship and parallel festivals. Jeroboam provides all of these.

Given the conditions under which the two kingdoms divided, Jeroboam's suspicions seem well founded, and his actions might even seem prudent.[13] For example, we know that Rehoboam, upon his return to Jerusalem, gathered his troops and was prepared to march north (1 Kgs 12:21). As Rehoboam is preparing for this expedition, Shemaiah, a "man of God," tells him not to proceed to fight against his relatives in Israel. The divided kingdom is the LORD's own doing. Even so, Rehoboam's activity does make it seem unwise for Jeroboam to allow the Northern tribes to continue to worship in Jerusalem. It seems perfectly prudent for Jeroboam to provide a viable alternative within his own boarders.

Although Jeroboam's actions are neither prudent nor faithful, it is important to understand that for Jeroboam to recognize that his kingship is from God requires a significant level of faith. Moreover, for Jeroboam to continue to allow Israelite worship to remain focused on Jerusalem seems to require even more than that. It requires a dramatic reorientation with regard to his own power and position, to his understanding of his place in God's dealings with Israel, and to his willingness to participate in those dealings without abandoning the proper worship of the LORD.

Jeroboam's actions are clearly idolatrous. It is interesting, however, to recognize that they are idolatrous in particular ways. For example, he does not directly abandon worship of the LORD.[14] Rather, his fears and suspicions about both God's promise to him and the people's loyalty lead him to set up an alternative set of institutions, symbols, and practices for the worship of the LORD who made him king. This is not because of any inherent flaw in the Jerusalem Temple and its priesthood; it is simply located outside the territory he controls and where he can count on a certain amount of loyalty. Rather, Jeroboam's policy appears to be a straightforward way of establishing national unity and security, by eliminating the risks inherent in keeping worship of the LORD focused on Jerusalem.[15] His fears and suspicions ultimately distort his perceptions such that he ends up in idolatry through the pursuit of an apparent good. My aim here is not to excuse Jeroboam's idolatry. Rather, I want to make it understandable. If we contemporary believers cannot see how prudent and even reasonable Jeroboam's fear-driven actions may have seemed at the time, we will not appreciate the threat that such fears pose for us.

FEAR, PREEMPTION, IDOLATRY

As Bader-Saye notes, in addition to suspicion, preemption is one of those vices that begins to emulate a virtue within an ethic of safety governed by disordered fear. As he describes it, preemption tends to result in premature or unnecessary flight or premature and presumptuous fighting.[16] In continuing to explore the ways in which disordered fear disposes the people of God toward idolatry, we find a version of preemptive fear leading to idolatry in Isaiah 28–31.

The narrative of divided Israel continues to unfold over the course of 1–2 Kings. In 2 Kings 17 we learn that under King Hoshea Israel becomes a vassal of the Assyrian king Shalmaneser. In hopes of breaking free of Assyrian domination, Hoshea seeks help from the Egyptians. This does not go well. Assyria invades Israel and carries the Israelites away (2 Kgs 17:1-6). From 17:7-23 we learn the causes of Israel's exile. There are no surprises here. Forgetting the LORD and following other gods is the primary cause of Israel's demise. The text reminds us that this outcome was set in motion by Jeroboam back in 1 Kings 12–13.

Assyria ultimately turns its sights on Judah. In 2 Kings 18-19 we read about the Assyrian king Sennacherib's invasion of Judah. The Judean king Hezekiah has aggressively attempted to purge the land of idols (2 Kgs 18:1-8).

Although Judah will eventually fall to the Babylonians, Hezekiah's reforms appear to forestall the LORD's immediate judgment.

These chapters from 2 Kings have a rough canonical correspondence with Isaiah 28–39. Isaiah's often poetic account of Judean politics and practice provides both a more complicated account than the rather terse narrative of 2 Kings and a further example of the ways in which fear may dispose the people of God to idolatry.

I will focus on passages in Isaiah 30 and 31 in particular. To help illumine some of the interpretive details of these passages, however, it may be useful to rehearse the movements that begin in Isaiah 28. Within Isaiah 28–35 there is a dizzying alternation between accounts of judgment and deliverance, destruction and restoration. Sometimes this alternation occurs as one passage of judgment follows immediately and without transition, a passage declaring God's love and deliverance of Israel (e.g., 29:9-24). Sometimes this alternation occurs within verses of a single passage (e.g., 31:4-5). Throughout, Isaiah relies on rich and subtle images, similes, metaphors, and ironic descriptions to account for Israel's life with the LORD, its blindness, corruption, splendor, and hope.

For the biblical critic trained to pick at textual seams, fissures, and rough edges in order to disentangle layers of redactional activity and then to map that activity onto events in Israel's history, these chapters provide a critical bonanza. The textual tensions and sudden alternations in these chapters tend to dissolve as scholars consign various textual conflicts and rough edges to distinct redactional periods. The results of this work are technically serious, but also equivocal and rarely assured. More importantly, these studies rarely clarify the text as it now stands in its canonical form.[17] Brevard Childs' commentary on Isaiah raised this point repeatedly. "The major point is that the Isaianic message does not consist of a tension between pessimistic and optimistic opinions of the prophet, or between competing redactional construals of earlier and later periods. Such a developmental trajectory renders an understanding of the true dimensions of the text virtually impossible. Rather, the issue is a complex theological one that emerged already in the prologue of the book (1:2-3). How is such a lack of understanding of God by Israel possible?"[18]

As Isaiah 28 begins, it appears that in the light of an imminent threat from Assyria, Judah's political leaders sought an alliance and protection from Egypt. In response to this, Isaiah proclaims that Judah's leaders have made a "covenant with death" (28:15). Perhaps this is a reference to the pagan god Mot, whose name means death.[19] It is more likely that this is God's evaluation of the Israelites' attempts to secure their future through an alliance with Egypt.[20] However one evaluates the treaty, the very act of making the treaty would have involved idolatrous practices. Nevertheless, this is not the LORD's primary line of attack. Rather, God claims that this move will fail on its own terms. Either Egypt will not come to Israel's rescue or Egypt's attempt at rescue will fail. Instead of securing their future, the leaders of Judah have ensured their failure, sheltering under lies and falsehoods.

This is a politics driven by fear. This politics requires a sort of double idolatry in order to purchase national security. The first act of idolatry begins with seeking security in something other than the LORD. The second occurs in the formal idolatry required in making treaties. Moreover, as Isaiah's word from the LORD makes clear, this policy will fail (28:18-29). In contrast to this, the one who trusts in the foundation laid by God "will not panic" (28:16).[21]

Isaiah returns to this issue of seeking help from Egypt against the Assyrians in chapter 30. The leaders of Judah are called rebellious children because they have not consulted with God and have formed a plan contrary to God's will. The Hebrew וְלִנְסֹךְ מַסֵּכָה ("to pour out a pouring") in 30:1 is translated as "make an alliance" by the NRSV and ESV. The Hebrew may indicate that a drink offering was typically used to seal a treaty. If so, it further implicates this entire fear-driven policy in idolatry.[22] In 30:1-5 the primary criticism of the policy with Egypt seems to be that it was carried out without any regard for the LORD and the LORD's plans. Indeed, if 29:15 is taken as a reference to this policy, it was a deliberate attempt to keep the LORD in the dark. Moreover, this policy sought from Egypt and Pharaoh the very things the LORD provides to Israel, "refuge" and a "shadow."[23] The accusation here is that secretly the leaders of Judah have attempted to replace the LORD with Pharaoh. The LORD's response to this seems to be to give the leaders of Judah precisely what they want. This substitute god, however, will not provide the refuge and security the Judeans seek. Instead, "The protection of Pharaoh shall become your shame and the shelter in the shadow of the Egypt your humiliation" (30:3). Israel's presumptuous and preemptive gestures toward Egypt will lead to disaster. The fear-driven policy of ignoring the LORD and the LORD's messengers in favor of the seemingly prudent and politically shrewd alliance with Egypt will result in Judah's downfall. Despite the intentions of Judah's leaders, they have allied themselves with oppression and deceit instead of the Holy One of Israel (cf. 30:12).

The Judean policy is driven by fear, implicates them in idolatry, and will not succeed. Nevertheless, it seems important to mention that Judah did face a very real threat from Assyria. Indeed, such a situation seems to be worth serious concern, if not fear. It may be the case that although the Assyrians were well worth some fear, the Judean political leaders were even more afraid of the LORD's alternative policy. We learn of this policy in 30:15, "For thus says the LORD God, the Holy One of Israel: In returning and rest you shall be saved: in quietness and in trust shall be your strength."[24] This recalls 28:16, where we are told that those who trust in God "will not panic." The Israelites are called to put their trust in God rather than in alliances with Egypt. Without question this is a demanding political policy. It hearkens back to Exodus 14:14, "The LORD will fight for you and you have only to be still."[25] This is an incredibly demanding and potentially terrifying political agenda. It requires great faith and patience in the face of a potential threat.[26] Given the real threat of Assyrian attack and the prospect of facing this attack by resting in the LORD, the fear of the Judean leadership is both recognizable and understandable.

Nevertheless, that fear drives them further from security, deeper into idolatry, and seals their fate as a nation. "The day that 10:20-21 had foretold when Israel will be forced to recognize how useless its idols are. Instead, Jerusalem's leaders are determined to adopt an idolatrous political course."[27] The Judean leaders act as if they ultimately agree with the Assyrian diplomat (the Rabshekah), who advises surrender by pointing to all of the nations the Assyrians have already conquered. He asks, "Who among all the gods of these countries have saved their communities out of my hand, that the LORD should save Jerusalem out of my hand?" (36:20).[28]

The alliance with Egypt comes into focus again in chapter 31. Again, Isaiah contrasts Judah's abandonment of trust in God with their reliance on horses and chariots from Egypt. They have fundamentally abandoned trust in God in favor of trust in humans (31:3). God will bring judgment both on Egypt and on Judah because of this (31:2, 4).[29]

Almost as quickly as one learns of Judah's judgment and destruction, however, one finds promises and anticipation of restoration (31:5). Returning to the LORD will entail destruction of the idols (31:6-7). Presumably this covers any and all idols, but particularly the idols and offerings that would have naturally come into Judah's public life through its foreign alliances. Such a return to the LORD also points to Assyria's ultimate defeat by God, who will reestablish Jerusalem (31:8).

When it comes to the beginning verses of chapter 31, the bulk of scholarly attention focuses on the relationship between 31:4 and 5. Because the imagery of 31:5 signifies the LORD's protection of Jerusalem, it is difficult to account for the imagery of v. 4, in which the LORD appears to battle against Judah.

The linguistic evidence here seems relatively clear. Isaiah 31:4 establishes the LORD as Judah's judge and opponent. In the next verse the LORD is Jerusalem's protector and rescuer. Given the alternations between judgment and restoration that have marked the previous three chapters, one can only say that this is different only to the extent that it occurs in such a compressed space.[30]

Given my interests in fear and idolatry, I am more intrigued with the argument of G. C. I. Wong regarding 31:2. He proposes that "turning to Egypt for human help and resources was opposed by Isaiah primarily because it represented a human effort to avoid or counter the divine intention of bringing judgment upon Jerusalem."[31] Wong's judgment hinges on the assumption that Isaiah understood the Assyrian threat as God's judgment on Jerusalem, a judgment Judah must face and not seek to avoid. In short, Wong posits a situation in which one can discern a setting and motivation for Isaiah's declaration, which then govern the interpretation of 31:1-3.[32]

Wong's suggestion raises the possibility that Judah's political moves may also blind the leadership to the causes of this policy's eventual failure. By throwing their lot in with the Egyptians, the Judeans muddy the waters to such a degree that when that policy fails, it will not immediately be clear that it is the LORD who has caused its failure. Further, if this policy threatens to obscure the connection between defeat and God's judgment, it may also break the causal bonds between God's action and Israel's redemption. This, too, may well be part of Isaiah's resistance to the alliance with Egypt. If so, it further supports my earlier claim that the fear of the Judean leaders may be driven as much by a fear of what the LORD may demand of them as by a fear of Assyria.

Whereas Proverbs indicates that the fear of the LORD is both the beginning of wisdom (9:10) and a fortress for the righteous (10:29 LXX), the leaders of Judah display a different type or a disordered form of the fear of the LORD. They have made securing the nation and retaining their power their overriding aim. In their eyes the LORD may be as big a threat to their hold on power as the Assyrians are. It is not then surprising that they are willing to take on the idolatrous practices required by an alliance with Egypt in order to achieve their vision of security.

My aim with regard to Isaiah 28–31 has been to indicate that Judah's fear-driven politics lead to a preemptive alliance with Egypt in the face of an Assyrian threat. Whether or not idolatry already drives this politics of fear, it clearly results in or deepens Judah's idolatry. This is so in the material sense that it requires offerings and sacrifices to Egyptian gods to seal the treaties. It is also the case in that Judah's actions, in a reversal of

Exodus, effectively displace the LORD in favor of Pharaoh as the one who determines the future of the people of God.

As with Jeroboam's idolatry, it is important to try to reckon with the fact that the leaders of Judah were hoping to secure their future, not corrupt the nation. No doubt they sought their own benefit before that of the nation. Like most rulers they probably assumed that power should be used to benefit the powerful and that there was only a negligible gap between their interests and the interests of the nation as a whole. Nevertheless, they did not seek idolatry as an end, though they ended up there. Instead, fear led them to see particular courses of action as prudent and beneficial. Fear inclined them to interpret the political situation in ways that disposed them to idolatrous policies.

FEAR, ACCUMULATION, IDOLATRY

Bader-Saye articulates three shadow virtues that rise to the surface in an ethic of security driven by fear. With regard to the shadow virtues of suspicion and preemption there were relatively clear biblical examples that directly linked fear and idolatry in the realm of politics. When it comes to the shadow virtue of accumulation, it is not difficult to find numerous biblical examples critical of various aspects and forms of wealth accumulation. As Luke Johnson notes, "It is out of deep fear that the acquisitive instinct grows monstrous."[33] Indeed, as I indicated with regard to Paul's identification of greed with idolatry, one sees that Christians have traditionally read those passages in Ephesians and Colossians in the light of Matthew 6:24, where Jesus asserts that one cannot serve God and Mammon or unrighteous wealth. Jesus indicates that the single-minded devotion that God requires is incompatible with anything that might distract from or compete with the single-minded, wholehearted love of God. One might infer from this that those things, such as wealth accumulation, that distract from or compete with this love of God might be thought of as idols. This inference, however, is not always clear or explicit in the NT. Moreover, it is important to note that something such as wealth accumulation does not need to demand levels of love and devotion comparable to the LORD's demands in order to be counted an idol. It need only deflect, detract, or distract from people's devotion to the LORD. Given these qualifications, I suggest, however, that some of the best examples that connect fear, accumulation, and idolatry will come from Luke's Gospel.

In Luke 12 we hear Jesus addressing a crowd of followers. Appropriately for my purposes, he begins in v. 4 with an admonition against fear. In particular, he warns against an undue fear of those who would persecute followers of Jesus (12:4-12). He reminds his followers of God's attentive care, of the long-term damage they do to themselves if they deny their Lord, and of the promise that the Spirit will support and sustain them in times of trial.

Without a pause, we are told that someone in the crowd wants Jesus to command a man to share his inheritance (12:13). Jesus steps back from such arbitration (12:14), but quickly offers some advice tied to this request, warning against "all forms of greed" (φυλάσσεσθε ἀπὸ πάσης πλεονεξίας). He further asserts that true life does not consist in an abundance of things (12:15-16). This leads Jesus to tell a parable about a man whose fields were very productive. Rather than a source of satisfaction and contentment, his accumulated goods simply cause anxiety for him, since he has no place to store them. He tears down his old barns and builds new ones. Only when his barns are complete and he believes that he has secured his future well-being does he begin to relax, telling himself he can rest, eat, drink, and be merry (12:16-19). Of course, in trying to secure his wealth, he has not taken either God or his own death into account. Those familiar with this story expect God's judgment on this man's foolishness. At the same time, we get no indication that this man has attained his bounty in an unworthy or unjust way. He is a successful farmer; he can genuinely treat his success as God's blessing. The real problem comes when such a blessing provokes anxiety and fear rather than generosity. The blessing is given to someone whose fear overwhelms any properly theocentric approach to possessions. The upshot of this story is to attend to being "rich in God" (εἰς θεὸν πλουτῶν), instead of cultivating treasure for oneself (ὁ θησαυρίζων ἑαυτῷ [12:21]). Jesus further elaborates on this theme by trying to short-circuit any fear the disciples might have for their own future well-being. He does this not by promising them riches, but by promising God's continual care and urging them to pursue the things of the kingdom above all else (12:22-31).[34] He concludes by encouraging his followers not to fear and to locate their treasure in God, because where their treasure is, that is where their heart will also reside (12:32-34).

Although as a whole 12:13-34 presume a close connection between fear and accumulation and acquisitiveness, these final words directly connect fear with accumulation. They do not explicitly lead to idolatry. They do, however, indicate that fear will lead disciples to treasure, to locate their heart, in something that is not God.

Several chapters later, Luke takes up the incompatibility of serving God and Mammon in the light of the parable of the dishonest steward in 16:1-13. The parable itself has several interpretive puzzles. Chief among these is the master's commendation of his embezzling steward, followed closely by Jesus' concluding comment on the parable, "Make friends for yourselves by means of unrighteous mammon, so that when it runs out, they will welcome you into their eternal homes" (16:9).

The parable begins without much backstory. The master learns that his steward has been squandering his wealth. We do not know exactly how or why. It is, however, interesting to note that the same Greek verb (διασκορπίζω) appears immediately preceding the parable of the prodigal son to describe the way the son treats the inheritance he is given (15:13).[35] Nevertheless, the steward recognizes that the jig is up. His response is certainly driven by fear, recognizing that he is too weak to survive by means of his own physical labor and is too proud to beg. He tries to pull one last swindle. Rather than directly siphoning off money, he offers to shave something off the debts that various people owe the master, so that when the steward is fired, as he must be, "they will receive me into their homes" (16:4).[36] He is not expecting to be given a job in these homes. Rather, the steward hopes to transform the debts these characters owe the master into debts and obligations they have toward him. He sets up a network of accountability among those who owe his master money. He relieves them of their accountability to the master so that they become accountable to him. This is what it means to "make friends by means of dishonest wealth" (16:9). The manager "shrewdly" opts to create and then depend upon these friendships.

In the light of his actions, the steward is identified as both dishonest or unrighteous (ἀδικία), on the one hand, and clever or wise or prudent (φρονίμως), on the other hand. Despite attempts to focus on the identity of the "master" and who is speaking in vv. 8-9, it is the tension that inheres in this identification of the steward as both unrighteous and shrewd that lies at the heart of the exegetical challenges of this parable.

Given this scenario, it seems the best way to interpret vv. 8-9, the master's commendation and Jesus' admonition, is to take one of these terms ironically.[37] It makes best sense to focus on the term "prudent" (φρονίμως). The steward is wise or shrewd in exactly the same way the Corinthians are "wise in Christ" relative to Paul's "foolishness" (1 Cor 4:10; 2 Cor 11:19).[38] In this light, it is clear that the children of this age are more "clever" than the children of light (16:9). One would be surprised if that were not the case. Of course, it is the wisdom of this age, rather than the wisdom of God. The real contrast here is between cleverness and faithfulness (cf. vv. 10-13).

In the case of the steward, his well-founded fears led to a "clever" course of action. As Jesus indicates, his initiatives in using unrighteous Mammon will lead him to be welcomed into the "eternal tents" of those he has befriended.

Should one really expect that the eternal tents of those who are friends made through unrighteous Mammon will be the places one wants to spend eternity? This ironic reading also supports the way in which Jesus turns this parable on the Pharisees in 16:15.

The ultimate conclusion of this parable is that one cannot serve two masters. Any attempt to do so will lead to deficient service to both. Although not directly about idolatry, for a Jew such as Jesus to make this assertion to fellow Jews, it would likely call to mind the single-minded devotion to the LORD required in Deuteronomy 6. In that light, one would have to say that if trying to serve two masters is not outright idolatry, any compromise of one's devotion to the LORD would be to head down the road toward forgetting the LORD and worshiping other gods.

Fear of not having enough or fear of losing what one has makes accumulation always seem like a wise strategy. Whether such practices of accumulation are just in themselves, as seems to be the case in Luke 12, or unjust, as in Luke 16, they share a common source in one's fear of not having enough. Although the movement from fear to idolatry in these passages is not as direct as in 1 Kings or Isaiah, Luke provides us with sufficient reason to think that those whose activities mirror either the rich man's who tears down his barns, or the unjust steward's, are well on their way to idolatry.

As with the other two fear-driven shadow virtues, accumulation in itself can seem like a reasonable strategy when one is faced with the financial challenges of everyday life. As Bader-Saye points out, fear-driven accumulation attempts to construct a wall of invulnerability around us that substitutes for dependence on God. In this respect it mirrors precisely the dangers inherent in eating one's fill in the promised land. We can forget our dependence on God, assuming that our own hard work, cleverness, or talent has gotten us what we have. It is the first step toward forgetting the LORD. Moreover, fear-driven accumulation will tend to render us less generous and hospitable. We will begin to see others, both friends and strangers, as potential threats to what we have accumulated, rather than as people with whom to share our goods.

In at least the ways I have surveyed here, fear is a disposition that inclines one toward idolatry. Through cultivating shadow virtues such as suspicion, preemption, and accumulation, fear has the capacity to make certain courses of action, and certain practices seem not only benign, but prudent and even necessary. When this happens, we will find that our moral and spiritual imaginations are severely truncated. Fear will drive us down an increasingly narrow way, but a narrow way that will not lead to life. In this light, it would seem that the best alternative for believers is to eliminate fear. As Bader-Saye has already reminded us, however, fear is intimately connected to love. Indeed, the surest way to eliminate fear is to stop loving, to become indifferent to loss, death, and deprivation. Given that Christians are called both to a whole-hearted love of God and to love their neighbors as themselves, this cannot be an option. Instead, believers who are called to lives of love and who also want to avoid the forms of fear that lead to idolatry will need to come to grips with the ways in which love and fear might be properly related.

FEAR AND LOVE

One way to begin to explicate the relationships between fear and love is to look at 1 John 4:16b-21. In 4:7-12 believers are called to love one another. This call is rooted in the unsurpassed quality of God's love for believers (4:11).[39] Indeed, believers' love for one another is the chief way of demonstrating that God lives in them and that this unsurpassed love is being perfected in them (4:12).[40]

Moreover, it is not simply the case that God lives in believers; believers also are called to "abide" in God. Indeed, the very notion of "abiding" requires two parties. In this case, believers and God abide in each other. The granting of the Spirit is the sign and affirmation that God is abiding with believers. The Spirit is granted to those who believe in God's foundational act of love, the Father's sending of the Son as savior of the world (4:13-16a).

The next passage begins by announcing that love is the basis for the mutual abiding of God and believers: "God is love and those who abide in love abide in God and God abides in them" (4:16b). It is important, however, to note that love is not some third thing that God and humans share as part of their mutual abiding. Rather, God is love. The initiation, foundation, and sustenance of this mutual abiding lie solely in God's identity.

As the passage continues John goes on to note that this mutual abiding is the context within which love is perfected or brought to its proper end in believers.[41] God's love does not need perfection, but believers' love does. Moreover, the passive voice of the verb reminds us that God is the agent accomplishing the perfection of that love, which is God's very identity, in us.[42]

As John sees it, one of the aims of bringing believers' love to its proper end is so that we might be bold and have confidence at the day of judgment. This is followed by an ambiguous phrase, "Because we are in this world just as that one is." Given the way καθὼς ἐκεῖνός is used in 2:6; 3:3, 7 to refer to Christ as an example, it seems likely that this is the way the phrase is being used here.[43] If one takes it this way, then the force of the claim is that Christ's

entry into and continued presence in "this world" would indicate that being
in "this world" is not an insuperable barrier to confidently facing the day of
judgment. Alternatively, if ἐκεῖνός is a reference to God, then the fact that
God abides with us in "this world" indicates that our presence in "this world"
should not preclude a confident anticipation of the day of judgment. In either
case, the claim relative to believers in this world is that the mutual abiding of
God and believers in this world will lead God to bring our love to its proper
end so that we may with confidence face the day of judgment.

When the God who is love brings the mutual abiding of God and believers to its proper end, then fear will be expelled. Perfected love and fear have
nothing to do with each other. Further, "the one who fears is not perfected
in love" (4:18). This verse is not speaking about the fear of the LORD that
really reflects the proper disposition of creatures to their creator. Rather,
this is the sort of fear I have been reflecting on in this chapter, the fear that
comes from losing or anticipating the loss of what one loves. In John's terms,
this is the fear of punishment, of not gaining what one has hoped to gain.
As 1 Kings, Isaiah, and Luke have all indicated, this type of fear disposes
believers toward idolatry.

On the one hand, Bader-Saye reminds us that one way to achieve fearless-
ness is to extinguish love. This is hardly an appealing option for Christians.
On the other hand, 1 John argues that when God brings our love to its proper
end, to its perfection, there will be no place for fear. This will be because there
will be no chance of loss, decay, or punishment separating us from our loves.
As appealing as this option is, it seems clearly to be an expectation that awaits
eschatological fulfillment when God will wipe all tears from our eyes. Further,
noting that the expulsion of fear is tied to the eschatological perfection of our
love is not a great deal of help for believers now. If fear disposes us toward
idolatry in any of the ways noted above, or in any other way, we are right to
desire something in addition to an eschatological hope. Moreover, this odd
phrase in 4:17, "Because we are in this world just as that one is," indicates that
from John's perspective there may be some things to say about how believers
might order their love and their fears prior to that time when our hopes are
fulfilled and our love is perfected.

First John seems immediately prepared to begin explaining that issue as
4:19-20 lays out two crucial components in the process of perfecting our love
in this world. First, we are freed from having to perfect our own love because
our love is dependent on God's prior love of us. This is the point of 4:19, "We
love, because God first loved us." The second aspect of this is that love of
God requires love of our brothers and sisters. This is not all that surprising

given the claim in 4:16 that the love of God, who is love, is part of the mutual abiding of God in us and us in God. This mutual abiding implicates us in abiding with and loving those brothers and sisters who are also participating in this love of God. Indeed, as the early Christian monk Dorotheos of Gaza pointed out, "Suppose we were to take a compass and insert the point and draw the outline of a circle. The center point is the same distance from any point on the circumference. . . . Let us suppose that this circle is the world and that God is the center; the straight lines drawn from the circumference to the center are the lives of [human beings]."[44] Dorotheos goes on to make the point that as one moves closer to God, one must inevitably move closer to one's brothers and sisters who are on a similar journey. Growth in love of God entails growth in love of one's brothers and sisters.

Moreover, it would seem then that as God moves believers toward that time when their love is perfected and fear is cast out, such abiding in communion with fellow lovers of God may provide a crucial context within which we learn to order our love and fear in ways that help avoid idolatry. There are several ways in which this may be so. First, the more isolated we are, the more likely it is that our fears will lead us to view others as threats. In such a case, an ethic of security and the shadow virtues of suspicion, preemption, and accumulation will appear more attractive.[45] Thus, a community of fellow believers on a common journey toward ever-deeper love of God and each other would be a necessary but not sufficient context for believers to perfect their love of God and each other. Perfecting our love a little more and casting fear a little further from our doorstep requires abiding in the communion of fellow lovers of God.

One must admit, however, that communities can also be captivated by fear rather than love; they, too, can lapse into idolatry and collective blindness and deafness to the claims of the gospel. Those communities can fall prey to fear resulting in idolatry. There is no method or procedure guaranteed to inoculate Christian communities from the same type of fear-driven moves that led Israel, Judah, and characters in Luke toward idolatry. The scriptural examples I discussed earlier would indicate that the fear that disposes believers toward idolatry is often accompanied by a blindness and deafness to those who are pointing out the idolatrous movements within the common life of the people of God. The likelihood that Christian communities will become subject to the types of fear that dispose them to idolatry increases to the extent that the borders of these communities become hardened and rigid, to the extent that such communities are only attending to their own voices and concerns. Christian communities that are outward-looking and expansive, with more

porous contours, seem better placed to resist such fear. Hence, expanding
the contours of the church through mission is one complex practice that is
more likely to develop and further perfect our love of God and help us expel
fear. Of course, the missionary activity of Christians has come under a lot
of critical scrutiny in recent decades. My aim is not to address those specific
criticisms in great detail. Rather, I will offer a particular account of Christian
mission, an account that seemed quite vibrant in the early centuries of the
church and may well be gaining new roots in the present.

LOVE AND MISSION

One way to begin this account is to reflect on Psalm 50:2, "Out of Zion, perfect
in its beauty, God reveals himself in glory." I am aware that this is not the
most formally correct translation of the Hebrew, though it does not misrepresent it. It also uses a masculine pronoun for God, which should generally
be avoided. It is, however, this translation, as we chanted it in church on one
of the Sundays of Advent, that stuck in my mind.

Zion is one of the Bible's ways of referring to the city of Jerusalem. The
thought here that is so striking is that God's glory is revealed in the beauty
of a city, the particular city Jerusalem. What is it that makes Zion beautiful?
How is God's glory revealed in this beauty? What would the result of such
an epiphany be?

What makes Zion beautiful? There are at least two possible ways to
answer this question. The first type of answer pins the source of Zion's beauty
on its impressive appearance, the magnificence of its buildings, most notably
the Temple. You do not have to go too far from Psalm 50 to find this view. In
Psalm 48, for example, we read: "Great is the LORD and greatly to be praised
in the city of our God. His holy mountain, beautiful in elevation, is the joy of
all the earth, Mount Zion, in the far north, the city of the great King. Within
its citadels God has shown himself a sure defense" (1-3). In the middle of the
psalm (48:9-11) there is mention of the Temple, and then the psalm ends with
these words: "Walk about Zion, go all around it, count its towers, consider
well its ramparts; go through its citadels, that you may tell the next generation that this is God, our God forever and ever. He will be our guide forever"
(48:12-15). (See also Pss 46, 76 for similar sentiments.)

It is clear from this psalm that the beauty of Zion is directly related to its
strength as a fortress. Its impregnable ramparts and citadels are the source
of its beauty. This, of course, is a very dangerous way for Israelites to think
about the beauty of Jerusalem. It is the flip side of the sort of fear that drove

Judah's rulers to seek an alliance with Egypt. The more one reflects on the beauty of fortress Jerusalem as a sign of God's care and defense of Israel in the face of her enemies, as this psalm does, the less likely it becomes that one can conceive of God subjecting Jerusalem to judgment. This leads to the incorrect assumption that God would do anything, including overlooking Israel's sin, to protect Jerusalem. The prophets, Jeremiah in particular, are quite clear that in the face of Israel's sin and injustice, fortress Jerusalem will be handed over by God to whichever nation God has decided to use to bring judgment on Israel. It is only the foolish who look at the beauty of fortress Jerusalem and assume that such beauty can overcome the darkness of Israel's sin.[46]

There is, however, another way of thinking about the beauty of Jerusalem. It is spoken of indirectly here in Psalm 50, but receives much more explicit discussion in other OT texts. As I indicated, Psalm 50 begins with this extraordinary assertion that the perfection of Zion's beauty reveals God's glory. One searches in vain, however, to find any discussion in the rest of the psalm of the magnificence of Jerusalem's buildings or fortifications. The Temple is mentioned, but not as a place of beauty. Rather, it is the site where sacrifice is offered continually. Ironically, God rejects these sacrifices because they are not accompanied by justice, fidelity, and truthful speech. In the light of God's expressed desire for justice, fidelity, and truthfulness, it would appear that the beauty of Zion is not a function of its buildings but of the sort of common life its inhabitants maintain with God and with each other. Indeed, as the prophets repeatedly note, without justice, fidelity, and truthfulness, there is no beauty in Jerusalem's buildings. Moreover, the absence of justice, fidelity, and truthfulness leads to God's imminent destruction of Jerusalem. The common life of Jerusalem, the quality of the community its inhabitants can sustain is the true source of the city's beauty, a beauty that is capable of revealing God's true glory.

It is not only Psalm 50, however, that ties the beauty of Zion to the common life of her inhabitants. One of the most striking passages to make this claim is found in Isaiah 2:2-5,

> In days to come the mountain of the LORD's house shall be established as the highest of the mountains, and shall be raised above the hills; all the nations shall stream to it. Many peoples shall come and say, "Come, let us go up to the mountain of the LORD, to the house of the God of Jacob; that he may teach us his ways and that we may walk in his paths." For out of Zion shall go forth instruction, and the word of the LORD from Jerusalem. He shall judge between the nations, and shall arbitrate for many peoples; they shall beat their swords into plowshares, and their spears into pruning hooks; nation shall not lift up sword against nation, neither shall they learn war anymore.

Although Zion is not directly called beautiful in this passage, Isaiah touches on the same theme we found in Psalm 50, developing it in several important ways. First, Psalm 50 speaks of the present perfection of Zion's beauty; Isaiah speaks of some future time when Zion's prominence will be established. Moreover, within the scope of the first two chapters of Isaiah, it is clear that Zion's prominence only comes out of the ashes of her devastation. Isaiah begins with a long litany of God's charges against Israel (1:1-20). They have forsaken God; they have perverted justice; they have oppressed those in their society least able to defend themselves. In the light of this infidelity, injustice, and oppression, God judges the Israelites, promising to hand them over to their enemies and to leave Jerusalem decimated (1:21-24).

Almost in the same breath, God quickly turns to promise redemption and forgiveness to repentant Israel. Jerusalem will be restored. In the words of 1:25, God promises to "smelt away your dross as with lye and remove all your alloy. I will restore your judges as at the first and your counselors as at the beginning. Afterward you shall be called the city of righteousness, the faithful city. Zion shall be redeemed by justice, and those in her who repent, by righteousness." If, as Psalm 50 indicates, Zion's perfect beauty inheres in the quality of her common life, God's promised restoration of a common life based on righteousness in Isaiah 1 leads nicely into the vision of the newly beautified Zion that begins chapter 2.

In Isaiah 2 we learn of restored Zion's beauty through its effects. Restored Zion enjoys a renewed intimacy with God. The common life of its inhabitants is marked by peaceableness. Weapons are turned into farming implements. When the nations see what God has done in the city, they are fascinated by it, attracted to it, compelled to come near, and ultimately drawn into the intimacy that God and Israel enjoy. They say, "Come, let us go up to the mountain of the LORD, to the house of the God of Jacob; that he may teach us his ways and that we might walk in his paths." The redemption and renewal of the city of Jerusalem is so astonishing, so attractive and fascinating, that the world is ultimately drawn to God by what they see going on there. God's glory is revealed in the beauty of redeemed Jerusalem, and the nations are drawn to God. This is one of the chief purposes for which God calls Abraham in the first place in Genesis 12. The establishment of Israel as the people of God is to bring a blessing to the nations. As the world sees both God's redeeming, loving relationship with Israel and the sort of common life this forms and sustains within Israel, all peoples are drawn to God. In this way the notion of Zion's perfect beauty—a beauty manifesting itself in lives that are reconciled with God and with others and in a common life founded on justice, fidelity, and truthfulness—is simply a compressed and rich way of reflecting on the divine economy of salvation. Recall that the point of Zion's beauty is to better reveal God's glory.

Moreover, tying the image of Zion's beauty to the economy of salvation links the salvation of the nations quite closely to Israel's manifestation of a particular common life. God forms and sustains a people whose life with God and each other exudes such a radiance that the world is drawn to God.[47]

Although I have more to say about this, it may already strike some as an odd account of mission. It focuses on the particularities of the common life of the redeemed people of God as a vehicle through which God's glory is revealed, captivating and drawing outsiders into the people of God. This image of mission in the light of the perfection of Zion's beauty supplements the perfecting of believers' love and the concomitant expulsion of fear needed to keep idolatry at bay.

Nevertheless, it seems fair to ask, How and in what ways does this theme of the beauty of redeemed Zion fit into the Gospels and Christian mission? One must admit that Jesus does not offer a very flattering evaluation of Jerusalem.[48] In the Gospels Jerusalem often comes to stand for opposition to Jesus. Hence, it is not possible to develop this theme about the compelling attractiveness of the common life of redeemed Zion through a close study of Jesus' own words about this city. Nevertheless, I will try to show that in the Gospels the life, death, and resurrection of Jesus bring the theme of Zion the beautiful to a climax. At the same time, Jesus' teaching leads to a modification of this theme in theologically crucial ways. Luke's Gospel, in particular, makes this clear. In addition, there are further lines of continuity running from images of the beautiful city of God in the OT to other parts of the NT. These lines of continuity are subsequently used in the patristic period to reflect on the nature of the church and its mission.

For Christians, the life, death, and resurrection of Jesus represent the climactic point in God's ongoing redemption of the people of Israel.[49] To elaborate on this claim I will focus on Luke's Gospel, though I think Matthew and Mark also reflect the views I will lay out here. At key moments in Luke, specific characters in the Gospel identify Jesus as the redeemer of Israel. The birth stories in particular are filled with foreshadowings of the redemptive role this yet-to-be-born child will play. Listen to what Gabriel tells Mary about the child she will bear: "The Lord God will give him the throne of his ancestor David, He will reign over the house of Jacob forever, and of his kingdom there will be no end" (1:32-34). In response to this news, Mary sings her song, the *Magnificat*, in which she praises God for "helping his servant

Israel, . . . according to the promise made to our ancestors, Abraham and his descendants forever" (1:55-56). In this light, it is impossible to make sense of these ways of thinking about the soon-to-be-born Jesus without tying him into God's deliverance of Israel. Then, when the newly born Jesus is presented in the Temple, Simeon proclaims that this child is the promised salvation of God. He will be "a light of revelation to the Gentiles and a glory to Israel" (2:32). The image here comes right from Isaiah.

Luke presents Jesus as the one who, through his life, work, and teaching, is redeeming Israel. Granted, Israel's redemption in Jesus does not take place in the ways that many of Jesus' Jewish contemporaries recognized. Nevertheless, at crucial points in the story we are given divine confirmation that Jesus is doing the Father's will and that God is well pleased.

The crucifixion, however, raises troubling questions about Jesus' status, even among his own followers. Think of that conversation that takes place between the resurrected Christ and two of his followers on the road to Emmaus in Luke 24. These two who are walking from Jerusalem are joined by the resurrected Christ, although they do not recognize him. He begins to question them about happenings in Jerusalem. They tell him about Jesus, his life, his work, and his recent death in Jerusalem. They conclude by saying, "we had hoped he was the one to redeem Israel" (24:21). From their perspective, the crucifixion has thwarted their hopes. In conversation with their strange companion, however, they learn that there is more to the story. Indeed, their hopes are given new life; their hearts are set ablaze as their fellow traveler opens the scriptures to them so that they see that the redeemer's death is not the last word of the story. Finally, there is that revelatory moment when they break bread together and he becomes known to them as the resurrected redeemer of Israel.

This is important for my earlier discussion about the compelling beauty of redeemed Zion. As Isaiah notes, Zion only becomes this welcoming beacon to the nations in "the latter days." It is only when the redemption of Israel has happened, when the redeemer or Messiah has come, that the common life between the inhabitants of Zion and God becomes so compelling that the nations observe this and are drawn to God. The problem, as any Jew will point out to you, is that the world is not redeemed. Within thirty-five years of the resurrection of Jesus, Jerusalem was in ruins. Zion was a pile of stones; the Temple was destroyed and has yet to be rebuilt to this day. If Jesus was the redeemer of Israel, why has Israel not been redeemed? Where is the beautiful city that will draw the nations to God?

These questions rang in the ears of the first Christians, too. At least partly in response to those questions, it becomes important to modify this notion of beautiful Zion. Christians must agree that the world still awaits the consummation of its redemption. The life, death, and resurrection of Jesus bring about the redemption of Israel and thus the world, yet it is a redemption that awaits its ultimate completion. Even so, when that consummation is spoken of in passages such as Revelation 21, the image is of a redeemed Jerusalem, beautiful in all of the ways mentioned in Psalm 50 and Isaiah 2. One aspect of the Christian answer to questions about the redemption of the world always recognizes that redemption has already happened, but has not yet been completed or consummated.

Nevertheless, from the very beginnings of Christianity it was clear to the followers of Jesus that to the extent redemption had already been accomplished, it would primarily be manifested in the communities formed by the followers of the crucified and resurrected one, those places where God's dwelling with believers through the Spirit enabled the perfecting of their love for God and each other. The church became the place to which Christians could point, saying, "Here is where you will find both a testimony to God's redemption of the world and a foretaste of what that redemption will look like." God's beautiful city was no longer spatially tied to Mount Zion. It was mobile. Indeed, it was found throughout the known world, though always embedded in particular places.[50]

In fact, in the first couple of centuries of the church, it was relatively common for theologians as diverse as Origen and Tertullian to point to the church as the fulfillment of Isaiah 2.[51] The Word of God, manifested in the visible and gathered body of Christ, becomes the site of the "mountain of the Lord." Other early Christian theologians, such as Justin Martyr and Ireneaus, make similar connections between Isaiah 2 and the church. They founded these connections on some of the following characteristics of the early church:

First, in the earliest Christian communities, at least for a time, gentiles were drawn to a predominantly Jewish body. Acts relates this most clearly. Indeed, the first seven chapters of Acts focus on the reconstitution of Israel in the light of the death and resurrection of the Messiah. Most of these transformations and restorations take place in and around Jerusalem. In time, however, the first followers of the resurrected Christ, all of whom were Jews, spread out from Jerusalem. In halting, sometimes faltering ways, these Jews are led by the Spirit to preach to gentiles. Much to their surprise, the gentiles receive the gospel in large numbers. Even Paul, the apostle to the gentiles, always begins by preaching to Jews first when he enters a new town. Acts, Romans, and Galatians in particular make it clear that Christianity is a Jewish movement to which gentiles are drawn. Moreover, the first theological controversy these followers of Jesus have to address is whether the gentiles who join these outposts of redeemed Israel need to become Jews. That is, do they need to be circumcised and observe such things as Jewish food laws? Despite the fact that Paul, among others, vociferously argues that gentiles need not become circumcised in order to be part of the body of Christ, he also is unequivocal in his commitment to seeing the church as being continuous with God's redemption of Israel. It is the gentiles who have been grafted into a Jewish group and not the other way around.

Having said that, it is equally important for these first Christians that they are a single body of Jews and Christians united in the body of Christ. Gentiles neither need to become Jews nor are they second-class citizens in God's redeemed Israel. Unless this is the case, as Paul so clearly saw, there would be no sense in which one could speak of Isaiah 2 finding its fulfillment in these local manifestations of redeemed Israel, which we know as the first churches. Paul saves his sharpest criticisms for those whose doctrines and practices threaten the actual concrete manifestation of a unified body of Jews and gentiles in Christ. Nowhere in the NT do we find the importance of the unity of Jew and gentile more clearly stated than in Ephesians 2. What makes this discussion in Ephesians 2 so significant is that by the time of its writing, these believers in Ephesus seem to have had very little contact with Jews. There do not appear to be any of the central issues and disputes between Jewish and gentile believers that animate Romans or Galatians. Rather, Paul, or whoever wrote Ephesians, understands the importance of predominantly (if not exclusively) gentile churches understanding themselves in relation to God's dealings with Israel.[52] This is crucial for contemporary Christian mission. Believers today are heirs of nearly two millennia of almost exclusively gentile Christianity. What do we make of the inclusion of gentiles into redeemed Israel when there are no longer many, if any, Jews in the church? Christians must always see themselves within the full scope of God's drama of salvation. We must understand that this drama does not begin with Jesus. Rather, it has its roots in creation and in the calling of Abraham. To use Paul's image, believers must constantly remind ourselves that it is we who have been grafted into the olive tree that is Israel. This should inspire a measure of humility and an appropriate sense of gratitude, if nothing else.

The second characteristic of these communities that led people to view them as fulfillments of Isaiah 2 was that they were places of peace. Remember that Isaiah 2 notes that when the nations are drawn to the beauty of redeemed Zion, people turn their weapons into tools. Moreover, they cease to learn war. The earliest Christians embodied this in two precise ways. First, they refused to fight in the Roman army. If they were in the army, they left. In addition, this refusal to fight often cost them their lives, a price many seemed more than willing to pay. In part, this refusal to serve in the army was because, as followers of Jesus, Christians are called to be nonviolent. It is also due to the fact that life in the Roman army was tied up with emperor worship and other sorts of idolatry.

If the first way in which the early churches were places of peace was in their refusal to participate in the empire's violence, the second way in which these outposts of redeemed Israel embodied peace was in their relationships with each other. This has to do with their practices of forgiveness and reconciliation. These first Christian communities were not morally perfect. One has only to read the Corinthian letters to see that. Rather, it is how these communities deal with their manifest failings, their practices of forgiveness and reconciliation, that mark them as communities of peace.[53] Through participating in the common life of these communities, people whose lives were enmeshed in cycles of sin and violence learned to speak truthfully about their sin; they learned to become skilled in asking for and offering forgiveness; they engaged in the hard work of reconciliation so that their restored relationships with God and each other testified to the fact that sin and brokenness were not the last words on their lives.

To the extent that the first churches manifested these practices so often associated with Isaiah 2, attracting and welcoming the nations, being places of peace and practicing forgiveness and reconciliation, they were able to offer concrete testimony to God's redemption of Israel through the life, death, and resurrection of Christ. Indeed, this beauty was not only evident to those who were drawn to God through the church. Even those who were enemies of the church recognized some of this beauty. Julian the Apostate, no friend of Christianity, writes, "Why do we not observe that it is their [the Christians'] benevolence to strangers, their care for the graves of the dead, and the pretended holiness of their lives that have done the most to increase atheism [i.e., Christianity]? ... When ... the impious Galileans support not only their own poor but ours as well, all men see that our own people lack aid from us."[54]

In these ways, early Christian communities became dispersed, yet spatially embedded, manifestations of redeemed and beautiful Zion, through which God's glory is revealed. It is important to reflect on this for a moment. Although there are many ways in which the earliest Christians could point to their communities as manifestations of redeemed Israel, anticipated by Isaiah, they could not avoid the fact that these outposts of redemption were separate from Zion, from Jerusalem. Whatever the centrality of Jerusalem for these early believers, they also understood that beautiful Zion could be found in Philippi or Corinth or Ephesus or any other place where the church took root. In this sense, Christians live in a sort of diaspora that is only resolved when the new Jerusalem comes down from heaven. Nevertheless, they also found that God's glory is revealed in these local settings of redeemed Zion. This recognition is important because it also comes with some risks. By loosing Zion from a specific place, Christians run the risk that they will become detached from the specificities of any place. In such a situation it would become significantly easier to spiritualize these characteristics of redeemed Zion and to fail to attend to the concrete manifestation of these characteristics in the embodied life of specific communities.[55]

There are countless examples of times in which the church failed to manifest a common life worthy of the gospel (Phil 1:27). Nobody can undo those parts of the Christian past or present. One should not pretend they did not happen. As people who are schooled in the story of God's ways with Israel and their climax in Christ, Christians must speak truthfully about our sin, ask for forgiveness, and engage in the hard work of reconciliation in the knowledge of God's forgiveness.

Thus far, I have tried to offer an account of mission that originates in Psalm 50:2, but is evident elsewhere in the OT. Further, I have tried to show that in the NT and into the early church, one can find this notion of mission in play. One might respond by arguing that whatever coherence this view of mission held in the first centuries of the church, believers today are in a very different situation.

I am not so sure. That form of Christendom in which Christianity was used to baptize the dominant cultures of our world is fast dying away. Global capitalism understands, in a way that nation-states did not always, that a world driven by hyperconsumption does not need to be underwritten by a thin form of Christianity. Despite the prevalence of belief in God among those who respond to such survey questions, many of the cultures in which Christians in the United States live and work are, for the most part, independent and ignorant of, if not antipathetic to, Christianity. One might argue that the church in the United States is moving ever closer to the situation of the church in the Roman Empire of the second and third centuries. An account of mission such as this one may turn out to be particularly relevant for our world.

Regardless of what the future has in store, I want to return to my assertion that if Christians are to resist the fear that leads to idolatry as God perfects their love through participation in communities of love, they will need this or some similar account of mission. Recall that this account stems from the recognition that fear is a disposition that inclines believers to idolatry and at the same time is intimately related to love. Further, as 1 John notes, because God first loved us, we are drawn into a life of love of God and our brothers and sisters in Christ. In this mutual love, we are assured of God's indwelling presence and of the ultimate perfection of our love. In addition, as our love is perfected, fear is dispelled from us and our common life. On its own, purely in terms of 1 John, however, such love is confined to the mutual love that believers have for God and each other. This is what makes some account of mission a crucial supplement to the idea that as fear disposes us to idolatry, love and mission provide the appropriate response to such fear.

An account such as this one will help believers sustain an expansive, outward-facing common life. Such a common life is needed as both a context within which the Spirit will perfect our love, keeping us from the fear that breeds idolatry, and to help to keep that context from becoming dangerously parochial, closed off from the voice of God that comes to us through outsiders.

Such a common life will welcome and delight in those who are most different from us.[56] Sustaining such a common life will require us to discern on a regular basis whether we are attentive enough to recognize the Spirit's work in their lives and welcome them into the body of Christ without making them become just as we are. It will lead us to ask of ourselves, "Can we come to yearn for the richness these people bring to our life together? Can we learn to extend the hospitality to others that God extends to us in the Eucharist?" This would be a sort of hospitality that welcomes outsiders in all of their difference.[57] At the same time, such hospitality would invite them into the body of Christ, where God is perfecting our love as we are in the process of being transformed into the image of Christ.

5

THE COMMUNITY OF THE CURIOUS

In the previous chapter I explored the ways in which fear and a fear-driven ethic of security can dispose the people of God to idolatry. Because fear depends on love, or at least forms of love, for its power, love is also the disposition that will cast out fear as it is perfected in believers. One danger that accompanies our engagements with love is that love, particularly as described in 1 John, can be insular and isolating if it is does not also lead to mission. I concluded that chapter with an extended reflection on mission, beginning with the idea that the perfection of Zion's beauty reveals the glory of God and draws the world back to God. I traced ways in which this theme might be developed through attention to Isaiah 2:1-4, where the nations flock to redeemed Israel because they are fascinated by what God has done among these people. This idea played a role in early Christian thinking as Christian communities were seen as outposts of redeemed Israel. In this way, Christian mission became connected to the manifestation of a common life that would draw the world to God. A crucial, and potentially problematic, move in this approach to mission is that it required a shift in thinking about Zion/ Jerusalem. Some early Christians adopted and adapted the notion that the common life of redeemed Zion would draw the world to God and located that common life in church. The beautiful life of redeemed Israel was no longer confined to a single place, Jerusalem. Rather, it resided in communities of believers. The perfection of its beauty and the revelation of God's glory were now dispersed in the church throughout the world.[1]

Given that argument, it is with some sense of irony, then, that I begin this chapter by reflecting on Deuteronomy 12, the chapter that commands the Israelites to centralize their worship in a single place when they enter the promised land. In addition, I will also follow a different approach in this chapter. Rather than begin by identifying a disposition that leads to idolatry and then offering a discussion of the ways that disposition is displayed in Scripture, I will begin by looking at scriptural scenarios in which the LORD warns the Israelites about lapsing into idolatry when they enter the land in Deuteronomy 12–13. I will argue that all of the idolatrous scenarios imagined in this section arise from a common disposition. It is not immediately clear, however, how one ought to describe that disposition. My claim will be that a traditionally Christian account of the vice of *curiositas* or curiosity offers the best way of accounting for the idolatrous tendencies addressed in Deuteronomy 12–13. I will then sharpen this notion somewhat by examining Paul's engagement with the Athenians in Acts 17. If these discussions work properly, it will be clearer why and how curiosity is a disposition that will incline believers towards idolatry.

To counter this disposition, I will suggest that Christians cultivate a "single" eye. Luke 11 and Luke's Gospel more generally will help me make this case. Finally, I will argue that the challenge for Christians today is to work, with the Spirit's help, to cultivate a "single" eye in a context that seeks to control and fragment our attention.

IDOLATRY IN DEUTERONOMY 12–13: THREE SCENARIOS

As the Israelites sojourned in the wilderness prior to entering the land, they worshiped the LORD in a variety of locations. In Deuteronomy 12 the LORD enjoins the Israelites to pursue two interrelated activities when they enter the land. First, they are to destroy all sites of Canaanite worship (12:2-4). Secondly, they are to centralize their own worship of the LORD in one place, yet to be determined (12:5-27).[2]

After some fairly detailed instructions about what this centralization will mean for the eating of animals slaughtered for food as opposed to animals to be sacrificed to God, the chapter returns to discussing the potential continuing allure of Canaanite religious practices. Despite the fact that Canaanite worship incorporates "every abhorrent thing that the LORD hates," including child sacrifice, the LORD is still concerned that the Israelites will want to imitate these practices (12:29-32). In 12:30 the LORD seems to be particularly concerned that long after the Israelites have destroyed all evidence of

Canaanite religious practice, they will still be entrapped[3] into asking, "How did these nations worship their gods? I also want to do the same." In this question and its response, one finds a particular disposition toward idolatry. Nevertheless, it is not immediately clear how best to describe this disposition.[4]

Before saying too much in this regard, it may be worthwhile to continue following the account of Deuteronomy 12 into Deuteronomy 13. There the LORD imagines three different scenarios wherein Israelites might be tempted to pursue the idolatrous practices of the Canaanites. One way of reading these passages is as more detailed and extended examples of the general disposition described in 12:30. In each of these scenarios the Hebrew verb שָׁמַע appears at crucial points. In 13:4, 9 it appears in the warnings not to listen to those who would ensnare one in idolatry. In 13:19 it describes hearing about the apostasy of a city. This repetition recalls the central role of שָׁמַע in Deuteronomy 6:4, calling Israel to the single-minded, wholehearted love of God.[5]

The extremity of the punishments the LORD imposes on those who turn to idols captivates the attention of many modern commentators.[6] Although these passages raise significant issues with regard to the character of God, they are not the only texts that do so. My concern is that addressing such issues at this point will distract from my own project, so I will leave them aside for now.

The first scenario is one in which prophets and or diviners of dreams offer signs that indicate that the Israelites should worship another god (13:1-5). Prophecy and dreams are two approved ways by which God communicates with people (cf. 1 Sam 28:6). They seem especially powerful when accompanied by "signs and portents" (Deut 13:2). For example, in Exodus 4:1-9 the LORD commands Moses to perform specific signs. These confirm to both Egyptians and Israelites that Moses and his mission are divinely authorized. At the same time, the magicians of Egypt can replicate many of the plagues (cf. Exod 7). Thus, signs are powerful, but they are not always unequivocal testimony of divine authorization. Prophets may not always speak for God; dreams can be hard to discern or deceptive, as many biblical characters can attest. Indeed, Deuteronomy is well acquainted with the struggle to discern true from false prophecy (cf. 18:20-22). In this case, however, one would think it should be a fairly straightforward matter. It should be self-evident that any sign or portent offered that encourages the Israelites to abandon the single-minded, wholehearted love of the LORD in favor of following another god would not be a sign from God. Instead, to the extent that such signs come from God, one must treat them as tests from God that probe the sincerity of Israel's love. Further, as this passage continues, it is clear that the LORD considers anyone who would encourage such activity to be a traitor and deserving of death.[7] Alternatively, if those who have heretofore been reliable messengers of God perform signs to support what they claim to be a word from the LORD, it is not hard to imagine that would have significant persuasive power.

The second scenario proposes that a close friend or relation might lure someone secretly to worship other gods (13:6-11).[8] In the first scenario, prophets and dream diviners rely on publicly displayed signs and portents to get people to worship other gods. Here, close friends and relations act in secret. Given the punishments involved, this secrecy is understandable. In this scenario it is the closeness of the relationship that provides the call to idolatry with added force.

The final scenario does not deal merely with the potential for idolatry. Rather, it addresses what to do if an entire town is led to worship other gods. Most of this passage has to do with establishing the truth of the matter and then how to proceed in the light of such apostasy. Those who lead the town astray are identified as בְּנֵי־בְלִיַּעַל. This is a much more negative identification than the NRSV's "scoundrels." These are sons of Belial. Unlike the close friend or relation who persuades in secret, these sons of Belial must operate in the open in order to persuade an entire town to worship other gods. Whatever the term "sons of Belial" conveys about motives and moral status, these must be civic leaders, people with sufficient status to entice an entire town to do something that should otherwise be self-evidently wrong.

In 12:30, the LORD warns the Israelites against becoming ensnared in an attempt to worship the gods of the Canaanites. Deuteronomy 13 offers some scenarios about how this might happen. This text anticipates that the desire and attempt to learn about and imitate the worship of the Canaanites will be a genuine problem for the Israelites when they enter the land. It is worth reflecting on why this may be so. Given the lack of information in the text, however, any answers will be speculative.

What sort of habits and dispositions would lead the Israelites to inquire about and then imitate Canaanite religious practices? Deuteronomy 13 makes it clear that however one describes this disposition to follow the gods of the Canaanites, even after their religious sites have been destroyed, this decision is often animated by particular relationships. These are relationships to prophets and their signs, to close friends and family, and to those who operate in civic life to direct the path of whole communities. These relationships are crucial because communities have their hopes, desires, and questions formed and nurtured through such particular relationships. Nevertheless, it is also clear that prophets, friends, family, and civic leaders all have the capacity to dispose the people of God toward idolatry.

In addition, although we learn little in these texts about the shape and nature of the particular disposition that might lead the Israelites into idolatry, things seem to go wrong beginning with this question in 12:30: "How did these people worship their gods? I want to do likewise." If this question is one way of displaying a disposition that leads to the people of God toward idolatry, then it becomes important to figure out how to describe and account for this disposition both in Deuteronomy and now.

Traditionally, Christians would have claimed that a question like the one in 12:30 arises out of the vice of "curiosity." At first, it may seem odd to characterize curiosity as a vice. For example, immediately after baptizing someone, we Episcopalians pray that God will give the person who has just been baptized an "inquiring and discerning heart." This would seem to ask God to give someone a curious spirit. Further, at Loyola every student for every class evaluates whether their professor "stimulated intellectual curiosity." In many, if not most, colloquial contexts today, curiosity is considered a virtue. How, then, could curiosity be a vice? Obviously, much depends here on what one means by "curiosity."

CURIOSITY

Christians have always recognized that humans, like no other creature, have a desire to know, an intellectual appetite.[9] This desire to know, however, was not considered to be free-floating or always directed for good. Our intellectual appetite, our desire to know, needs to be cultivated and shaped. In this respect, early Christians were not different from their Jewish and pagan neighbors. Although they held these views for different reasons, neither ancient pagans, nor Jews, nor Christians assumed that this desire to know would naturally direct itself in the ways it should go. The intellectual appetite required training, disciplining, catechizing. One sees this nicely laid out in Proverbs 9:1-18, where we read that Wisdom and Folly have each in their own ways prepared feasts. Each calls out to those in need of formation and growth, offering to shape and direct the intellectual appetite in particular ways. The passage makes it clear that the feast one chooses to attend will determine the difference between a long and fruitful life or death.

Wisdom and life, on the one hand, and Folly and death, on the other, represent ideals toward which one cultivates and trains the intellect. Of course, in real life the choice is rarely presented this clearly. Even in Proverbs 9 both Wisdom and Folly offer something that at least appears to be attractive. If this were not so, no one would ever choose folly. Cultivating the capacity to discern the good and true from what is merely apparent is one of the aims of all forms of intellectual and moral cultivation. There are a variety of views about how best to achieve this cultivated state. Paul Griffiths explains, "But at every point on the gamut there was (and largely, still is) agreement that some methods of disciplining the appetite for knowledge malform it, while some form it as it should be formed. 'Curiosity' was the Christian term of art for the former, and 'studiousness' for the latter."[10] Of course, "curiosity" was not strictly the word. Rather, it was the Latin *curiositas*. This term stood in contrast with *studiositas*. Griffiths again: "For Christians, however, the word [*curiositas*] almost always labeled an appetite always potentially vicious and usually actively so; and their discussions of it were polemical, aimed at separating their catechetically formed identity from that of their pagan interlocutors by offering a critique of the disciplinary regimes that produced *curiositas* by contrasting them with those that produced *studiositas*."[11] This recognition should remind believers that the formation of our intellectual appetites, and of all of our lives, is a matter of lifelong attentive formation. Such formation is not a one-time achievement. Further, as I will note later, we are always being formed by someone or something, even if we do not always recognize it. *Studiositas* is first and foremost a matter of ongoing attentiveness.

As Griffiths and others have recently reminded us, there is a rich vein of Christian reflection on *curiositas* as a vice.[12] Without rehearsing that history, and without attempting to offer the fullest account of *curiositas*, I would like to mention three interrelated aspects of this vice that seem relevant to Deuteronomy 12:29–13:19 and idolatry.[13]

The three relevant characteristics of an intellectual appetite formed and driven by *curiositas* are its desire for novelty, its approach to knowledge as a form of possession, and its disconnected habit of knowing. As Griffiths argues, "The desire for novelty (*novitas*) is an essential concomitant of curiosity."[14] The curious person wants to know what has not yet been known, what has yet to be seen. This quest for novelty inevitably leads to a measure of impatience and restlessness. What is new will not remain new for long. The curious must, therefore, move on. Griffiths again: "The novelty seeker, therefore, is one whose gaze never stays long upon any one thing. The gaze becomes a glance, and the novel object sought becomes of no further interest as soon as it is found."[15] This type of disposition tends to perpetuate itself. Moreover, the need for novelty tends to shape one's capacities so that one attends only to those things that one imagines to be capable of being apprehended quickly so as to be prepared to move on to the next new thing. That which requires deep study and contemplation holds little interest for the curious intellect.[16] One ends up knowing a large number of things superficially.

In addition, the curious person desires knowledge to possess it. There are several aspects to this lust for possession. First, it will tend to appropriate for oneself things that should be common. Second, because knowing is complex, the curious person who seeks to possess knowledge, as if it were composed merely of discrete things, will also tend to atomize pieces of knowledge, disconnecting them from their contexts and from other elements. This will render the illusion of possession much more plausible. At the same time, this desire of the curious to possess knowledge actually renders true knowledge much more difficult. Griffiths continues, "For curiosity's grasp at ownership to succeed, then, is for what is grasped immediately to be lost. It is no longer held and known as what it is—a participant in being's excess—but instead as an inert thing, objectified and gazed at as though it existed *in se*, by itself alone."[17]

With regard to idolatry, it is equally important to recognize a potential irony in the curious person's desire to possess what is known. That is, as one seeks to possess what is known, the object comes to possess the person. Augustine displays this with regard to his good friend Alypius in *Confessions* 6.8. Having disdained the gladiatorial games for most of his life, one day Alypius is finally persuaded by his friends to accompany them. He proclaims that though he will attend in body, his eyes and heart will be elsewhere. He thus thinks he will overcome both his friends and the spectacle. For the most part, he is successful, until, at the climactic point in the contest, the crowd roars. Alypius is "overcome by curiosity" (*curiositate victus*). The sound that entered his ears "unlocked his eyes," and from that point on the curious Alypius is captivated by the games, returning repeatedly, until God plucks him out of his compulsion. In addition to this episode, several of the examples of idolatry I have already explored in this volume provide analogous examples of curiosity. Although Scripture as a whole tends to say very little about the motives for human actions, it appears that one of the motives for fabricating images—even of the LORD—is to render God more manageable, more capable of human manipulation, and ultimately to domesticate God. Rather than being possessed by God, the idolater seeks to possess God or, sometimes, many gods through the fabrication of an image.

Finally, the curious do not direct their desire to know toward God, and do not seek to know things in their relation to God. "The curious man misidentifies (and so misprizes) what his appetite seeks. He understands the knowledge he seeks to be capable of ownership by himself because he thinks it is not already inextricably subject to God."[18] Those familiar with Augustine's thought will not find this surprising. For him, all of our appetites misfire, misdirect, and fail to find rest and fulfillment until they are properly ordered relative to our desire for God.[19]

Curiosity as a Key to Deuteronomy 12–13

If one takes "curiosity" to be the disposition that inclines believers to idolatry in Deuteronomy 12:30–13:18, several insights emerge. First, recall that the move to imitate and follow the religious practices of the Canaanites after these have been removed from the land is driven by the curious question "How did these nations worship their gods?" This question reflects all of the characteristics of the vice of curiosity. It seeks the unknown and the new in the sense that these practices are unknown and new to the Israelites. Obviously, these practices have their own past, even if they have been suppressed.[20] Further, it would appear that curious Israelites desire this knowledge in order to follow Canaanite religious practice. They do not seek this knowledge in order to protect themselves or to better avoid these practices. They want to possess this knowledge in order to use it. They may not plan to abandon worship of the LORD completely, but they are certainly diluting their single-minded attention to and love of the LORD in favor of a new set of experiences.

Further, as the verb "ensnare" in 12:30 indicates, despite the fact that the Israelites may seek this knowledge as something to possess and control, it is really a trap. They will end up being controlled by, rather than controlling, this knowledge. This becomes clear as the books of Kings and Chronicles narrate the subsequent history. Rather than simply possessing this knowledge, it comes to possess them in much the same way Alypius becomes captivated by gladiatorial contests. Finally, it should be clear that this knowledge is sought independently of God. Indeed, it is in direct disobedience to the LORD. At this point it appears that there is now some purchase on the suggestion that curiosity becomes one more disposition that inclines the people of God toward idolatry.

In addition, if one takes Deuteronomy 13 to develop further aspects of the disposition to curiosity reflected in the question found in 12:30, it becomes clear that this form of curiosity operates in a communal context. The signs and portents of a prophet can direct the curious. Likewise, the pull of friends and family and the suasions of civic leaders can lead the curious into idolatry. This would indicate that one's relationships with a whole host of others can be crucial in shaping one's intellectual appetites in one way rather than another. This important observation is not particularly surprising. Our connections to others play a significant role in shaping our desires, perceptions, and actions.

CURIOSITY AND IDOLATRY IN ACTS 17

Before moving to discuss dispositions that might address believers' tendencies toward curiosity and idolatry, I want to look at one further passage that relates curiosity and idolatry, Acts 17:16-34. This passage recounts Paul's speech to the Athenians. Given my previous discussions about the differences between the idolatry of unbelievers and that of believers, it may seem odd to bring this passage into the discussion. In this passage Paul is clearly addressing unbelievers, people whose idolatry, though vexing to Paul, is not surprising. In many respects the narrative reflects many of the standard Jewish and Christian criticisms of pagan idolatry found in Wisdom 12–15 and Romans 1. If, however, one of the larger rhetorical aims of Acts is both to contrast a nascent Christian culture with the dominant Greco-Roman culture and to contribute resources that would enable Christian readers to construct and maintain their own identity and culture within that world, then this episode may fall closer to the interests of this volume.[21]

To set the scene: Paul is in Athens waiting for the arrival of his friends Silas and Timothy. He is distressed to find that the city is full of idols.[22] He is thus provoked into debating with Jews in the synagogues and Greek philosophers in the markets. The Athenians take him to be "proclaiming strange (or foreign) divinities" (ξένων δαιμονίων). As Luke relates this, it appears that Paul's audience takes his proclamation about Jesus and the resurrection to be referring to two gods, Jesus and his consort Anastasis (ὅτι τὸν Ἰησοῦν καὶ τὴν ἀνάστασιν εὐηγγελίζετο).

The possibility that Paul may be proclaiming some religious novelty gains him a hearing with the Athenians. As Luke has set the context, a number of different overtones are audible as Paul begins his speech. Paul, from his side, is vexed by Athenian idolatry. Paul's initial audience in the market treats him as a babbler or a scandalmonger.[23] Those who hear Paul "grab hold of him" (ἐπιλαβόμενοί [17:19]) and lead him to the hill of Ares.[24] One may also recall that Socrates was killed by the Athenians for introducing new gods into the city. It seems clear that the Athenians at this time do not consider Paul a threat to the city in the way their predecessors viewed Socrates. Nevertheless, as Luke describes this situation, it is anything but an abstract exchange of views in a neutral intellectual context.[25]

Further, Luke describes the Athenians as those "who like nothing better than hearing and speaking about new things" (17:20-21). Indeed, Luke uses the comparative form of the adjective "new." In this way, he firmly locates at least part of the Athenians' motives squarely in the realm of a *curiositas* that seeks ever-new ideas to possess as discrete items of interest.

Paul begins his speech by noting that the Athenians are δεισιδαιμονεστέρους. This term can imply that they are extremely religious, on the one hand. On the other hand, it can also serve to criticize them as being extremely superstitious. From one perspective, it would seem odd to begin one's attempt to convince an audience of the truth of one's views by insulting them. Alternatively, if this speech might be read as a part of a larger rhetorical project directed at believers reading or hearing Acts, opposing Christianity to a dangerous and inferior Greco-Roman culture, then it makes sense to read this passage as a criticism of Athenian idolatry. Of course, the audience in Athens may well hear Paul flattering their religious observance, while the reader of Acts sees this as a sharp criticism of Athenian idolatry.[26] These are not mutually exclusive options.

For my purposes, it is sufficient to note that from Luke's perspective Athenian idolatry appears to be founded on their curious quest for novel ideas and is underwritten by an unwillingness or an inability to "studiously" move from what knowledge they do have to knowledge of the one living God.[27] We also get some confirmation of this view when we learn that Paul's audience hardly lets him finish. When he mentions the resurrection of the dead, Paul's audience scoffs. If they expected that ἀνάστασις was Jesus' divine consort, they may have been looking forward to a story with salacious detail.[28] When it becomes clear that Paul is speaking about something very different, his audience seems to lose interest. Most do not listen long enough to learn about Jesus' resurrection. They are not interested in the truly new, radical, and transformative event of resurrection. They are not interested in recognizing and correcting their ignorance or repenting of their sin. As Patrick Gray points out, "the curious man is loath to dwell on his own sins. The sins of others are far more interesting, but the call to repentance in v. 30 forces the individual to turn inward."[29]

This brings up another interesting irony with the curious. Their curiosity for novelty is of a very limited type. Their interest in the new is limited to new things that can already fit comfortably within the current limits of their imagination. They really seek new versions of the same, since that would not require interior reflection and transformation.[30] In this respect curiosity is simply a shadow form of genuine inquiry or reflection.

One can find a further example of the connection between *curiositas* and idolatry in 17:24-29. There Luke has Paul note that although the Athenians have some sense of the connection between God and creation, they fundamentally misunderstand the nature of that connection. They attempt to know things in relation to God, but because they fail properly to know God, they cannot avoid idolatry.[31] In many respects this account is a slightly more sympathetic version of the accounts of pagan idolatry in both Wisdom 12–15 and Romans 1.

In both Deuteronomy 12:30–13:19 and Acts 17:15-34 we see the close connection between forms of *curiositas* and idolatry. In the case of Deuteronomy the LORD is concerned that, if the people of God are not careful, their curiosity will lead them into idolatry. The Deuteronomy passage functions as an internal warning to the people of God.

In the case of Acts, Luke makes it plain that Athenian idolatry, which Paul finds so distressing, is rooted in their curiosity. They are eager for novelty, but cannot entertain the radically transformative claims about Jesus' resurrection. Moreover, they fail to understand the proper relationships between created things and the one God. For Luke, this passage is part of a pervasive criticism of pagan idolatry, indicating that Christianity offers something radically different from and superior to its contemporary alternatives. Given the readership of Acts, the point of this criticism is not primarily to convert unbelievers, but to help form a culture among believers capable of resisting parallel forms of the curiosity that plagues the people of God in Deuteronomy 12–13.

Thus, *curiositas* is a disposition that will incline believers to idolatry. Moreover, as Augustine understands it, curiosity is a disposition of the "eyes." As Griffiths notes, the key biblical text Augustine ties to curiosity is 1 John 2:16, where the ἡ ἐπιθυμία τῶν ὀφθαλμῶν is translated by *concupiscentia oculorum*, "the possessive desire of the gaze."[32] This verse is part of a typically Johannine contrast between "the world" and God. This Johannine way of presenting things offers a clear contrast between the things of the world and the things of God. This is combined with firm admonitions to abandon the world in favor of God. As John presents it, this is a zero-sum game. One side only gains at the expense of the other. This is important guidance for Christians. There are numerous occasions when Christians have been far too willing to blur lines between "the world" and God that should have otherwise been clear and bright. The Johannine perspective is a clear reminder that a significant part of the Christian life is the Christ-focused, Spirit-directed formation and reformation of our perceptual habits, whether visual, auditory, tactile, or otherwise.[33]

I would, however, like to qualify and supplement this Johannine perspective in several respects. First, however, one must also say, when drawing distinctions between the world and God, that it is important that believers draw such distinctions under the guidance of love for rather than disdain for or hatred of the world. Moreover, 1 John in particular offers important, but limited, guidance about how to distinguish between the desires of the world and the desires of God. 1 John 2:8-11 indicates that loving one's brothers and sisters in Christ will help one remain in the light. No doubt this is correct, but it may not offer enough guidance in specific situations. Thus, I would like to offer a Lucan supplement to the Johannine perspective. In Luke Jesus calls his followers to have a "single" or "healthy" eye. By examining this idea in Luke, I hope to offer a further alternative to the *curiositas* that disposes believers to idolatry.

COUNTERING CURIOSITY WITH A "SINGLE" EYE

Although it is clear from Deuteronomy 13 and Acts 17 that one can exercise *curiositas* through the ears (and other senses as well), Augustine's point seems to be that *curiositas* is dependent upon patterns, habits, and manners of perception. In contrast to these patterns, habits, and forms of perception that shape and are shaped by a curious disposition, Jesus offers an alternative when he commands his followers to develop a "single" eye. "Your eye is the lamp of your body; when your eye is single (ἁπλοῦς) then your body is full of light; but when it is not sound (πονηρὸς), then your whole body is full of darkness. Therefore, be vigilant lest the light in you (prove to) be darkness" (Luke 11:34-35). Jesus offers this admonition after he has been accused in 11:14-26 of casting out demons by the power of Satan. In response to this accusation, he notes, first of all, that a kingdom divided against itself cannot survive (11:17-18). The implication of this is that if Jesus is casting out demons by God's power ("by the finger of God"),[34] then these exorcisms serve as a sign of God's inbreaking rule (11:20). Such signs call for a singular response—follow Jesus, the stronger man of v. 22. Any other response is taken to be a form of opposition (11:23).

After this episode, a woman interjects, "Blessed is the womb that bore you and the breasts which you sucked!" Jesus corrects this assertion, noting that the response he seeks is not admiration of him (or his mother), but "keeping and doing the word of God."[35] Again, there is an emphasis on the appropriate, single-minded response Jesus demands as he marches to Jerusalem.[36]

Immediately following this, Jesus addresses the crowd from which the woman in v. 27 shouted to him. He criticizes them both for seeking a (further?) sign from him. This crowd's request for a sign could be taken to reflect a form of *curiositas*. Because they have not perceived and responded to wisdom greater than Solomon's and preaching greater than Jonah's, they will be judged. As with Acts 17, the curiosity that drives the crowds to ask for a sign also renders them blind to something that is truly, radically different. Thus, they cannot understand Jesus and respond appropriately. Moreover, as vv. 34-36 make clear, they are responsible for this blindness because they are responsible for keeping their eye "sound," "single," or well-focused. The term used to characterize the sort of vision one should have is ἁπλοῦς. This word normally is used to mean "single" rather than, say, "double." This reading, however, is not particularly informative as an account of human sight. Susan Garrett, following C. Edlund, has persuasively argued that in this context keeping one's eye ἁπλοῦς has to do with focusing one's attention on God alone. "The expression would have conveyed the notion that a given individual *focuses his or her eye on God alone*. No worldly pleasures, no competing masters, no evil spirits can cause a person of 'the single eye' to compromise his or her integrity toward the Lord."[37] Garrett bases her view on a study of the ways ἁπλοῦς and its related nominal and adverbial forms are used in the LXX and the Testament of the Twelve Patriarchs. In particular, one finds in Testament of Issachar 4:1-6 a number of occurrences of ἁπλοῦς to designate the virtue of integrity. In Testament of Issachar 4:1-6 the occurrences of ἁπλοῦς present integrity as a virtue whose practice is tied up with one's vision. For example, in 4:6 we are told that the person of integrity "lives his life straightforwardly, and views all things single-mindedly (πορεύεται γὰρ ἐν εὐθύτητι ζωῆς, καὶ πάντα ὁρᾷ ἐν ἁπλότητι), not admitting with the eyes evils that come from the world's error, lest he look perversely upon any of the Lord's commands."[38] Garrett further notes that in the Testament of the Twelve Patriarchs Belial strongly opposes the practice of such single-minded integrity.[39] This is particularly interesting in the light of the dispute regarding Jesus' relationship to Satan at the beginning of Luke 11.

Given this way of reading ἁπλοῦς (I will use the English "single" from here on), in Luke 11:34 Jesus appears to be expanding his specific critique of the crowds' moral and spiritual blindness in 11:29-32 into a more general admonition.[40] The eye comes to stand, synecdochally, for all of one's powers of perception and judgment, for the way one's intellectual appetites are formed. If these powers are single-mindedly focused on Jesus, then one is full of light. An absence of such single-minded attention on Jesus is the sign of a defective (πονηρὸς) eye, resulting in spiritual darkness.

This is followed in 11:35 by a warning. One must beware lest the "light" in you be darkness. This seems to be a warning against being deceived (either by

Satan, or by someone else, or by oneself) into thinking that one is full of light when in fact one is in darkness. Such deception would come about by diverting one's single-minded attention from Jesus.[41] The admonition of 11:34-35 indicates that being able to make an appropriate and sustained response to an encounter with Jesus requires that one pay attention to the state of one's "eye." This is because keeping the body illuminated with true light requires maintaining the eye as a single-minded instrument focused on God.[42] This task requires ongoing attention; it is not a once-for-all achievement. Indeed, as 11:36 cryptically notes, this task will be completed at the eschaton, when all darkness will be removed from those with a single eye.[43]

Those who follow Jesus, then, are enjoined to attend to the character of their eye. That is, they are to attend to the faculties by which they come to perceive Jesus and make judgments about him. To perceive Jesus properly, to judge rightly about him, requires one to maintain a single-minded focus on him. One can see that success in this will tend to breed more success. Properly perceiving Jesus will, with the Spirit's help, allow one to cultivate a deeper relationship with him. This will entail both growth in one's love and knowledge of Jesus as well as a turning away from one's sins. In the course of this one learns how to perceive him in new, deeper, and more profound ways. This will, in turn, allow one again, under the guidance of the Spirit, to further cultivate one's perceptive capacities. Moreover, we can assume that such growth in one's perceptual faculties will not simply be limited to the ways in which one perceives Jesus. Rather, it will shape the way one views the entirety of one's life in the world, thus providing an alternative to the manner of perceiving things that funds *curiositas*.

To fail in this regard is to open oneself to darkness. As 11:35 indicates, the most dangerous type of failure is to fall into that deception by which one comes to think that darkness is light. That is, one's eye can become so distorted that it confuses darkness with light. This type of failure is particularly poignant because it can only befall those who are seeking to be filled with light.[44]

Although the term ἁπλοῦς does not appear again, Luke's Gospel displays numerous characters that either succeed or fail in exercising the single-minded vision called for in 11:34-36. An examination of some of them may help to display the character of the vigilance called for here. For example, in 18:9-14 we find a brief parable told to those who "are confident of their own righteousness [δίκαιοι] and who scorned others."[45] This passage, which relates the prayers of a Pharisee and a tax collector, may well be the most explicit narrative example of the issues addressed in 11:35. The Pharisee's prayer is a thanksgiving for all of the ways he is filled with "light." His prayer does not so much thank God for granting him such virtue as it boasts that he had attained it (unlike others).[46] Interestingly, attention to the sins of others, such as this Pharisee displays, is a distinctive feature of monastic accounts of *curiositas*.[47] Alternatively, the tax collector is simply able to identify himself as a sinner and to ask God for mercy. This passage recalls both 7:36-50 and 16:14-15, where Jesus upbraids the Pharisees for their failure both to see themselves properly and rightly to identify God's desires for sinful people. It is not surprising that Jesus offers the judgment that it is the tax collector who leaves justified (δεδικαιωμένος).

The story of the rich ruler found in 18:18-24 can also be read as an example of failure to develop and maintain a single eye. This becomes clearer when this story is contrasted with the single-minded focus on Jesus demonstrated by Zaccheus in 19:1-10.[48] The ruler comes to Jesus wanting to know how he might inherit eternal life (18:18). He admits to having observed the commandments from his youth (18:21). According to Jesus, the only thing remaining for him to do is to sell all of his riches, give it to the poor, and become a disciple (18:22). At that point the ruler goes away. He does not dispute the truth of what Jesus says. Rather, we get the clear impression that he is unable to do the one thing that would provide him with the life he sought. He is curious in the way that does not allow him to receive something that is actually new and life changing.

Zacchaeus, on the other hand, merely wants to see Jesus (19:3). He ends up finding salvation (σωτηρία [19:9]), the very thing sought by the rich ruler. Zacchaeus, the rich tax collector, seems to move easily into the kingdom, a move which seemed so impossible to the ruler. Based on his observance of the commandments (18:20-21), the ruler presumably considered himself a child of Abraham. His encounter with Jesus, however, leaves us in doubt of this. Alternatively, Zacchaeus, a widely recognized and self-confessed sinner (19:7-8),[49] turns out to be a "son of Abraham" based on the manner in which he receives Jesus. The ruler fails to attain that which he sought because he is unable to do the one final thing Jesus asked of him—give up his riches. Zacchaeus, with no prompting from Jesus, cannot seem to get rid of his riches fast enough. The rich ruler is too hesitant, too circumspect. Zacchaeus, rather, presents a picture of one who single-mindedly abandons anything which previously might have kept him from finding salvation. The story begins with him wanting to see Jesus. He does so in a way that shows that his eye is single. The ruler demonstrates that very dangerous position of the curious, mistaking darkness for light; lacking a single eye, he fails to embrace a new type of light when it is offered to him.

Consider also the story of the "woman who was a sinner" and Simon the Pharisee in 7:36-50. The sinful woman's single-minded attention to Jesus focuses on washing and anointing his feet (7:37-38). Simon also has an interest in Jesus, but it is of a different, curious, sort.[50] Simon seems more interested in determining whether or not Jesus is a prophet (7:39) than in attending to him in the way a more hospitable host might have done (7:44-46). Again, the "sinner" manifests the single eye.[51]

What is striking about those who fail to demonstrate the sort of single-minded attention required of those who would be filled with light is that they are all interested in Jesus. It is not the case that they are ignorant of or indifferent to him. They are curious. Nevertheless, they are not attentive in the appropriate way or to a sufficient degree. Moreover, they lack the self-knowledge shown by those who respond to Jesus appropriately. In Luke's gospel, those who respond best to Jesus are those who can identify themselves as sinners. In fact, it would seem that to keep one's eye single-mindedly fixed on Jesus requires the ability to see oneself as a sinner whose redemption is through a single-minded attention to Jesus.

If my reading of Deuteronomy and Acts brings out the idea that *curiositas* is a disposition that will incline believers (and unbelievers such as the Athenians) toward idolatry, then the cultivation of a devoted attentiveness to Jesus characterized by the phrase ὁ ὀφθαλμός ἁπλοῦς, "the single eye," will help incline believers toward fidelity. The single eye will result in a proper attention to one's own sins rather than those of others; it will stand in contrast to the ἡ ἐπιθυμία τῶν ὀφθαλμῶν, "the possessive desire of the eyes," which Augustine argued was the foundation of curiosity.

Keeping a Single Eye in Our Distracted Age

It should be clear both that *curiositas*, as Christians have traditionally understood it, is a vice and that it is one that will incline believers toward idolatry. Moreover, the forms of attention required to resist *curiositas* are not easily won or retained. This is especially the case in our current distracted age. I am not sure that anyone highlights the difficulties surrounding the formation of Christian attention in our current environment better than Michael Budde. Beginning with his book *The (Magic) Kingdom of God* and continuing through a series of essays and articles, Budde lays out the stark contrast between the traditional patterns and practices of Christian formation and the current patterns and practices through which "global culture industries" form people in the United States.

One of the hardest elements for contemporary Christians to grasp is that even though they may not be directly engaged in active Christian formation, this does not mean that they are not being formed. Given our current form of capitalism, in which the cultivation of increasing levels of consumption has replaced the quest to balance supply and demand characteristic of earlier forms of capitalism, it should not come as a surprise that there are very powerful interests at work seeking to form us into being good and active consumers. One of the chief aspects of this formation is focused on the control of our attention.

Budde notes that from the earliest days of the church the formation of new members was a matter of great seriousness. The formation of new members required such elements as substantial investments of time from both the individual and the community; "a process of *sequential learning*, with knowledge building upon knowledge and practice upon practice" in order to develop sufficient levels of competence to live and worship faithfully as a Christian; "an apprenticeship with a church member" who would both guide the neophyte and act as exemplar; "materials of instruction"; "a formal examination with rejection a live possibility"; real and binding obligations on the community to continue to support and nurture new believers; and a capacity to pray as a Christian.[52]

In contrast with these patterns and practices by which new believers are formed to take their place in the body of Christ, Budde discusses the patterns and practices employed by the global culture industries in order to form us to take our place in the global economy. The ultimate aim here is the orchestration of our attention.[53] It is not simply the case that "the possessive desire of our eyes" is given free reign. Rather, that desire is both heightened and directed in specific ways rather than others. Modern technological advances have made this an extremely sophisticated and subtle set of processes. Images and messages from previous times and places are plundered, removed from their original contexts, and combined with new images and messages in order to create levels of desire and dissatisfaction in us so that we continue to consume.[54] We are presented with a world that appears to require no serious interpretation; that can be accessed fully and immediately without prior training; that is always available.

Such formation works to undermine our patience so that we disdain the difficult, abandon whatever does not entertain us, and demand ever new experiences. As I already noted above, however, these experiences are not so much new as new versions of the same.[55] Though Augustine could hardly have imagined it, one would have to work hard to devise a more supportive environment for the development of curious people. Ironically, as the current political climate reveals, people who are "curious" in just this way are also deeply susceptible to disinformation, "fake news," and news headlines that confirm deeply held prejudices regardless of the facts.

Budde's book is somewhat dated in that it focuses on television as the medium through which the "global culture industries" most readily shape us. Today the internet and social media are more likely to play that role. Nevertheless, his basic point still holds: the patterns and practices of formation that Christianity requires in order to sustain itself, to live and worship faithfully, are starkly at odds with those patterns and practices through which the global culture industries seek to form us to be ever more dissatisfied (and hence better) consumers. Moreover, when the average churchgoer in the United States spends more time engaging the online world than in church-related activities by a factor of ten, the church appears to be wildly overmatched in the battle for our attention. Thus, believers living in these situations are much more likely to fall victim to *curiositas* and idolatry than they are to develop a "single" eye.

On top of this, Budde outlines a series of ways in which the approach most churches take to these global culture industries manifests an astonishing inability to perceive how these industries form people and how dangerously close the church is to becoming simply one more global culture industry.[56] "Unless Catholics and other Christians make their lives as a called, gathered community of disciples, a people 'on the way,' their *primary* point of reference and identity, the gospel will remain emaciated and marginalized by the effects of culture industries, militarized patriotism, capitalism, and other systems of exclusion and domination."[57]

If cultivating a "single eye" results in the disposition that will most directly counter our tendencies toward *curiositas* and hence idolatry, then Budde's work provides believers with a very sobering recognition of how difficult that will be in the current age. In addition, in lessons from Deuteronomy 13 through to the present, it is clear that our dispositions toward either *curiositas* or a single-minded attention to Jesus are shaped in community. Recall the three contexts in Deuteronomy 13 in which the Israelites are going to be tempted to exercise their curiosity and worship other gods. The first is through prophets and mediums who would deploy signs and portents. The second is through the urgings of close friends and family. The final is through those who shape the views and practices of whole towns, the civic leaders. We find further evidence for the communal context of *curiositas* in the particular concern medieval monastic communities devote to the examination and prevention of *curiositas* in their communities.[58] If *curiositas* thrives in communal contexts, this would also suggest that the cultivation of a "single eye" may also be tied to the quality of communal relations that Christians are able to sustain over time. In overcoming a distracted age and developing the proper attentiveness to Jesus, believers will need to rely on their brothers and sisters for support, encouragement, forms of exemplary behavior, and admonition if the inquiring and discerning hearts we pray for in baptism are to lead us toward the LORD rather than toward other gods.

This brings the discussion back to baptism. Recall that when I began to discuss curiosity I noted that at baptism a prayer is offered for the baptized that they would have "an inquiring and discerning heart, the courage to will and to persevere, a spirit to know and to love [God], and the gift of joy and wonder in all [God's] works."[59] Presumably this "inquiring and discerning heart" is perfectly compatible with "joy and wonder" in all of God's works and with the attentiveness characteristic of the "single eye." Nevertheless, on its own, an inquiring and discerning heart could easily lapse into a curious and distracted heart. Indeed, under the formative power of global capitalism, we should expect no other result. This would be one reason why this prayer is offered after both the community in general, and godparents and sponsors in particular, have already made promises that commit them to the formation of baptized people into lifelong disciples. Moreover, this prayer comes after the actual baptism. The baptized have been joined to the covenant people of God. This sacrament of new birth has indissolubly made them citizens of the realm of Christ. The question that abides here is whether these communities that baptize will also, with God's help, have the capacities and willingness to help form people in the Christian faith and life so that they grow into the full stature of Christ. If not, then our hopes for resisting a disposition toward *curiositas*, and then idolatry, will be slim.

CONCLUSION

In the previous chapters I offered readings of a variety of scriptural texts with the aim of displaying some of the habits and practices that, if left unchecked, are likely to lead the people of God into idolatry. I also offered readings of texts that displayed habits and practices that, if cultivated individually and communally, might help keep believers from moving into idolatry. A set of assumptions about idolatry lay behind each of these readings. I tried to account for these assumptions in the first chapter.

Perhaps the most important of these assumptions is that idolatry is less like a one-time event and more like a process. It is a process through which believers move further away from the single-minded, wholehearted love of God commanded in Deuteronomy 6:4 and reconfirmed by Jesus until at some point it makes sense to speak of them as idolaters. By that point the habits and practices that lead believers into idolatry have become so settled in them that the term "idolater" is an apt and fair description of them. There does not appear to be a clear way of knowing when one has reached that point. The images of blindness and deafness are so deeply woven into descriptions of Israel's idolatry that it gives one reason to think that determining the precise point at which one becomes an idolater might not be worth the effort. Instead, I have stressed that one should avoid even getting close to this position.

I recognize that I have not offered a complete list of the habits and practices that may lead believers either toward idolatry or into deeper, more sustained love of God and neighbor. I do not know what such a complete list might look like, nor would I know how to determine it was complete. Rather than display further discussions of those dispositions that lead toward or away from idolatry, I want to conclude this volume with further reflections on the nature of idolatry for believers, especially Christians in the United States today. These build upon and presume the discussions of the previous chapters.

CAUTIONS ABOUT IDOLATRY IN THE PRESENT

When people learn I am working on a book on idolatry, they assume that there currently are numerous examples of idolatry in the churches of the United States. They also assume my work will describe these in rich prophetic detail. If they have a background in theology, they may remind me of Calvin's claim that the human heart/mind is a perpetual forge or factory for idols.[1] After making this claim, Calvin goes on to say, "The human mind, stuffed as it is with presumptuous rashness, dares to imagine a god suited to its own capacity; as it labors under dullness, nay, is sunk in the grossest ignorance, it substitutes vanity and an empty phantom in the place of God." At the beginning of this paragraph Calvin explicitly alludes to Wisdom of Solomon's account of idolatry in Wisdom 12–15. In chapter 1, I discussed these chapters in Wisdom. Wisdom's account notes that people have a basis for belief in the one true God through their apprehension and appreciation of the good things of creation. Ideally, they should have extended their imaginations to probe behind these things to find their creator and Lord (Wis 13:1-5). They did not. Too often people treated the beauty and delights of creation as ends, worshiping them as gods.

Unlike Calvin's more universal claims about humanity, Wisdom is offering an account of idolatry that describes the idolatry of unbelievers. It accounts for how they misperceive aspects of the created order and end up worshiping the creature rather than the creator. Looking at idolatry from this perspective, idolatry is easy. In fact, it seems almost unavoidable. This makes me uneasy on several levels.

The first is relatively minor and is tied to Calvin's deeply polemical context. Despite Calvin's universal claims about the human propensity toward idolatry, one should also note that Calvin is particularly interested in making his claims about idolatry with regard to the Roman Catholic Church's commitment to images, a commitment Calvin takes to be a sign of the church's idolatrous corruption. Hence, the first qualification concerns images and the material world. Calvin's discussion draws on the iconoclastic controversies of the eighth and ninth centuries. His charges and assertions against Catholicism might lead one to believe that the material world in general, and the use of images by Christians in particular, inevitably incline believers toward idolatry. The discussion of Deuteronomy 6 in chapter 2 and the other chapters of this volume repeatedly make the point that God favors the use of the material world in worship and devotion. Keeping "these words" as signs on people, houses, and public buildings is a crucial practice to remembering the LORD (cf. Deut 6:6-9). The bounty of the promised land can be an occasion for forgetting the LORD, but it is also an occasion for blessing God's goodness (cf. the discussion of Num 9:25 in chapter 2). The material world on its own inclines one neither toward nor away from idolatry. Ironically, living in a context that does not purposely fabricate idols may require that believers have a deeper attentiveness to their engagements with the material world since almost any created phenomenon might distract one from the single-minded, wholehearted love of God. This is where the discussion of temperance, generosity, and so on in chapter 2 particularly comes into play.

The second way in which Calvin's position makes me uneasy is that, by claiming the human heart is a perpetual idol factory, it tends to assume that idolatry is the default condition of all humans at all times. It allows for no distinctions between believers and unbelievers in this matter. It cannot account for growth in holiness. Calvin (and he is not alone in this) draws on the discussion of the idolatry of unbelievers in Wisdom 12–15 (maybe also Rom 1) and applies it to believers. Yes, it may be the case that the hearts of unbelievers are perpetual idol factories. Nevertheless, as troubling as this may be, given the account in Wisdom 12–15, it is not altogether surprising. The claim that the human heart is a perpetual idol factory does not account for believers whose hearts must be in some ways transformed from their unbelieving state. There must, at least in principle, if not always in practice, be a difference from those baptized into the death and resurrection of Christ, whose hearts are, over time, and in the light of specific dispositions, gradually distracted away from the single-minded love of God and neighbor. This, at least, seems to be assumed in Paul's letters. As my students, whose questions got this project underway, already understood, this type of idolatry, the idolatry of believers, raises much more troubling issues. Calling all human hearts perpetual idol factories does not really get at this important difference.

As I indicated in chapter 1, I think it is important to distinguish between accounts of idolatry such as Wisdom 12–15 and Romans 1, each of which describes the idolatry of unbelievers on the one hand, and the idolatry of those who are believers, which is the focus of this volume, on the other hand. Secondly, even though it is possible that believers can and do reach the point where "idolater" is a fair and apt description of them, I hesitate to make such definitive claims about my fellow Christians in the United States today. This is primarily because the witness of the prophets is that once one is clearly an idolater there are very few who turn back from that path. The blindness and deafness that accompany idolatry make it ever more difficult to recognize and repent of one's idolatry. One should never doubt the capacities of the Spirit to break through and lead us back to repentance. Alternatively, the track record of the prophets, led by that same Spirit, is not good. To address idolatry in the ways that I have in the course of the volume means that identifying any of my fellow Christians as idolaters is to render a bleak judgment. It may be true, but I leave it to others to make that claim.

I also recognize that stopping at this point is not sufficient. I do believe there are some elements in contemporary church life in the United States—at least the churches I am familiar with—that one might well understand in terms of the account of idolatry offered in this volume. In these elements I find many of the habits, practices, and dispositions that I have argued above can lead believers into idolatry if left unchecked. I want to conclude by reflecting on one of the most pressing challenges, if not the single most pressing one, facing churches in the United States when it comes to grappling with idolatry and the lessons of this volume. There is no single term for this disposition or set of dispositions, but it often goes under the name of *white privilege* or *whiteness*. (Nationalism might be another example, but this is far less common in the churches I most often find myself in.)

Whiteness and Idolatry

Whiteness summarizes a collection of dispositions, practices, and habits pervasive in the United States. The sum of these dispositions, practices, and habits represents a systemic tilting of the playing field in a way that provides a set of advantages for white people while at the same time making the tilting of the field seem normal. In this light, accounts of white people who struggle on many levels in our society, as well as accounts of people of color who succeed on many levels, largely miss the point and help to reinforce our inability to see the systemic nature of this situation. Whiteness is not a guarantee of success for all white people all the time.

Nevertheless, whiteness is as deeply ingrained and normalized in the United States today as the worship of gods was in first-century Corinth. It touches virtually all aspects of life; I and others like me have been habituated into this way of thinking, acting, and perceiving to such a degree that it is what counts as normal for us. This construction of the normal is what makes whiteness so hard for people like me to see and makes calls for change and repentance so hard to hear. Moreover, it is sustained by many of the dispositions such as fear, forgetful distraction, and greed that in Scripture lead to idolatry. I recognize, however, that this analogy is not altogether apt. A Christian in Corinth can turn from idols to worship the one true God. I cannot stop being white. I can, however, learn to repent of participating in whiteness.

Whiteness is founded on and sustained by types of forgetfulness similar to those described above in chapter 2. This forgetfulness was not simply a failure of memory. Rather, forgetfulness depended on the decline or demise of many of the concrete practices that Deuteronomy 6 described as essential for the Israelites to love the Lord when they entered the promised land. Apart from maintaining these practices, practices related to how believers engage people, places, and things, it would be all too easy to eat our fill, forget the LORD, and begin to worship other gods.

Consider, for example, the disputes over removing Confederate monuments from public spaces. I suspect that many, like me, were surprised to learn that the vast majority of these monuments were not dedicated in the immediate aftermath of the Civil War. Instead, there were two particular times when there was a sharp increase in the dedication of Civil War monuments. These were the first two decades of the twentieth century, when states were beginning to enact Jim Crow laws, and during the civil rights movement in the 1950s and 1960s. The spike in dedication of Confederate monuments is thus closely tied to periods when southern states were seeking to solidify and defend white supremacy, as noted in the Southern Poverty Law Center's 2016 report "Whose Heritage? Public Symbols of the Confederacy." Remembering this context distinctively and differently shapes the way one understands the role these monuments were designed to play.

One can also see that specific forms of disordered fear, such as suspicion and preemption, underwrite and sustain whiteness. Recall that in chapter 4 I noted that, within an ethic of safety governed by disordered fear, suspicion and preemption can appear as necessary dispositions. Kelly Brown Douglas argues that these dispositions lie at the heart of a "stand your ground" culture that inevitably normalizes the treatment of black bodies as a threat.[2]

Recall that chapter 3 made the case that the greed Paul identifies as idolatry in Ephesians and Colossians is a disordered desire that rejects, and thus breaks, the communion between God and humans (as well as the communion between God, humans, and the rest of creation). Greed does not transgress a social standard of what is appropriate; it distorts and damages a relationship of communion either by desiring something other than God or by subverting that desire for God. Further, our capacities for fellowship with God shape and are shaped by our capacities for fellowship with others. First John 4:20-21 states this in typically sharp Johannine terms. Recall the image that Dorotheos of Gaza uses to describe the Christian life. In that image individual believers are points on a circle moving closer to God in the center of the circle. As one moves closer to God one must inevitably move closer to other believers.

Thus, if greed inheres in rejecting and thereby distorting communion with God in favor of something that is not God, then it is inevitable that damaged communion with God will also damage our communion with others.

In this light, whiteness enshrines a pattern of damaged communion. At its root, whiteness requires others to conform to its constructed norms in order to be welcomed. In this respect, to its detriment, Christianity reflects and participates in the logic of colonialism. As Willie James Jennings argues, "Other peoples and their ways of life had to adapt, become fluid, even morph into the colonial order of things, and such a situation drew Christianity and its theologians inside habits of mind and life that internalized and normalized that order of things."[3] Given these imposed requirements on communion, it is not at all surprising that 11 a.m. on Sundays is still the most segregated hour of the week.

Admittedly, the disposition I name as curiosity does not connect to the practices of whiteness quite as directly as the others mentioned above. There are, however, a few ways in which one might see these connections. Even for white Christians concerned with matters of race, there are numerous forces that might distract our attention from this issue. Such distractibility is not identical with curiosity, but these two dispositions overlap. Moreover, there are numerous voices within the church who argue that this issue is not as serious it might appear, that its dangers are less significant than one might think. This attitude does seem to reflect some of those displayed in Deuteronomy 12–13 that formed the basis for my discussion of curiosity.

In his "Letter from Birmingham Jail," Martin Luther King Jr. ironically glosses the question in Deuteronomy 12:30, "How did these nations worship?" in his comments about white moderates:

> I have traveled the length and breadth of Alabama and Mississippi and all the other southern states. On sweltering summer days and crisp autumn mornings I have looked at her beautiful churches with their lofty spires pointing heavenward. I have beheld the impressive outlay of her massive religious education buildings. Over and over again I have found myself asking: "What kind of people worship here? Who is their God? Where were their voices when the lips of

Governor Barnett dripped with words of interposition and nullification? Where were they when Governor Wallace gave the clarion call for defiance and hatred? Where were their voices of support when tired, bruised and weary Negro men and women decided to rise from the dark dungeons of complacency to the bright hills of creative protest?"[4]

Although King's questions about white church buildings and the god worshiped in those buildings allude to Deuteronomy 12:30, his question is not a curious question that might lead to idolatry. Rather, it reflects a bewildered wonder that those who worship in these buildings ought to be standing with him rather than opposing him. This ironic gloss on Deuteronomy 12:30 may itself be an indication that those worshiping in these buildings have already succumbed to the idolatry of whiteness.

Recall that chapter 5 relies on Luke's Gospel to argue that the cultivation of a "single eye" as a form of attentiveness focused on Jesus might counter the disposition of the curious toward idolatry. In this light, it would seem that in posing alternative ways forward, the "single eye" which serves as the antithesis to curiosity is an essential component for helping Christians in the United States begin to subvert our participation in whiteness. In chapter 5 I argued that the orchestrated distractions of the global culture industries pose the most significant threat to contemporary Christians' capacities to cultivate and maintain a "single eye." With regard to whiteness, the problem is not so much distraction as the fact that whiteness is already so deeply ingrained in us that it is the standard for what counts as normal. Coming to see how the "normal" and "natural" for most of us is formed and shaped by assumptions about white priority and privilege will be a significant initial step in our repentance. This is as much about unlearning as about overcoming distraction.

I do not presume to have offered a full account of whiteness or white supremacy. Others have done a much better job of that. Neither have I reviewed all of the arguments I make in this volume. Nevertheless, I hope I have done enough here to show that the habits, practices, and attitudes of whiteness incorporate many of the central dispositions that incline believers toward idolatry. As a way of concluding this volume, I suggest that believers can find resources for repenting of the habits, practices, and attitudes of whiteness in the cultivation of some of those dispositions that can counter believers' inclinations towards idolatry. To begin, it may be useful to see the parallels between our contemporary situation and that of the people of God as related in Jeremiah.

THE CHALLENGE OF TOO MANY PROPHETS

When it comes to matters of idolatry in U.S. churches, whether it concerns whiteness or any other matter, there is no shortage of theologians, pastors, and others from all sides eager to take up the prophetic mantle, each pointing out the idolatries of the other, each calling the other to abandon their ways and repent. Rather than a complete absence of prophets, we have a surfeit of prophets calling the church in conflicting directions. To whom should one listen? This situation is not all that different from the context in which Jeremiah delivers his prophetic call to the people of Judea. It is easy to forget that in his time Jeremiah was not the only prophet working in Jerusalem. Many prophets adopted the view that God would never let Jerusalem, and the Temple in particular, fall into pagan hands. The Temple was the dwelling place of God, and God would never willingly become homeless. Hence, God's deliverance and peace must be just at hand. Against this message Jeremiah argued that God will not and cannot overlook Judah's persistent sin forever. Conforming to God's desires meant submitting to God's impending judgment at the hands of the Babylonians.

This contrast of prophetic voices is neatly displayed in Jeremiah 28 in the conflicting accounts offered by Hananiah and Jeremiah. Hananiah asserts, against Jeremiah, that the LORD has already decreed that the successes enjoyed by the king of Babylon will be reversed and things will soon be restored to their rightful order (Jer 28:1-4). Jeremiah certainly would like this vision to be true (Jer 28:6). But this is not what God has in store for the Judeans. God will bring the Judeans into exile, and because he has led the people to trust in a lie, Hananiah will die within the year.

In the midst of a cacophony of prophetic voices, I do not propose to try to separate the Jeremiahs from the Hananiahs of our day. Instead, if white Christians in the United States are to begin to unlearn and repent of our whiteness, I think we may initially find guidance by looking to the letter that Jeremiah sends to the exiles in Babylon in Jeremiah 29.

This letter makes it clear that exile is part of God's plan for those in Babylon. In 29:11, we read that God's plan is intentional, not haphazard, and that it is ultimately a plan for shalom, "to give you a future with hope" (29:11). The instructions to the exiles are quite clear and seemingly mundane. Unlike the Israelites in Deuteronomy, they will not walk into houses they did not build, eat from gardens they did not plant, or drink from wells and vineyards made by others. Instead, they are to build their own houses and inhabit them; plant gardens and eat from them; marry and multiply. In short, they are to "seek the shalom of the city where I have sent you and pray to the Lord on its behalf, for in its shalom you will find your shalom" (29:7).

Should this command have any import for Christians, and particularly white Christians, in America? On the one hand, if one takes Jesus' peripatetic ministry, his claim to have no place to lay his head, the evangelistic impulse in Christianity that led Paul and others to engage in extensive missionary travels, and the NT's language about Christians as pilgrims and citizens of no earthly kingdom, it is not difficult to think that Christians, unlike the exiles in Babylon, are not and should not be rooted to any particular place. On the other hand, even if, or perhaps because, Christians are resident aliens, or, exiles, or pilgrims, we, like the exiles in Jeremiah, are called to seek the shalom of the place where God has put us. We Christians are pilgrims, but pilgrims who inhabit places as those who are rooted there because that is how God wants us to inhabit any and all places we might find ourselves. This is the only way to establish solidarity with and love of our neighbors. This will inevitably require us to know our place and to know ourselves as people of a place.

To seek the welfare or shalom of the cities where God has placed us today, Christians in the United States will need to understand those places. Whether God has placed us somewhere for a long time, or temporarily, Christians cannot seek the shalom of any place unless they understand it as a particular someplace, somewhere with a past that has influenced both its present and how one might imagine its future. If forgetting is a disposition that inclines the people of God toward idolatry, then beginning to understand where God has put us will be a central practice of remembering.

This sort of remembering will be crucial for the task at hand because, as Jennings has argued, one of the key conceptual and practical moves that enabled and sustained racialized identities and colonial domination was when Europeans came to think of Africans apart from their specific place. This enabled racialized identities to arise, with disastrous results. "Without place as the articulator of identity, human skin was asked to fly solo and speak for itself."[5]

Further, learning about one's place may not be as simple as reading a history book or studying demographic surveys, though it may well involve those things. More profoundly, learning about a place is likely to involve recognizing those people and stories that have not typically been seen or heard, those missed in the surveys and ignored in the histories. This will require a sharpening of our perceptual capacities so that we do not simply see or hear what is immediately in front of us, but also recognize what we are not, but should be, hearing and seeing. It may require a redrawing of the boundaries of the place where we find ourselves so that they are different, perhaps more flexible and more porous. Only to the extent that believers come to a renewed understanding of the place where God has led them can they genuinely seek its shalom. In addition, as I indicated in chapter 2, a transformation in the way one thinks of places will also change the way one thinks of people and things in relation to God. Moreover, this would reflect the type of "single-eyed" attentiveness that will keep *curiositas* at bay.

Recall that in response to the dispositions of fear and greed that incline the people of God toward idolatry, I proposed love and thanksgiving as counterdispositions. With regard to whiteness, I think love and thanksgiving take on a particular form. I want to describe these in light of Jennings' work and my own work on Ephesians.

Continuing the emphasis on place that begins his book, Jennings rightly indicates in his final chapter that the threat of thinking of Christian identity apart from place may ultimately arise from our sinful habit of forgetting that Christian identity must not be disconnected from its roots in God's election of and dealings with Israel.

For example, it is essential to recall both that God freely and graciously elects and that God freely and graciously elects Israel. If God's freedom in election becomes disconnected from the particular election of Israel, then it becomes much easier to use biblical texts and theological notions of election to provide Christian support for a whole range of nationalist ideologies, including, but not limited to, whiteness.[6]

When we who are gentiles remember God's gracious election of a particular people, we will recognize that we are, at root, outsiders to this story. Like Jennings, I find that Ephesians 2:11-22 is a crucial text here.[7] In 2:11-22 Paul reflects on the relationships between Jews and gentiles in Christ. In both Romans and Galatians one finds similar concerns. In those two epistles one gets the clear impression that there is significant tension within each of these communities over how to resolve issues of Jewish and gentile unity in Christ. These issues are not evident in Ephesians. There does not seem to be any pressure on Ephesian gentile believers to take on circumcision or Torah observance. There is no sense in which gentile Christians are treating their Jewish brothers and sisters as second-class citizens in God's kingdom. Indeed, it does not seem that the Ephesian Christians have much, if any, contact with Jewish Christians. As a result, the discussion in Ephesians is different from those in Romans and Galatians. As a result, it may prove more directly relevant to contemporary American Christians.

Ephesians 2:11 begins with an admonition, "Therefore, remember that you formerly were gentiles in the flesh, called the uncircumcision by those called the circumcision—a circumcision in the flesh, made by hands." This "therefore" in 2:11 must, at least, draw on the previous verse, where Paul indicates that God has "created us in Christ Jesus for good works." Thus, the immediate good work that seems to be in view is the work of memory.[8] In this respect, one can think of "remembering" as an example of being "transformed by the renewing of your minds" such as Paul advocates in Romans 12:2. That is, one of the primary good works that God has prepared beforehand for believers to walk in is the reconstruction or repair of our memories. This is so that both Ephesian and contemporary believers come to see their past (and their present and future) from the perspective of God's saving activity.

In 2:11 the Ephesians are called to remember their identity as gentiles. This is not as straightforward as it might seem. Romans, Greeks, and other non-Jews in Ephesus (or elsewhere) would never refer to themselves as gentiles. That designation only has currency within Judaism. Indeed, one might say that there are only gentiles because there are Jews. From the perspective of being in Christ, Romans, Greeks, Scythians, or any other inhabitant of Ephesus need to learn that they are gentiles. They need to remember (or reconceive) their past as a gentile past. They need to learn both what being a gentile meant when they were outside of Christ and what it means now that they are in Christ.

As 2:11 indicates, being a gentile meant most obviously that one was uncircumcised. Yet Paul here seems to relativize the importance of circumcision for gentile identity. That is, the most visible way of identifying gentiles might not be the most significant way.

Having indicated that circumcision is not the most significant thing to remembering one's gentile past, Paul goes on to note those things he takes to be crucial to gentile identity in v. 12.[9] Interestingly, being a gentile does not begin with understanding oneself in relation to Jews, but in relation to Christ, the Messiah of Israel.[10] Being a gentile is not primarily about circumcision, but about alienation from the Messiah. The next element of gentile identity is their exclusion from the commonwealth of Israel.[11] Remembering one's gentile past, then, entails understanding oneself as physically and spiritually excluded from this commonwealth. Moreover, gentiles were strangers to the "covenants of promise" (cf. Rom 9:4).[12] Because being a gentile means alienation from the "commonwealth of Israel and the covenants of promise," it also means that gentiles are "without hope and without God in the world."

From the perspective of being in Christ, the Ephesians are called to recognize how hopeless their situation as gentiles was.[13]

In v. 13 Paul makes the transition from what was "once" the case (vv. 11-12) to what is "now" the case. The Ephesians are reminded that they were "far off." This spatial designation summarizes the full scope of the alienation of their gentile past, as noted in vv. 11-12.[14] Although the Ephesian gentiles were "far off," now that they are in Christ they have been brought near.[15] As vv. 11-12 illustrated, the gentiles' alienation from God was also an alienation from Israel. On the one hand, vv. 15-22 indicate that by coming near, the gentiles have not come to occupy exactly the same space as Israel. Israel, too, is "near" (cf. Ps 148:14), and they have not been supplanted by gentile believers. Rather, in Christ both Jews and gentiles have been brought near to God.[16] On the other hand, coming near to God must involve also coming near to Israel.[17]

The passive voice of the phrase "you have been brought near" makes it clear that the gentiles did not move themselves closer to God or to Israe Rather, they were moved. Christ's death and resurrection is the agent that brings the gentiles near, reinstating and healing their memory so that they can truly understand who they were, where they were, where they now are, and how that relates to Israel.[18] Jesus has made peace between these two groups and brought them near to God, uniting them in one body. The making of two into one is described in ways that make it clear that the two are not dissolved into one. Peacemaking here is not homogenizing. Nevertheless, it does draw both parties into something new. Participation in this new creation requires changes from both of them. Pagans must come to understand themselves as gentiles; Jews must come to understand their Judaism in Christ, the telos of the Torah. It is only in this way that peace is truly made.[19]

In the face of whiteness, it is important for people like me to avoid the interpretive step of allegorizing oneself into the place of Jews in this passage. White Christians should read themselves as gentiles. The challenge to white Christians in the United States is not to welcome others (gentiles) into their churches, asking or requiring to adopt the patterns and habits of whiteness in order to be welcomed. That is precisely the approach to gentile inclusion rejected by the NT churches.

Christ's work incarnates a new person, and Christ invites Jew and gentile to participate in it. Jennings rightly notes, however, that this participation entails the Spirit-infused desire to be near each other—and to be near without preconditions. This is the love that counters fear-driven idolatry. This is the desire for communion that undermines greed. To the extent that white Christians conceptually recognize the work of Christ, but do not desire nearness and communion, we remain captured by the fear-driven habits of whiteness that lead to idolatry. As Jennings describes this, "Imagine a people defined by their cultural differences yet who turn their histories and cultural logics toward a new determination, a new social performance of identity. In so doing, they enfold the old cultural logics and practices inside the new ones of others, and they enfold the cultural logics and practices of others inside their own. This mutual enfolding promises cultural continuity measured only by the desire of belonging."[20]

Participating in the desire for nearness creates new networks of relationships, new patterns of being together, new forms of communion. "What characterizes the communion of this new space is not the absence of strife, contention or division but its complete capture. Just as Jesus drew into himself the energy of a violent world in order to heal that energy and turn it toward the good, so the communion envisioned by his body draws into itself the agon of peoples in order to turn strife into desire."[21]

Jennings concludes his work by advocating for "spaces of communion." These spaces "announce the healing of the nations through the story of Israel bound up in Jesus, spaces situated anywhere and everywhere the disciples of Jesus live together."[22] The dispositions and practices that work to pull believers back from idolatry and toward a more wholehearted, single-minded love of God must, at the end of the day, be drawn into some type of unity. They cannot really be manifested in isolation from each other. Moreover, we will naturally expect that those who exhibit some measure of success in remembering the LORD will also demonstrate the patterns of love and thanksgiving that counter fear and greed. This is not to say that progress with regard to each of these must be uniform. Nevertheless, one will expect some level of progress and growth with respect to these and other dispositions and practices that incline believers away from idolatry and toward the LORD.

Jennings' description of spaces of communion carries with it the implication that dispositions and practices that incline believers away from idolatry, away from the idolatry of whiteness, are never simply manifested by individuals. Rather, they also are the dispositions and practices of communities, concrete communities, occupying real places, such as the exiles in Babylon. In my place, deeply embedded within the systems of whiteness, I take it that I am called to desire such spaces. To the extent that this is true, it should serve as a constant reminder that my capacity to repent of and resist this particular inclination toward idolatry depends not only on God's mercy, but also on the mercy of others who will join me in these spaces of communion[23] where our struggles and conflicts are not eliminated, but "captured by Christ."

NOTES

Introduction

1   Stephen E. Fowl, *Engaging Scripture* (Oxford: Blackwell, 1998), 13–21.

2   Dale Martin, *Biblical Truths: The Meaning of Scripture in the Twenty-first Century* (New Haven: Yale University Press, 2017), especially the introduction.

3   Martin, *Biblical Truths*, 28.

4   For a theologically nuanced example, see Christopher J. H. Wright, *The Mission of God* (Downers Grove, Ill.: InterVarsity Press, 2006), chap. 5. Despite Wright's important insights about ancient idolatry, he is more interested in describing ancient forms of idolatry and less interested in discussing how and why the people of God move into idolatry. In *We Become What We Worship: A Biblical Theology of Idolatry* (Downers Grove, Ill.: InterVarsity Press, 2008), G. K. Beale organizes biblical material regarding idolatry around tropes of blindness and deafness to argue a thesis about idolatry in the Bible. I find that his readings are often based on arguments about vocabulary that I find unpersuasive.

5   These points are made in such various volumes as Benjamin Sommer, *The Bodies of God and the World of Ancient Israel* (Cambridge: Cambridge University Press, 2009), and Nathan MacDonald, *Deuteronomy and the Meaning of Monotheism* (Tübingen: Mohr Siebeck, 2012).

Chapter 1: Thinking about Idolatry

1   In their magisterial study *Idolatry*, trans. Naomi Goldblum (Cambridge, Mass.: Harvard University Press, 1992), Moshe Halbertal and Avishai Margalit begin by asking, "What is idolatry and why is it viewed as an unspeakable

sin?" (1). All who write on idolatry in the wake of this volume are in debt to Halbertal and Margalit's analysis. For the most part, however, they are not directly interested in the questions that drive this volume. Moreover, they do not address the specific ways idolatry is handled in the New Testament.

2   I am not claiming that there is direct literary influence from Wis 12–15 on Rom 1. I am not making strong claims about texts that influenced Paul's thinking. Rather, I simply note that the pattern of reasoning in Wis 12–15 is reflected in the pattern of reasoning in Rom 1. In this regard, I side much more with Dale Martin's approach to this text than Richard Hays'. See Dale Martin, "Heterosexism and the Interpretation of Romans 1:18-32," *BibInt* 3, no. 3 (1995): 332–55, and Richard B. Hays, *The Moral Vision of the New Testament* (San Francisco: HarperCollins, 1996), chap. 16. Hays had published a number of essays on aspects of Rom 1 prior to the publication of *The Moral Vision*.

3   The context here makes it clear that the claim in 14:27 is not a claim about the etiology of evil. Rather, it is to link all current evils, including those not already articulated, to the rise of idols.

4   Again, this is not a claim about direct literary influence. For example, both Ps 106:20 and Jer 2:11 speak of Israelite idolatry in terms of exchanging the glory of God for an image (Rom 1:25). The appearance of a common vocabulary, however, should not necessarily be taken as evidence of a common pattern of reasoning. Both Ps 106 and Jer 2 are talking about Israelite idolatry, whose origins and consequences are different from the gentile idolatry addressed in Wis 12–15 and Rom 1.

5   See Walter Brueggemann, *A Commentary on Jeremiah* (Grand Rapids: Eerdmans, 1998), 38, who seems to take Judah's claims here as willful self-delusion without offering any explanation other than Judah's refusal to obey God.

6   M. Daniel Carroll R., "Imagining the Unthinkable: Exposing the Idolatry of National Security in Amos," *ExAud* 24 (2008): 43.

7   This is the approach of Halbertal and Margalit, who tend to treat prophetic criticisms of idolatry as versions of these themes.

8   See Deut 6:20-24:

> [20] When your children ask you in time to come, "What is the meaning of the decrees and the statutes and the ordinances that the LORD our God has commanded you?" [21] then you shall say to your children, "We were Pharaoh's slaves in Egypt, but the LORD brought us out of Egypt with a mighty hand. [22] The LORD displayed before our eyes great and awesome signs and wonders against Egypt, against Pharaoh and all his household. [23] He brought us out from there in order to bring us in, to give us the land that he promised on oath to our ancestors. [24] Then the LORD commanded us to observe all these statutes, to fear the LORD our God, for our lasting good, so as to keep us alive, as is now the case."

The commandments cannot easily be separated from the great deeds of Exodus.

9   In Deut 4:11-15 God recounts that, when the law was given to the Israelites, they saw no image of God. Therefore, they should not make any images of God.

10   For example, there are issues concerning how Moses learns about the calf in vv. 7-15; the relationships between Moses' intercession in v. 11; the promise of forgiveness in v. 14 and the punishment in vv. 25ff; the relationship between the drinking of the water in v. 20 and the plague in v. 35 as different punishments. There are also debates about the compositional makeup of the text. One can find these discussed in most critical commentaries. See, for example, Brevard S. Childs, *Exodus* (Philadelphia: Westminster, 1974), 555–62; and William C. H. Propp, *Exodus 19–40*, AB (New York: Doubleday, 2006), 541–65.

11   Cassuto's commentary goes to some length to explain that although Aaron sinned, he did not commit idolatry in this instance. He begins by noting that the ark has cherubim carved on it, serving as a throne for God. Why are carved cherubim allowed in the tabernacle, but the calf is considered a forbidden image? In the first instance, this is because the prohibition is focused on earthly, visible creatures. Carved cherubim, being the work of someone's imagination, were never likely to induce people to worship them. "In the view of Scripture, Aaron's intention, when he made the calf, was only to fashion a vacant throne for the Godhead, like the throne of the cherubim, which, at this very time, Moses had been commanded to make. He made the calf in order to satisfy the need of the multitude to see at least a tangible symbol of the Deity's presence, the same need the Torah sought to gratify when it permitted the cherubim and even enjoined their construction." See U. Cassuto, *A Commentary on the Book of Exodus*, trans. I. Abrahams (Jerusalem: Hebrew University Press, 1967), 408.

12   Halbertal and Margalit, in *Idolatry*, 2, wonder about the ban on representing God: "and why are linguistic representations of God apparently permitted while visual representations are forbidden?" I certainly do not presume that my answers here are the only possible answers. I only aim to offer reasonable responses to this question. In Stephen's speech in Acts 7:41 he seems to link the forming of the image, the offering of sacrifices, and the taking of joy in "the works of their hands" as elements in a single complex act of idolatry.

13   Nathan MacDonald, "Rescuing the Golden Calf: The Imaginative Potential of the Old Testament's Portrayal of Idolatry," in *Idolatry: False Worship in the Bible, Early Judaism, and Christianity*, ed. Stephen Barton (New York: T&T Clark, 2007), 25. MacDonald nicely shows that as the golden calf is contextualized in the light of the rest of the OT, it provides the basis for a rich and multifaceted account of idolatry. One consequence

of this argument is that MacDonald offers an account of idolatry in the OT that undermines the developmental model proposed by Halbertal and Margalit.

14 Calvin gets at this when he comments on Exod 32, "But when Aaron said that those were the gods by whom they had been set free from the land of Egypt, they boldly assented [Ex 32:4], obviously meaning that they wished to retain that liberating God, provided they could see him going before them in the calf" (*Inst* 1.11.9, trans. Henry Beveridge, Christian Classics Ethereal Library, https://www.ccel.org/ccel/calvin/institutes.i.html).

15 Philo, *Agr.* 98.

16 As David Stubbs notes, it is fitting that the bronze serpent, which symbolizes both Israel's suffering as the result of her sin and God's victory, should become a symbol of the crucifixion. *Numbers*, Brazos Theological Commentary (Grand Rapids: Brazos, 2009), 169.

17 In the light of the way the story runs, there may be some irony in the fact that the name Micah refers to the incomprehensibility of the LORD. See Tammi Schneider, *Judges*, Berit Olam (Collegeville: Michael Glazier, 200), 231.

18 I will leave to one side the question of whether Micah's mother was, in fact, Delilah. There are some indications of this, but it is not relevant to my discussion.

19 The Hebrew term here is פֶּסֶל; the Greek is γλυπτὸν.

20 Daniel Block notes that some interpreters have taken this phrase literally to refer to such things as amulets or tattoos on the breast. "But the issue in context is the internalization of idolatry, not its external expression." The passage here presents idolatry as "an intentionally fixed 'state of mind.'" See *The Book of Ezekiel*, NICOT (Grand Rapids: Eerdmans, 1997), 425.

21 First 1 Thessalonians 1:9 notes that the Thessalonians "turned away" from serving idols to serve the living God.

22 In what follows I depend to a significant degree on Derek Newton's *Deity and Diet: The Dilemma of Sacrificial Food in Corinth*, JSNTS 169 (Sheffield: Sheffield Academic Press, 1998); as well as David Horrell, "Idol-Food, Idolatry, and Ethics in Paul," in Barton, *Idolatry*, 120–40.

23 Newton, *Deity and Diet*, 171–74.

24 Newton, *Deity and Diet*, 261.

25 These would have included such things as funerals, or celebrations after athletic games.

26 Newton, *Deity and Diet*, 298–305, 310. "The whole 'problem' of Greco-Roman cultic belief and practice regarding sacrificial food was that it displayed a fundamental ambivalence, a range of intractable boundary issues and wealth of conflicting conceptual differences" (378).

27 Newton, *Deity and Diet*, 312–13. Newton argues that Paul's grudging permission of it as long as it does not cause other believers "to stumble" is

primarily a rhetorical one since it would have been extremely difficult for "strong" believers in such a crowded context to know who may or may not be watching. Horrell ("Idol-Food," 126), however, seems to be correct in claiming that the ἡ ἐξουσία of the strong (8:9) must be real and legitimate in order to make sense of the argument of chapter 9.

28 Although the rhetoric is different, this is very much in accord with the argument Paul makes in Phil 1:12-26.

29 Newton, *Deity and Diet*, 340.

30 Newton, *Deity and Diet*, 369.

31 As an aside in 10:29b-30, Paul recognizes that believers cannot always and in all places defer to weak consciences. "Ridiculous proportions could be reached if weak consciences were allowed to dictate all the boundaries of Christian freedom in a wide range of behavioural situations." Newton, *Deity and Diet*, 377–78.

32 This also seems to be the case for Jews in this period. See Helen K. Bond, "Standards, Shields, and Coins: Jewish Reactions to Aspects of the Roman Cult in the Time of Pilate," in Barton, *Idolatry*, 88–106.

33 See Andrew F. Walls, "The Gospel as Prisoner and Liberator of Culture," in *The Missionary Movement in Christian History: Studies in the Transmission of Faith* (Maryknoll, N.Y.: Orbis, 1996), 3–15. "The impossibility of separating an individual from his social relationships and thus from his society leads to one unvarying feature in Christian history: the desire to 'indigenize,' to live as a Christian and yet as a member of one's own society, to make the Church . . . *A Place to Feel at Home*" (7).

34 See David Morgan, *Visual Piety: A History and Theory of Popular Religious Images* (Berkeley: University of California Press, 1998). Morgan reinforces the point that for most believers the faith is learned and encountered visually through images rather than through writing. This then influences popular religious practice and piety.

35 See Carlos Eire, *War against the Idols: The Reformation of Worship from Erasmus to Calvin* (Cambridge: Cambridge University Press, 1986), chap. 6.

36 Jean-Luc Marion, *God without Being*, trans. Thomas A. Carlson (Chicago: University of Chicago Press, 1991).

37 Marion, *God without Being*, 10–11.

38 "The idol thus acts as a mirror, not as a portrait: a mirror the reflects the gaze's image, or more exactly, the image of its aims and of the scope of that aim." Marion, *God without Being*, 12.

39 "The icon, on the contrary, attempts to render visible the invisible as such, hence to allow that the visible not cease to refer to an other than itself, without, however, that other ever being reproduced in the visible." Marion, *God without Being*, 18.

40   I am aware that even today, believers around the world live in contexts where the fabrication of idols still happens. Whatever else one might say about these contexts, believers living in those contexts have ample ways of employing biblical images, language, and tropes related to idolatry.

41   For example, when speaking of a pervasive human capacity to misunderstand, misperceive, and misdirect attention toward God, John Calvin argues that the human heart/mind is a perpetual forge or factory for idols (*Inst.* 1.11.8). Calvin's comments are about the origins of idol worship and follow the basic outline of Wis 12–15.

42   Tertullian, *On Idolatry* 1. I think this is a different claim from Wis 14:27, which cites idolatry as the beginning, cause, and end of all evil. In that same context, Wisdom claims that this has not always been the case. Hence the claim of 14:27 cannot be taken to be an account of the etiology of evil.

43   It also seems to me that such an account cannot reckon with the very clear difference in Scripture between the idolatry of believers and that of unbelievers.

44   I recognize that for different types of theological projects it may be important to think of sin as damaging the image of God in oneself and others. In that respect, all sin might be thought to be a form of idolatry. The many merits of such an account would seem most beneficial to a theological anthropology rather than a theological account of idolatry among believers.

45   For Tertullian, some activities or professions are inextricably tied to idolatry. Those whose work included the fabrication of idols (*On Idolatry* 4), the selling of frankincense to pagan temples (*On Idolatry* 11), and teaching about pagan gods (*On Idolatry* 9) could hardly escape complicity in idolatry. It would be much harder, though not impossible, to make a similar case today.

46   See, for example, Jacques Ellul, *The New Demons*, trans. C. Edward Hopkin (New York: Seabury Press, 1975), and *The Technological Society*, trans. J. Wilkinson (New York: Knopf, 1964). See also Andrew Goddard, "Jacques Ellul on Idolatry," in Barton, *Idolatry*, 228–45.

47   See, for example, Paul Marshall, "Is Technology Out of Control?" *Crux* 20, no. 3 (1984): 3–9.

48   In this respect I differ with scholars such as Luke Johnson and others who press on the issue of the focus of one's "ultimate concern" as the way to identify idolatry. See, for example, "Idolatry, in simple terms, is the choice of treating as ultimate and absolute that which is neither absolute nor ultimate." Luke Timothy Johnson, *Sharing Possessions: What Faith Demands*, 2nd ed. (Grand Rapids: Eerdmans, 2011), 44. Whether or not this accounts for the idolatry of unbelievers, I would suggest that idolatry for believers is the result of the dissolution and distraction or our love and attention. One might well characterize this view as the refusal to treat anything as ultimate.

CHAPTER 2: FORGETTING AND ATTENDING

1   The LXX of Deut 6:4 begins by reminding the Israelites of the command-
     ments that the Lord gave them after leaving Egypt. It then claims: ἄκουε
     Ισραηλ κύριος ὁ θεὸς ἡμῶν κύριος εἷς ἐστιν.

2   Jeffrey H. Tigay, *Deuteronomy: The Traditional Hebrew Text with the New
     JPS Translation* (Philadelphia: Jewish Publication Society, 1996). Tigay
     cites Zech 14:9 as evidence of such an understanding of the *Shema*.

3   Indeed, such an understanding would seem to grant that other gods exist.

4   These points are made in such various volumes as Benjamin Sommer, *The
     Bodies of God and the World of Ancient Israel* (Cambridge: Cambridge Univer-
     sity Press, 2009), and Nathan MacDonald, *Deuteronomy and the Meaning of
     Monotheism* (Tübingen: Mohr Siebeck, 2012).

5   R. W. L. Moberly, *Old Testament Theology: Reading the Hebrew Bible as Chris-
     tian Scripture* (Grand Rapids: Baker Academic, 2013), 10–18, makes this
     point quite well.

6   Moberly, *Old Testament Theology*, 18–19, citing Deut 8:5, 10:19, and 30:19b
     as similar constructions. Also Moshe Weinfeld, *Deuteronomy 1–11*, AB (New
     York: Doubleday, 1991), 350.

7   Moberly, *Old Testament Theology*, 19.

8   Moberly, *Old Testament Theology*, 20; Weinfeld, *Deuteronomy*, 351.

9   Moberly, *Old Testament Theology*, 20.

10   Moberly, *Old Testament Theology*, 24.

11   In b. Ber. 61b the Shema gets interpreted in the light of martyrdom. That is,
     martyrdom is the ultimate way of demonstrating the wholehearted love of
     God called forth in the Shema.

12   Cited in Tigay, *Deuteronomy*, 77.

13   Weinfeld, *Deuteronomy*, 354, notes similarities between the Shema and
     ancient Near Eastern vassal treaties to press the notion of love of God in
     terms similar to obedience to one's overlord. Moberly, *Old Testament Theol-
     ogy*, 22–23, notes that this interpretation tends to neglect the very clear
     political and contextual differences between Deut 6 and a treaty imposed
     on a conquered people.

14   Tigay, *Deuteronomy*, 77; also Moberly, *Old Testament Theology*, 22.

15   "Activity directed toward virtue causes its capacity to grow through exertion;
     this kind of activity alone does not slacken its intensity by the effort, but
     increases it." Gregory of Nyssa, *Life of Moses*, trans. Abraham J. Malherbe
     and Everett Ferguson (New York: Paulist Press, 1978), para. 226.

16   When this call to wholehearted love of God is repeated in Deut 13:3, it is
     followed in v. 4 by these verbs commanding actions related to God: follow,
     fear, obey, serve, and hold fast.

17   See Moberly, *Old Testament Theology*, 25.

18   Moberly, *Old Testament Theology*, 26. See also the discussion of idolatry and
      control over space in the previous chapter.

19   Moberly, *Old Testament Theology*, 27, citing Joseph Lienhard, *Exodus, Levit-
      icus, Numbers, Deuteronomy* (Downers Grove, Ill.: InterVarsity Press, 2001).

20   "Whoever, therefore, thinks that he understands the divine Scriptures or
      any part of them so that it does not build the double love of God and of our
      neighbor does not understand it at all." Augustine, *On Christian Doctrine*,
      trans. D. W. Robertson (New York: Macmillan, 1987), 30 (1.40).

21   Moberly, *Old Testament Theology*, 28.

22   Moberly, *Old Testament Theology*, 28–30. In addition, churches and some
      other buildings are sometimes adorned with scriptural texts carved into
      them at various points. Indeed, at Seattle Pacific University, where I am writ-
      ing this chapter, almost all of the buildings and many other public places on
      campus have biblical verses inscribed on them. By contrast, Loyola Univer-
      sity, where I teach, has crucifixes in each classroom.

23   Moberly, *Old Testament Theology*, 31.

24   For similar arguments along these lines, see David Yeago, "The New Testa-
      ment and Nicene Dogma: A Contribution to the Recovery of Theological
      Exegesis," in *The Theological Interpretation of Scripture: Classic and Contem-
      porary Readings*, ed. Stephen E. Fowl (Oxford: Blackwell, 1997), 87–100;
      and Lewis Ayres, *Nicaea and Its Legacy: An Approach to Fourth-Century Trin-
      itarian Theology* (New York: Oxford University Press, 2004), esp. 414–20.

25   See the section on "symbolic predators" in Michael Budde, *The (Magic)
      Kingdom of God* (Boulder: Westview Press, 1997), 90–94.

26   Nicholas Lash, "What Authority Has Our Past?" in *Theology on the Way to
      Emmaus* (London: SCM, 1986), 54.

27   "Post-Fordist" refers to that form of capitalism arising in response to the
      struggles and crises of that stage of capitalism characterized by Henry Ford's
      assembly line and all that developed in its wake, where the alignment of
      supply and demand was a crucial concern. Rather than use the term post-
      Fordist, some may refer to the present period as global capitalism or finan-
      cialized capitalism. Regardless of the appropriate name, for my purposes it
      is crucial to note that one of the characteristics of this stage of capitalism is
      the shift from regulating supply and demand to the creation of ever greater
      demand through various forms of marketing.

28   To view the image, visit this page on the *Ads of the World* site: https://www
      .adsoftheworld.com/media/print/episcopal_new_church_center.

29   Yes, some of our buildings are named for donors and benefactors, but that
      was not relevant in this case.

30   There is one more troubling issue to raise here. This arises in the light of
      arguments raised by Willie Jennings in his book *The Christian Imagination:
      Theology and the Origins of Race* (New Haven: Yale University Press, 2010),

but not only there. The argument would be that the Christian imagination may be so corrupted by racism that what it perpetuates is something profoundly disconnected from the gospel. Thus, one might claim that no matter how well a Christian community maintains its catechetical practices, the faith that is being passed on is fundamentally distorted by racism. In the conclusion of this volume I will engage with the larger issue of whiteness and idolatry. The issue more immediately at hand here is how Christianity or any tradition-bound form of belief and practice responds to its own tendencies toward corruption. In this regard, one should avoid making "all or nothing" claims. It is not clear how one would even know if a tradition were absolutely corrupted. Instead, the questions have to be focused on "how," "to what degree," and "in what ways" a tradition is corrupted and how the tradition should respond. In some respects the arguments of this volume are attempts to figure out some of these issues in scriptural terms. Of course, this debate echoes the arguments between Hans-Georg Gadamer and Jürgen Habermas in hermeneutics and arguments advanced by Alasdair MacIntyre with regard to traditions.

31   See also the command to put fringes on Israelite garments as a way to remember the commandments in Num 15:37-40.

32   In this regard Moberly, in *Old Testament Theology*, 39, notes, "The point is that the tempting but misleading reality that can endanger allegiance to God is not some putative invisible entity (i.e., a deity, in a certain 'traditional' conception) but rather those things encountered within the life of the world that can draw the human heart away from the one true God."

33   Telford Work, *Deuteronomy* (Grand Rapids: Brazos, 2009), 98.

34   Tigay, *Deuteronomy*, 79. Also Weinfeld, *Deuteronomy*, 344, and Prov 30:8-9: "Give me neither poverty nor riches, but provide me with my daily bread, lest, being sated, I renounce, saying, 'Who is the LORD?'"

35   Hosea 13:1-8 explicitly links eating one's fill to making the heart proud and forgetting the LORD (13:4-6). The surrounding context might lead one also to see that forgetting the LORD under these conditions also leads to following other gods.

36   *Confessions* 1.12.19, trans. Henry Chadwick (Oxford: Oxford University Press, 1991).

37   See, in particular, the philosophical argument for the priority of intelligible to unintelligible actions in Alasdair MacIntyre's *After Virtue*, 3rd ed. (Notre Dame: University of Notre Dame Press, 2007), 208–10.

38   In 8:14 the phrase describing self-exaltation could more literally be translated "magnify your hearts."

39   See the later discussion of curiosity in chapter 5.

40   Although he is not speaking of slipping into idolatry, Augustine may be on the right track here when he claims, "The consequence of a distorted will is

passion. By servitude to passion, habit is formed, and habit to which there is no resistance becomes necessity." *Confessions* 8.5.10.

41 For one view of this image, see https://mamabyfire.files.wordpress.com/2014/09/img_1476.jpg?w=650.

42 Budde, *The (Magic) Kingdom of God*, 26.

43 Budde, *The Magic Kingdom of God*, 26.

44 See David McCarthy, *The Good Life: Genuine Christianity for the Middle Class* (Grand Rapids: Brazos, 2004), 108.

45 "What we need to live well is a suitable and respectable place among others, and what we need to live without shame depends on the nature of our society and our place." McCarthy, *The Good Life*, 109.

46 I simply cannot see that 1 Cor 7:17-24, despite its history of interpretation and application within the church, can be invoked here to justify acquiescing to or remaining in any of these situations as if they were the place "God has called" one to.

47 "We need enough to live well and to care for our families, close neighbors, and friends. We need enough to share and to give hospitality to the stranger—to put our property to the higher use of common life." McCarthy, *The Good Life*, 113.

48 McCarthy, *The Good Life*, 124.

49 McCarthy, *The Good Life*, 122.

50 As Matthew Crawford asks in *Shop Class as Soulcraft* (New York: Pilgrim Press, 2009), "Why do some current Mercedes models have no dipstick, for example? What are the attractions of being disburdened for involvement with our own stuff?" (7). Earlier he notes, "What ordinary people once made, they buy; and what they once fixed for themselves, they replace entirely or hire an expert to repair, whose expert fix often involves replacing an entire system because some minute component has failed" (2).

51 It is a deep irony that this culture also requires that information about our patterns of consumption be made available to an ever-wider and increasingly sophisticated circle of marketers.

52 "Perhaps most significantly, the sharing of food epitomizes the way in which God meets his people's deepest need, now and eternally." Samuel Wells, *God's Companions* (Oxford: Blackwell, 2006), 43.

53 "Food is a development of the notion of friendship because the preparation, sharing and clearing of meals provide a paradigm of the dynamic, nourishing, purposeful practices of the kingdom." Wells, *God's Companions*, 42.

Chapter 3: Bounded and Unbounded Desire

1 Pauline authorship of both Ephesians and Colossians is disputed. I have addressed both the historical arguments for and against Pauline authorship as well as indicated that for most interpretive and theological interests the

question of authorship is not directly relevant. See Stephen E. Fowl, *Ephesians*, NTL (Louisville: Westminster John Knox, 2012), 9–28. Regardless of how one answers the questions of authorship for these epistles, they are part of Christian Scripture and therefore worthy of theological engagement. I will use the name Paul to refer to the inscribed author of these texts without prejudicing historical arguments about the authorship of these epistles.

2   One explanation is that Paul is referring to all of the vices listed in Eph 5:3-5 and Col 3:5 as idolatry and not simply greed. This seems to be the approach of Beale, *We Become What We Worship*, 266. As I will indicate, particularly in Ephesians, there are strong grammatical reasons for limiting the identification of idolatry to greed alone.

3   Brian Rosner, *Greed as Idolatry: The Origin and Meaning of a Pauline Metaphor* (Grand Rapids: Eerdmans, 2007), offers a thorough survey of Christian interpretations of Eph 5:5 and Col 3:5. He also provides a detailed account of both greed and idolatry in Hellenistic Jewish texts. He then employs a theory of metaphor to account for the clearly metaphorical identification Paul draws between greed and idolatry in these two passages. There is a great deal to learn from Rosner's work here. To the extent that I differ from it, that difference lies primarily in the way he develops the metaphorical relationships between greed and idolatry. Too often he ends up making claims about greed that seem to me more properly made of wealth in order to forge connections to idolatry. Obviously greed and wealth are connected to each other. It appears to me, however, that greed is fundamentally a disposition toward things—including but not limited to wealth. Greed displays how one views one's place in the world relative to God, to others, and to things. Keeping this idea front and center will result in a different set of connections to idolatry from those Rosner draws on pp. 159–65.

4   Although the neuter singular relative pronoun agrees with neither πλεονέκτης nor εἰδωλολάτρης, the fact that it is singular should limit its reference to the greedy person and not to all three types of people mentioned in 5:5. See Harold W. Hoehner, *Ephesians: An Exegetical Commentary* (Grand Rapids: Baker Academic, 2002), 660. The pronoun in Col 3:5 is also singular, although it does agree with its antecedent.

5   In certain military contexts the word refers to a strategic advantage. See Josephus, *J.W.* 3.477; 4.43, 189, 358, 580; 5.66, 95, 143, 338, 429 et al.

6   For example, in 1 Thess 4:6 the verb πλεονεκτεῖν is associated with taking advantage of one's brother or sister in Christ with regard to sexual practices. In 2 Cor 2:11 the verb πλεονεκτηθῶμεν is used to describe being outfoxed by Satan. In 2 Macc 4:50 greed is focused on power. Josephus, *Ant.* 3.29, and Philo, *Leg.* 3.166, both use greed to refer to overgathering the manna that God sends in Exodus. In *Spec.* 2.225 Philo contrasts greed with temperance in all matters, as also in Letter of Aristeas 1.277.

7   In *Spec.* 4.215 greed is associated with a failure to observe the natural rhythms established by the Sabbath year. In *Jos.* 1.30 greed desires more than nature has apportioned to someone.

8   Josephus, *Ant.* 4.225.

9   Josephus, *Ant.* 18.172; Philo, *Spec.* 4.158, 213.

10   Josephus, *Ant.* 13.225; *C. Ap.* 2.272; T. Gad 5:1.

11   See Andrew T. Lincoln, *Ephesians* (Waco: Word, 1990), 322; Ernest Best, *Ephesians*, ICC (Edinburgh: T&T Clark, 2001), 477; Hoehner, *Ephesians*, 653.

12   See the similar notion expressed in Ezek 36:22-24 as well as in the Pastoral Epistles (e.g., 1 Tim 3:7; 5:14; 6:1; Titus 2:5, 8, 10). Aquinas, in *Commentary on Ephesians* (trans. Matthew Lamb [Albany: Magi Books, 1966], 198), takes the verse this way.

13   For a more detailed discussion of these terms see Fowl, *Ephesians*, 106.

14   In T. Judah 19:1 φιλαργυρία is mentioned as leading to idolatry because it mistakenly takes as God that which is not God (cf. also the discussion in 18:1-6). In T. Levi 17:11 love of money is listed with idolatry along with other vices. Of course, the passages in Deuteronomy covered in the previous chapter make similar connections.

15   Although texts such as 1 Cor 6:12-20 link prostitution and idolatry, and images of prostitution are often used to describe Israel's attraction to other gods, the syntax of Eph 5:5 limits the identification of idolatry solely to covetousness. See Best, *Ephesians*, 481; Hoehner, *Ephesians*, 661.

16   Rosner, *Greed as Idolatry*, 160–66. It is less obviously connected to Luke 16:13, where Jesus says the same thing about the impossibility of serving God and Mammon as a way of concluding the story about the unjust steward.

17   See Jon D. Levenson, *Creation and the Persistence of Evil* (Princeton: Princeton University Press, 1994). In rejecting the Christian doctrine of creation *ex nihilo*, Levenson argues that the OT presents creation as God's mastery of chaos. This way of treating Genesis and a doctrine of creation more generally comes with its own challenges. It is easy to see how this view might develop into the Manichean position that captivated Augustine for more than a decade.

18   Carol Harrison, "Taking Creation for the Creator: Use and Enjoyment in Augustine's Theological Aesthetics," in Barton, *Idolatry*, 180.

19   Harrison, "Taking Creation for the Creator," 181. Harrison uses this as the basis for understanding Augustine's reading of Rom 1:20-25, arguing that for Augustine the foundation of all idolatry lies in the creature's refusal to recognize its total dependence on God.

20   See in particular here Gregory of Nyssa's *Commentary on the Song of Songs*, trans. Casimir McCambley (Brookline, Mass.: Hellenic College Press, 1987), *Homily* 4 (p. 99). See also the comments of Morwenna Ludlow, *Universal Salvation: Eschatology in the Thought of Gregory of Nyssa and Karl Rahner* (Oxford: Oxford University Press, 2000), 56–58, and Martin Laird, "Under

Solomon's Tutelage: The Education of Desire in the Homilies on the Song
of Songs," *Modern Theology* 18, no. 4 (2002): 517.

21 Alexander Schmemann, *For the Life of the World* (Crestwood, N.Y.: St. Vladimir's Seminary Press, 2002), 14. Schmemann further notes that although all creation depends on food, only humans can bless God for the food they receive.

22 See also Apoc. Mos. 11.1: Τότε τὸ θηρίον ἐβόησε λέγον· ὦ Εὔα, οὐ πρὸς ἡμᾶς ἡ πλεονεξία σου οὔτε ὁ κλαυθμός σου, ἀλλὰ πρὸς σέ, ἐπειδὴ ἡ ἀρχὴ τῶν θηρίων ἐκ σοῦ ἐγένετο ("Then the beast cried, saying: 'It is not our concern, Eve, your greed and your wailing, but your own; for [it is] from you that the rule of the beasts has happened'").

23 Although I cannot develop this claim here, it would seem that a properly bounded concern to live within and maintain God's gift of communion would require appropriate uses of the gifts of God's creation and the earth that sustain rather than diminish or exploit those gifts.

24 Commenting on Nyssa's Homilies/Commentary on the Song of Songs, Laird notes, "The problem with desire, therefore, is not that it is concerned with the body *per se* but that the soul seeks ultimacy in what is not God." "Under Solomon's Tutelage," 508.

25 Laird, "Under Solomon's Tutelage," 509.

26 See the arguments of Thomas Piketty in *Capital in the Twenty-First Century* (Cambridge, Mass.: Belknap Press of Harvard University Press, 2014). Piketty shows how the rate of return on investments exceeds the rate of economic growth over long historical periods. To the extent that his has been and remains true, the gap between those who have capital to invest will always grow faster than the wealth of the general population. Although Piketty sees that both this economic phenomenon and the ways in which the phenomenon is described and understood involve a set of moral choices, his own moral vocabulary is shaped by a basic utilitarianism that would not be able to make recourse to language about greed.

27 Not surprisingly, the striking contrast to this approach is Pope Francis, who repeatedly urges people to a transformation of desire that would then lead people to act decisively against poverty and extreme forms of income inequality. See, for example, *Evangelii Gaudium*, esp. paras. 59–60.

28 Translation from St. Basil the Great, *On Social Justice*, trans. C. Paul Schroeder (Crestwood, N.Y.: St. Vladimir's Seminary Press, 2009), 61.

29 "Truly this is the worst kind of avarice: not even to share perishable goods with those in need." Basil, *On Social Justice*, 69.

30 "Though we have a God who is generous and lacks nothing, we have become grudging and unsociable towards the poor. . . . This is why God does not open his hand: because we have closed up our hearts towards our brothers and sisters. This is why fields are arid: because love has dried up." This comes

from the homily "In Time of Famine and Draught," in Basil, *On Social Justice*, 76. He has similar criticisms for those who lend money at interest. He notes that they see the poor as opportunities for increasing their wealth. The poor come seeking an ally and they find an enemy (see *On Social Justice*, 91).

31 See also Best, *Ephesians*, 479.

32 Galatians would be the exception to this general rule.

33 Jerry L. Sumney, *Colossians* (Louisville: Westminster John Knox, 2008), 54, asserts that "in the light" must refer to the place where God dwells. This possibility might enhance the idea that Paul is speaking about the restoration of communion with God. The contrast between a believers' movement from darkness to light in passages such as Acts 26:18 or 1 Pet 2:9 probably indicates that "in the light" should not be taken as narrowly as Sumney does.

34 These images of taking off and putting on begin in 2:11-15, where they are connected to circumcision and baptism.

35 Marianne Meye Thompson argues that "thanksgiving is the vertical correlate of the horizontal virtues found in this section." *Colossians and Philemon* (Grand Rapids: Eerdmans, 2005), 85. While affirming this, I also want to develop the role that thanksgiving plays in thwarting the greed that is idolatry.

36 The imperative verb is assumed here, and supplied in most English translations. It is not in the Greek.

37 As Thompson argues, "This peace is not first a personal, subjective, inner peace, but rather the unity, the wholeness, given by Christ to the community." *Colossians and Philemon*, 85. Although it is the case that one of the aims of allowing the peace of Christ to arbitrate in their hearts is to enable the Colossians to embody the unity to which God calls them, it does seem that, by allowing the peace of Christ to arbitrate in their hearts, Paul is calling the Colossians to practices that relate to their inner life. Indeed, there is little reason to think that allowing the peace of Christ to arbitrate among the conflicting desires of one's heart will be anything but a difficult transformative experience of rooting out some desires and radically redirecting others.

38 The only other time this verb is used in the Bible is Wis 10:12. There, wisdom is cast at the arbiter in the contest between Jacob and the angel (Gen 32:34). In addition, Paul used the cognate term καταβραβευέτω in 2:18 to mean "disqualify." See also *LSJ*, 327. Even when a term like "rule" might be appropriate, it is in the context of a conflict or unruliness. See also Robert M. Wilson, *Colossians and Philemon* (Edinburgh: T&T Clark, 2005), 264.

39 This latter phrase is found in several places in the Book of Common Prayer of the Episcopal Church, including in the Penitential Order Rite 1, p. 320.

40 Wilson, *Colossians and Philemon*, 266, says of these imperatives that "this is not something the Colossians are to achieve, but something they are to allow to happen, and not hinder."

41 Both Thompson, *Colossians and Philemon*, 85, and Sumney, *Colossians*, 223, argue that wise teaching and thankful praise are the ways in which the Colossians show that the word of Christ is dwelling in them. The relationship between the participles and the main verb in this verse is ambiguous enough that it allows one to take wise teaching and thankful praise as both enabled by the indwelling of Christ's word (as above) and a sign of that indwelling.

42 There seems little reason to take the "word of Christ" as either Christ's word or a word about Christ, i.e., the gospel. It can be "both/and." So Wilson, *Colossians and Philemon*, 266.

43 This seems to be similar to the wisdom needed to practice Augustine's distinction between use and enjoyment.

44 This is the upshot of Brian Rosner's *Greed as Idolatry*. I have not engaged Rosner's work very much in this chapter. Rosner stands much more squarely within the interpretive tradition that reads Eph 5:3-5 and Col 3:5 through passages like Matt 6:24, tying greed to wealth. I discuss what I take to be the shortcomings of that interpretive tradition early in this chapter. Hence, although I take Rosner's work to be an exemplary contribution to that tradition, it is also subject to its failings.

Chapter 4: Insecurity, Love, and Mission

1 This point is made clearly in G. Simon Harak, S.J., *Virtuous Passions* (New York: Paulist Press, 1993), 2.

2 Scott Bader-Saye, *Following Jesus in a Culture of Fear* (Grand Rapids: Brazos, 2007), 25–26.

3 Bader-Saye, *Following Jesus*, 26.

4 Bader-Saye, *Following Jesus*, 40, quoting Aquinas, *Summa Theologiae* II-II, q. 19, art. 3.

5 Bader-Saye, *Following Jesus*, 40.

6 Augustine, *Confessions* 4.4.7.

7 Augustine, *Confessions* 4.6.11.

8 This is not all that different from Augustine, who concludes his reflection on the death of his friend by noting that the passage of time gradually helped to repair "me with delights such as I used to enjoy, and to them my grief yielded. . . . The greatest source of repair and restoration was the solace of other friends, with whom I loved what I loved as a substitute for you." *Confessions* 4.7.12.

9 Augustine, *Confessions* 4.7.12.

10 Bader-Saye, *Following Jesus*, 29.

11 M. Daniel Carroll R. does not invoke the relationship between fear and shadow virtues, but he makes some parallel observations about how making national security an overarching goal leads the people of Israel into idolatry. See "Imagining the Unthinkable."

12   "Solomon may indeed be admired for his energy and ambition, but hardly for any sensitivity to human values. Like every other ruler in the ancient world, he believed in the exploitation of his fellow human beings." See Simon DeVries, *1 Kings*, WBC 12 (Waco: Word, 1985), 133.

13   "One gains the impression of a king who, like Solomon, gets right down to the important business of religious obligation—minus the extravagance and excesses for which his predecessor was known. Moreover, Jeroboam's flurry of activities in establishing these alternative national shrines is indicative of his political wisdom. Fostering national religious identity through the establishment of cultic centers and identification with a particular deity were all decisive political moves in the buildup of statehood." Gina Hens-Piazza, *1 and 2 Kings*, Abingdon OT Commentaries (Nashville: Abingdon Press, 2006), 128.

14   "When Jeroboam lead [sic] the succession from Rehobam, he recognized the need to establish an alternative substitute religion, since he was appealing to the same God—Yahweh—that Judah would use to substantiate its government and social system." Carroll R., "Imagining the Unthinkable," 44. See also DeVries, *1 Kings*, 162.

15   As Ephraim Radner has shown, this story of division and the establishment of parallel idolatrous worship of the LORD was read figurally by both sides during the Reformation as a way of underwriting the legitimacy of their views. As Radner, notes, however, ultimately, both Judah and Israel are destroyed. See Ephraim Radner, *The End of the Church: A Pneumatology of Christian Division in the West* (Grand Rapids: Eerdmans, 1998), 35–37.

16   Bader-Saye, *Following Jesus*, 33–35.

17   For my purposes, it is not important to resolve differences between the various canonical forms of Isaiah, be it the Masoretic text or the Septuagint (or any authorized vernacular translations). My judgment that redactional studies of Isaiah yield little interpretive light on the canonical forms of the text applies regardless.

18   Brevard S. Childs, *Isaiah*, OTL (Louisville: Westminster John Knox, 2001), 233. Childs is in particular addressing 31:4-5. It is interesting that this question is precisely the one raised by my students that I discuss in the introduction to this book.

19   This option is noted by Otto Kaiser, *Isaiah 13–39*, trans. R. A. Wilson, OTL (Philadelphia: Westminster, 1974), 251

20   See Joseph Jensen, OSB, *Isaiah 1–39*, Old Testament Message (Wilmington, Del.: Michael Glazier, 1984), 219.

21   "Will not panic" is the NRSV's rendering of the Hebrew יָחִישׁ. The ESV translates the verb as "will not be in haste." The LXX uses the very different καταισχυνθῇ ("will not be put to shame"). Either English version is possible,

but the NRSV rightly captures the connection in this passage between haste and fear, or fear-driven haste.

22 See Kaiser, *Isaiah 13–39*, 285.

23 "There is deliberate and heavy irony in Isaiah's depicting of Judah making Pharaoh their *refuge* and *shadow*, for this is terminology regularly used of the Lord in the protection he grants to those who look to him (see, e.g., Ps 27:1; 28:8; 31:3; 37:39; 43:2; 52:7; 90:1; 121:5; sometimes the expression is 'shadow of his wings': Ps 17:8; 57:1; 63:7). This is to say that they are putting Pharaoh and Egypt in the place of God (and 31:3 will say that the 'Egyptians are men and not God')." Jensen, *Isaiah 1–39*, 234.

24 The LXX moves in a different direction, suggesting that when Israel repents, they will both be saved and will become aware of just how far they had strayed from the Lord.

25 Jensen, *Isaiah 1–39*, 239.

26 Jeremiah 42 relates a similar type of situation.

27 J. D. W. Watts, *Isaiah 1–33*, rev. ed., WBC 24 (Nashville: Thomas Nelson, 2005), 479.

28 "The controversy is over the wielding of power. Israel's leaders appear to agree with the nations that the only real force lies in military strength. Israel's leaders thus share a basically pagan perspective, which resonates with the speech of the Rabshakeh in chapters 36–37. Are not all the gods impotent?" Childs, *Isaiah*, 231–32.

29 G. C. I. Wong, "Isaiah's Opposition to Egypt in Isaiah XXXI 1-3," *VT* 46, no. 3 (1996): 399. Wong's primary goal is to get scholars to see that 31:2 is the key to understanding Isaiah's views about Egypt.

30 See Childs, *Isaiah*, 233.

31 Wong, "Isaiah's Opposition to Egypt," 396. This is similar to the judgment rendered against those resisting the Babylonian capture of Jerusalem in Jeremiah.

32 Wong is quite clear about this. "Isaiah's Opposition to Egypt," 399.

33 Luke Timothy Johnson, *The Gospel of Luke*, SP (Collegeville: Liturgical Press, 1991), 201. See also Johnson's *Sharing Possessions: What Faith Demands*, 2nd ed. (Grand Rapids: Eerdmans, 2011), 40–50.

34 As Joel Green notes, in this way, the parable and its interpretation in 12:22-31 provide a connection between 12:4-12, where Jesus promises God's care to those who are faithful witnesses and the interruption from the crowd regarding greed and inheritance in 12:13-15. See Joel B. Green, *The Gospel of Luke*, NICNT (Grand Rapids: Eerdmans, 1997), 485–87.

35 Also noted by Johnson, *Luke*, 243.

36 In two detailed studies, J. Duncan M. Derrett has noted that the steward here has the right to act for the master. By changing the receipts he is basically eliminating the interest owed the master. See "Fresh Light on St. Luke XVI:1.

The Parable of the Unjust Steward," *NTS* 7 (1961): 198–219, and "'Take Thy Bond . . . and Write Fifty' (Luke XVI:6): The Nature of the Bond," *JTS* 23 (1972): 438–40. Joseph A. Fitzmyer, S.J., "The Story of the Dishonest Manager (Luke 16:1-13)," *TS* 25 (1964): 23–42, argues, based on Derrett's work, that the steward was simply giving up his own commission and not, therefore, cheating his master. Several points should be made here. First, this is not a finding indicated by Derrett's work. Second, this may account for why the steward is commended as "prudent," but it cannot account for his identification as "unrighteous." Finally, this reading seems to be driven by a need to make sense of 16:8 and not by the historical evidence Derrett cites. The exegetical key here is to be able to offer a reading that accounts for how the steward can be both ἀδικία and φρονίμως at the same time.

37 See Stanley E. Porter, "The Parable of the Unjust Steward (Luke 16.1-13): Irony is the Key," in *The Bible in Three Dimensions: Essays in Celebration of Forty Years of Biblical Studies in the University of Sheffield*, ed. David J. A. Clines, Stephen E. Fowl, and Stanley E. Porter (Sheffield: JSOT Press, 1990), 127–53. I do not follow all of Porter's exegetical moves, but I am indebted to him for opening this way of reading the parable.

38 Although there are many biblical examples in which human wisdom turns out to be folly, this is one of the passages where a form of the same Greek word, φρονίμως, is also used ironically.

39 As John Christopher Thomas notes, "In this verse the focus of the discussion is not primarily upon the nature of God's love. Rather, it is upon the implications of love's origin in God for the readers." *The Pentecostal Commentary on 1 John, 2 John, 3 John* (Cleveland: Pilgrim Press, 2004), 216.

40 In 1 John 2:8, 10 it is clear that loving one's brothers and sisters demonstrates that one is "in the light" and, as 1:5 indicates, "God is light."

41 I am, thus, taking "In this way" (Ἐν τούτῳ) in 4:17 to refer back to 4:16 and the mutual indwelling in live of believers and God. See the arguments for this in Judith M. Lieu, *I, II, and III John: A Commentary*, NTL (Louisville: Westminster John Knox, 2008), 193, and Robert W. Yarbrough, *1–3 John*, BECNT (Grand Rapids: Baker, 2008), 257. Thomas, *Pentecostal Commentary*, 233, makes the point that while it certainly refers back to 4:16, the phrase can also serve to point forward into vv. 17-18.

42 The perfect form of the verb τετελείωται here and elsewhere is not predominantly an indication of time, but of the nature or type of the action. The case that Greek verbs in the NT period are aspect predominant rather than tense predominant is decisively made by Stanley E. Porter, *Verbal Aspect in the Greek of the New Testament, with Reference to Tense and Mood*, 2nd ed. (New York: Peter Lang, 1993).

43 See Lieu, *I, II, and III John*, 194.

44 Quoted in Roberta C. Bondi, *To Pray and to Love: Conversations on Prayer with the Early Church* (Minneapolis: Fortress, 1991), 14.

45 See Bader-Saye, *Following Jesus*, 63.

46 Carroll R., "Imagining the Unthinkable," 50, makes a parallel observation with regard to Amos.

47 This point is not new. It is one of the primary arguments made by Gerhard Lohfink in *Jesus and Community*, trans. John P. Galvin (Minneapolis: Fortress, 1984). Lohfink refers to the Christian communities of the NT and early church as God's "contrast societies," manifesting a particular common life that drew in outsiders.

48 It is the city which martyrs the prophets and ignores God's messengers. Instead of the peaceableness of beautiful Zion, Jesus laments in Luke 19:42 that Jerusalem cannot recognize the things that make for peace. Jesus is subsequently arrested in Jerusalem and crucified right outside the city.

49 Jennings, in *The Christian Imagination*, esp. 252–64, offers a stunning account of the various ways that Christian imagination and practice are deformed when Christians separate their understanding of mission from their connection to Israel.

50 See Andrew F. Walls, "The Gospel as Prisoner and Liberator of Culture," in *The Missionary Movement in Christian History* (Maryknoll, N.Y.: Orbis, 1996), 3–15.

51 For example, in response to Celsus' charge that Christians are nothing more than the rebellious offspring of a rebellious Jew, Origen notes:

> "In the last days," when our Jesus came, each one of us has come "to the visible mountain of the Lord," to the Word far above every word, and to the house of God which is "the church of the living God," "a pillar and ground of truth." . . . And all the nations are coming to it and many nations go, and we exhort one another to the worship of God which has shone out in the last days through Jesus Christ, saying, "Come, and let us go up to the mountain of the Lord and to the house of the God of Jacob, and he will proclaim to us his way and we will walk in it. . . . No longer do we take the sword against any nation, nor do we learn war any more, since we have become children of peace." (Origen, *Cels.* 5.34. I have made some small revisions to the translation of Henry Chadwick.)

52 The first step in this process is for the Ephesians to learn what it means for them to be gentiles. This is a good reminder that "gentile" is not a term that non-Jews use to identify themselves. See Stephen E. Fowl, "Learning to Be a Gentile: Christ's Transformation and Redemption of Our Past," in *Christology and Scripture*, ed. Andrew Lincoln and Angus Paddison (Edinburgh: T&T Clark, 2008), 22–40; Jennings, *Christian Imagination*, 252–58.

53 See Michael J. Gorman, *The Death of the Messiah and the Birth of the New Covenant* (Eugene, Ore.: Cascade Books, 2014), chaps. 6 and 7.

54 *Letter to Arsarcius, High Priest of Galatia* (LCL).

55 Daniel Boyarin, in *A Radical Jew: Paul and the Politics of Identity* (Berkeley: University of California Press, 1994), already sees this tendency in Paul's writings.

56 "The plot of the moral life is to move beyond the security but hopelessness of egotism to the risk but enrichment of hospitality, and this is one thing friendship achieves." Paul J. Wadell, *Friendship and the Moral Life* (Notre Dame: University of Notre Dame Press, 1989), 147.

57 As Paul Wadell notes, "What is remarkable about the moral life is not that morality is friendship, but that all our friends were once strangers. What is remarkable about friends is what a risk it is to let a stranger become one." *Friendship and the Moral Life*, 148.

CHAPTER 5: THE COMMUNITY OF THE CURIOUS

1 In Acts the resurrected Christ both redeems and reconstitutes Israel, on the one hand, and disperses his followers throughout all nations, on the other hand, providing the impetus for a nonexilic dispersion of renewed Israel in order to draw the nations to God. Although I do not follow his reading of Paul, Daniel Boyarin offers some very insightful comments on "deterritorialized" Judaism in *A Radical Jew*, 251–59. To the extent Boyarin is right, the idea that Christians make redeemed Israel a "deterritorialized" reality may not be as threatening to Jewish identity as it might first seem. Of course, when Christians have political control over vast amounts of territory, it becomes a different story.

2 This seems to correlate with the reforms of Hezekiah (2 Kgs 18:3-6) and Josiah (2 Kgs 23:4-19). As a result, scholars tend to date this section of Deuteronomy to those time periods.

3 Tigay, *Deuteronomy*, 127, makes the point that the Hebrew פֶּן־תִּנָּקֵשׁ is not a reference to being enticed but to falling into a trap (see Deut 7:25; Exod 23:3; Josh 23:13; Judg 2:3). This makes it seem like it is less a situation of yielding to temptation and more a situation of blundering into a trap.

4 An alternative approach to the one I outline above is to argue that the Israelites will be ensnared in Canaanite religious practices because they want to be like other nations. That is, it is their unwillingness to stand against the crowd that leads them into idolatry. Certainly, there are a number of episodes in the OT when the Israelites seek to be like the nations among whom they live (cf. 1 Sam 8:4-5). According to the logic of Deut 12, however, the Israelites are to eliminate all vestiges of Canaanite religion. There would then be nothing to which they might be tempted to conform. I do agree that the way believers are disposed toward difference and conformity can lead to idolatry. I hope that I have touched on these in the course of this volume. I do not think that is the issue at the heart of Deut 12:29–13:18.

5   Tigay, *Deuteronomy*, 128, notes the occurrence of שְׁמַע without tying it to 6:4.

6   See, for example, Jeffries M. Hamilton, "How to Read an Abhorrent Text: Deuteronomy 13 and the Nature of Authority," *HBT* 20, no. 1 (1998): 12–32; also Deanna A. Thompson, *Deuteronomy*, Belief Commentary on the Bible (Louisville: Westminster John Knox Press, 2014), 119–21.

7   These verses present idolatry as a political crime, rejecting God's kingship. Halbertal and Margalit, *Idolatry, 214–16.*

8   With the lone exception of Job 36:16, the Hebrew verb סות is never used to incite or entice people to something good or true (see, for example, 1 Kgs 21:25; 2 Kgs 18:32; 1 Chr 21:1; 2 Chr 18:2; Jer 43:3).

9   Christians are not unique in this. Aristotle also thought the desire to know was a defining human characteristic.

10 Paul J. Griffiths, *Intellectual Appetite: A Theological Grammar* (Washington, D.C.: Catholic University of America Press, 2009), 14.

11 Griffiths, *Intellectual Appetite*, 13.

12 I will rely here both on *Intellectual Appetite* and Griffiths' earlier essay, "The Vice of Curiosity," *ProEccl* 15, no. 1 (2006): 47–63. See also R. R. Reno's perceptive review of *Intellectual Appetites* in *First Things* (February 2010): 33–37.

13 As Griffiths makes clear, his account depends heavily on Augustine. "It is no exaggeration to say that European thought about curiosity is Augustinian from the fifth century to the fifteenth." Griffiths, "The Vice of Curiosity," 49.

14 Griffiths, "The Vice of Curiosity," 52.

15 Griffiths, "The Vice of Curiosity," 52.

16 "The curious gaze is restless, insanely so, in fact." Griffiths, "The Vice of Curiosity," 52.

17 Griffiths, "The Vice of Curiosity," 55.

18 Griffiths, "The Vice of Curiosity," 56.

19 As Griffiths unfolds an Augustinian notion of curiosity, it is clear that this notion draws its force from 1 John 2:16. Here one's attachment to the "desire of the eyes" displays one's fundamental allegiance to the things of the world as opposed to the things of the Father.

20 For my argument, it is not necessary that the Israelites actually suppressed Canaanite religious practices once they were in the promised land. The fact that such suppression was never as comprehensive as Deuteronomy commands simply increased the prospects of lapsing into idolatry.

21 This, in a highly compact form, is one of the claims of Kavin Rowe's *World Upside Down: Reading Acts in the Graeco-Roman Age* (Oxford: Oxford University Press, 2009).

22 However one translates the term παρωξύνετο, it is clear that Paul does not see Athens in a neutral, academic way. Rather, it is one more idol-saturated space, and this distresses him. See Rowe, *World Upside Down*, 29.

23 The Epicurean and Stoic philosophers call Paul a σπερμολόγος. In Stocism, this is generally used as a term of abuse to refer to a "babbler" or a "scandal-monger." See Rowe, *World Upside Down*, 28.

24 Although Luke does use ἐπιλαβόμενος in Acts 9:27 to refer to a friendly attachment. In 16:19, 18:17, and 21:30 Luke uses this term to speak of Paul (and others) being seized by hostile characters. It seems best to take the term that way here. See Rowe, *World Upside Down*, 29.

25 As Rowe summarizes matters, "A careful reading of vv. 16-21 thus creates a distinct *Vorverständnis* with which the reader then hears Paul's speech. Instead of a romantic view of Athens as the place of university-like debate, Luke portrays the city's rampant idolatry—Paul is rightly vexed—as the context in which the Christian preaching of the resurrection of Jesus (1) is distorted and (2) results in a potentially life-threatening situation for Paul." *World Upside Down*, 33.

26 Rowe, *World Upside Down*, 34.

27 See Patrick Gray, "Athenian Curiosity (Acts 17:21)," *NovT* 47, no. 2 (2005): 109–16. Gray derives his conception of curiosity from Plutarch's essay *De curiositate*. Plutarch's account of "busybodies" bears most of the marks of the Augustinian vice of curiosity.

28 "That the Athenians misconstrue his preaching about 'Jesus and the resur-rection' as a deity and his female consort—like Venus and Adonis or Zeus and Dione—is in line with the busybody's prurient interest in sex." Gray, "Athenian Curiosity," 113.

29 Gray, "Athenian Curiosity," 115.

30 To this end, note that in Plutarch's account of curiosity, the curious cannot endure the solitude of the countryside. They must have news of others' trou-bles (see *Moralia*, "On Being a Busybody" 518F).

31 "Thus in Acts 17:24-25 Luke aligns Paul with the broadly philosophical critique of the interface between the gods and their images. At the same time, the narrative furthers the reshaping of the readers' religious imagination by placing its theological foundation in the transcendence of the Creator God over the world of images." Rowe, *World Upside Down*, 36.

32 "Augustine's expositions of curiosity on the basis of 1 John 2:16 are so frequent that it would be pointless to offer a list. Representative examples may be found at *Sermones* 72.15; 284.5, 306C, 311.7, 335C.13, 313A; *De vera religion* 38.69–71; *De catechizandis rudibus* 26.52; *Confessiones* 10.35, 54–57 (the whole of the second half of Book 10 is structured by the three-fold schema of 1 John 2:16); *Ennaratio in Psalmum* 8.13." Griffiths, "The Vice of Curiosity," 51n10.

33 I note a similar set of admonitions in Philippians in "Believing Forms Seeing: Formation for Martyrdom in Philippians," in *Character and Scripture*, ed. William P. Brown (Grand Rapids: Eerdmans, 2002), 317–30.

34   The allusion here must be to Exod 8:19, when, after matching Moses and Aaron sign for sign and plague for plague, the magicians of Egypt are forced to admit, when they cannot summon up gnats, that "this is the finger of God."

35   Of course, Luke has already presented, and will consistently present, Mary as someone who hears the word of God and does it. See Johnson, *The Gospel of Luke*, 186.

36   Jesus' journey to Jerusalem begins with a similar set of encounters stressing the need for a singular, single-minded response to his proclamation of the rule of God (9:57-62).

37   See S. R. Garrett, "'Lest the Light in You Be Darkness': Luke 11:33-36 and the Question of Commitment," *JBL* 110, no. 1 (1991): 99.

38   See the discussion in Garrett, "'Lest the Light,'" 96–99. Also T. Iss. 3:4, where Issachar tells his children that he lived his life with a "singleness of vision" (εν ἁπλότητι οφθαλμών).

39   Garrett, "'Lest the Light,'" 99; also T. Iss. 6:1; 7:7; T. Ben. 6:7; and T. Job 26:7-8. Recall also that in Deut 13:13 the civic leaders who draw a whole town into idolatry are called "sons of Belial."

40   "I suggest that Luke included the sayings about 'light' and 'eyes' at just this point because of a notion that the onlookers' testing pointed to the *absence* of a [ἁπλοῦς] eye or heart." Garrett, "'Lest the Light,'" 102.

41   My reading here is consonant with Garrett's, "'Lest the Light,'" 101. She, however, really only allows that Satan is the agent who diverts or corrupts one's "single" eye.

42   In this respect, Jesus' admonition here can be read as a gloss on the Deut 6:4, where the singular character of the LORD calls forth and demands a single-minded response from Israel (6:5). Jesus mentions Deut 6:5 in Luke 10:27. See also Michael Wyschogrod, "The One God of Abraham and the Unity of God in Jewish Philosophy," paper delivered to the Society for Scriptural Reasoning, New Orleans, November 1996, and also his "The 'Shema Israel' in Judaism and the New Testament," in *The Roots of Our Common Faith*, ed. H.-G. Link, Faith and Order Paper 119 (Geneva: WCC, 1983).

43   See Garrett, "'Lest the Light,'" 103, who follows Ferdinand Hahn, "Die Worte vom Licht Lk 11,33-36," in *Orientierung an Jesus: Zur Theologie der Synoptiker*, ed. Paul Hoffmann, Norbert Brox, and Wilhelm Pesch (Freiburg: Herder and Herder, 1973).

44   This type of attention stands in sharp contrast to discussions of *curiositas* in the monastic life. Richard Newhauser, relying on accounts ranging from John Cassian to Gregory the Great to Galand of Reigny to Bernard of Clarvaux, emphasizes that monastic life in particular requires the "humility of self-self-knowledge." Without this, it was difficult if not impossible to stand against proud curiosity. Curiosity was a "rejection of the most important virtue leading to a recognition of one's own need of correction." Richard

Newhauser, "The Sin of Curiosity and the Cistercians," in *Erudition at God's Service*, ed. John Sommerfeldt, Studies in Medieval Cistercian History 11 (Kalamazoo: Cistercian Publications, 1987), 74.

45 David Neale points out that this is not an attempt to identify a specific historical group of people. Rather, it is an "assessment of the intended target audience." See *None but the Sinners* (Sheffield: JSOT Press, 1991), 169.

46 The ambiguity about whom this prayer is actually addressed to is nicely shown by the use of the preposition πρός. On this see Johnson, *The Gospel of Luke*, 271.

47 See Newhauser, "The Sin of Curiosity," 72, who quotes from an allegory of Galand of Reigny, who puts the following words into the mouth of the character *Curiositas*: "And why do I make them investigate others' sins while they neglect their own? Because the more they censure those sins, the more they forget their own."

48 I have argued elsewhere that these two stories might be read together as examples of failing and succeeding in receiving the kingdom of God as a child. Most of what is related here replicates the points made there in more detail. See "Receiving the Kingdom as a Child: Children and Riches in Luke 18:15ff.," *NTS* 39 (1993): 153–58.

49 The traditional view of 19:8 is that Zacchaeus is committing himself to a future course of action as an implicit sign of repentance. There is a recent body of interpretation, however, that reads 19:8 as Zacchaeus' defense to Jesus against the crowd's complaint that he is a sinner. One advocate of this view is Alan C. Mitchell, "Zacchaeus Revisited: Luke 19:18 as a Defense," *Bib* 71, no. 2 (1990): 153–76. On this view, Zacchaeus is not pledging a change in his behavior. Rather, he is referring to his usual custom as a sort of *apologia*. I am not sure that my reading depends on taking a side in this debate. Nevertheless, it seems that the logic of the story leads one to read 19:8 in the traditional manner. For example, if Zacchaeus is in the regular habit of giving half his goods to the poor, he could hardly qualify as "rich" (19:2). Secondly, Jesus' claim to have come to seek and save the lost in 19:10 seems to draw its force from the fact that Zacchaeus really was in some sense lost. For a recent defense of this traditional view, see Dennis Hamm, S.J., "Luke 19:8 Once Again: Does Zacchaeus Defend or Resolve?" *JBL* 107 (1988): 431–37. Neale, *None but the Sinners*, 185–88, also defends this traditional view.

50 "The contrast between the sinful woman and Simon is a profoundly ideological one: The true and godly sentiment of repentance encounters the ultimate in self-righteousness." Neale, *None but the Sinners*, 144.

51 See also the story of Peter's first encounter with Jesus related in 5:1-11. After a fruitless night of fishing, Peter is instructed by Jesus to lower his nets in a particular place. When Peter is confronted with a massive load of fish, a

catch he clearly attributes to Jesus' intervention, his first response is "depart from me for I am a sinful man" (5:8). After being reassured by Jesus, however, Peter, along with James and John, leaves everything and follows Jesus (5:11).

52 Budde, *The (Magic) Kingdom of God*, 69–70.

53 Budde, *The (Magic) Kingdom of God*, 135.

54 Over time, this has created some rather ironic patterns. "At a time when for-profit culture industries orchestrate human attention to an unprecedented degree, we now witness a strange kind of institutional overlap where religious groups adopt the latest in advertising and marketing techniques and corporations sell their wares by exploiting deeply treasured religious symbols, images and stories." See Michael Budde and Robert Brimlow, *Christianity Incorporated: How Big Business Is Buying the Church* (Grand Rapids: Brazos, 2002), 55.

55 This synthesizes chapters 3 and 5 of Budde, *The (Magic) Kingdom of God*.

56 See Budde, *The (Magic) Kingdom of God*, chap. 6 and the various stories that populate Budde's subsequent essays. The strategies for marketing Pope John Paul II and the various lawsuits that ensued between dioceses and marketing firms as each tried to cash in on the pope's popularity do not provide a basis for optimism. With the equally intriguing Pope Francis, only time will tell.

57 Budde, *The (Magic) Kingdom of God*, 125.

58 Newhauser, "The Sin of Curiosity," 72–74.

59 Book of Common Prayer of the Episcopal Church, 308.

Conclusion

1 Calvin, *Inst.* 11.8.

2 Kelly Brown Douglas, *Stand Your Ground: Black Bodies and the Justice of God* (Maryknoll, N.Y.: Orbis, 2015).

3 Willie James Jennings, *The Christian Imagination: Theology and the Origins of Race* (New Haven: Yale University Press, 2011), 8.

4 Martin Luther King, Jr., "Letter from Birmingham City Jail," in *A Testament of Hope: The Essential Writings and Speeches of Martin Luther King, Jr.*, ed. James Melvin Washington (San Francisco: Harper & Row, 1986), 299.

5 Jennings, *The Christian Imagination*, 64.

6 Jennings, *The Christian Imagination*, 253. It is crucial to note, however, that Christian attentiveness to the election of biblical Israel need not, and often should not, lead Christians to support many of the forms of Zionism often supported by fundamentalist Christians in the United States. If nothing else, Christian attentiveness to Israel's election should sharpen awareness of the gaps that exist between biblical Israel and the modern nation state of the same name.

7 See Fowl, "Learning to Be a Gentile," in Lincoln and Paddison, *Christology and Scripture*, 22–40.

8   For other references that link the act of remembering to good works, see Exod 13:3; 20:8; Deut 24:22; Ps 22:27.

9   Many commentators note parallels between this list and Rom 9:4 where Paul lists the advantages of the Jew. There are some overlaps here, but it is important to remember that here the focus is on Gentile identity rather than Jewish advantage.

10 Lincoln, *Ephesians*, 137.

11 The verb translated as "excluded" only appears in the NT here and in 4:18 as well as in Col 1:21. In each case it can be translated as alienated or excluded. In each of these contexts the verb is used to describe one's state prior to being reconciled with God.

12 This probably refers to the covenants with Abraham in Gen 12:1-14; reiterated and expanded in 13:14; 15:21; 17:21; with Isaac in Gen 26:2-5; with Jacob in Gen 28:13-15; with David in 2 Sam 7. Lincoln, *Ephesians*, 137; Rudolf Schnackenburg, *The Epistle to the Ephesians*, trans. Helen Heron (Edinburgh: T&T Clark, 1991), 110. Given the negative comments in 2:15 about the "law of commandments and decrees," Paul is probably not referring to the Mosaic covenant. Aside from the negative example of 2:15, however, there is little in the text or its context that would specify which covenants are in question here.

13 This is the only time in the NT that the term ἄθεοι (without God) is used. In Greek literature the term can refer to someone who does not believe in a god or gods either willfully or out of ignorance. The term can also apply to the impious who believe in the gods but disdain them, or to someone forsaken by God or the gods (see LSJ). In this particular case, Paul probably means to indicate that Gentiles are forsaken by God (Lincoln, *Ephesians*, 139; Ernest Best, *Ephesians*, ICC [Edinburgh: T&T Clark, 1998], 243). The early Christians were often accused by the Romans of being "atheists" in just this sense of not believing in the god or gods of the empire.

14 In the OT the term "far off" is sometimes used of Gentiles (Deut 28:49; 29:22; 1 Kgs 8:14; Isa 5:26; Jer 5:15). These are all literal references to distant Gentile lands. Aquinas, in *Commentary on Ephesians*, 155, however, notes the parallel with Ps 119 [118 LXX]: "Salvation is far from the wicked, for they do not seek your statutes."

15 In rabbinic and Qumran literature the verb *to come near* is used of proselytes (e.g., 1QS 6.13-22; 7.21; 8.18; 9.15; Shabb. 31a; Num. Rab. 8.4 and J. A. Loader, "An Explanation of the Term *prosēlutos*," *NovT* 15, no. 4 [1973]: 270–77).

16 It is clear that Paul assumes that Israel has always been near to God, but his image says nothing about whether that near spatial location changes at all in the light of Christ. Even if Israel's spatial location remains unchanged, it is clear that walls have been broken down.

17 So Best, *Ephesians*, 245.
18 This claim, thus, builds upon and elaborates on the assertion of 1:7 that believers have redemption "in his blood."
19 "What we know of our collective selves, of our peoples, and of our ways of life is not eradicated in the presences of Israel's God, but that knowledge is up for review." Jennings, *Christian Imagination*, 258.
20 Jennings, *Christian Imagination*, 273.
21 Jennings, *Christian Imagination*, 274.
22 Jennings, *Christian Imagination*, 293.
23 At this point I can only point out that one implication of this is that on the whole I would argue that these spaces of communion cannot be congregations that are solely white. To unpack this further would draw me too far afield from the aims of this volume.

BIBLIOGRAPHY

Aquinas, Thomas. *Commentary on Ephesians*. Translated by Matthew Lamb. Albany: Magi Books, 1966.

Augustine of Hippo. *On Christian Doctrine*. Translated by D. W. Roberston. New York: Liberal Arts Press, 1958.

———. *Confessions*. Translated by Henry Chadwick. Oxford: Oxford University Press, 1991.

Bader-Saye, Scott. *Following Jesus in a Culture of Fear: Christian Practice of Everyday Life*. Grand Rapids: Brazos, 2007.

Basil of Caesarea. *On Social Justice*. Translated by C. Paul Schroeder. Crestwood, N.Y.: St. Vladimir's Seminary Press, 2009.

Beale, Gregory K. *We Become What We Worship: A Biblical Theology of Idolatry*. Downers Grove: InterVarsity Press, 2007.

Best, Ernest. *Ephesians*. International Critical Commentary. Edinburgh: T&T Clark, 1998.

Block, Daniel. *The Book of Ezekiel*. New International Commentary on the Old Testament. Grand Rapids: Eerdmans, 1997.

Bond, Helen K. "Standards, Shields and Coins: Jewish Reactions to Aspects of the Roman Cult in the Time of Pilate." In *Idolatry*, edited by Stephen Barton, 88–106. London: T&T Clark, 2007.

Bondi, Roberta. *To Pray and To Love*. Minneapolis: Fortress, 1991.

Boyarin, Daniel. *A Radical Jew: Paul and the Politics of Identity*. Berkeley: University of California Press, 1994.

Brueggemann, Walter. *A Commentary on Jeremiah*. Grand Rapids: Eerdmans, 1998.

———. *Israel's Praise : Doxology against Idolatry and Ideology*. Philadelphia: Fortress, 1988.

Budde, Michael. *The (Magic) Kingdom of God: Christianity and Global Culture Industries*. Boulder, Col.: Westview Press, 1997.

Budde, Michael, and Brimlow, Robert. *Christianity Incorporated: How Big Business is Buying the Church*. Grand Rapids: Brazos, 2002.

Carroll R., M. Daniel. "Imagining the Unthinkable: Exposing the Idolatry of National Security in Amos." *Ex Auditu* 24 (2008): 37–54.

Cassuto, Umberto. *A Commentary on the Book of Exodus*. Translated by Israel Abrahams. Jerusalem: Magnes Press, 1967.

Childs, Brevard S. *The Book of Exodus: A Critical, Theological Commentary*. Philadelphia: Westminster, 1974.

———. *Isaiah*. Old Testament Library. Louisville: Westminster John Knox, 2001.

Crawford, Matthew. *Shop Class as Soulcraft*. New York: Pilgrim Press, 2009.

Derrett, J. Duncan M. "Fresh Light on St. Luke XVI:1. The Parable of the Unjust Steward." *New Testament Studies* 7 (1961): 198–219.

———. "'Take Thy Bond . . . And Write Fifty' (Luke XVI:6), The Nature of the Bond." *The Journal of Theological Studies* 23 (1972): 438–40.

DeVries, Simon John. *1 Kings*. Waco: Word, 1985.

Douglas, Kelly Brown. *Stand Your Ground: Black Bodies and the Justice of God*. Maryknoll, N.Y.: Orbis, 2015.

Eire, Carlos M. N. *War Against the Idols: The Reformation of Worship from Erasmus to Calvin*. Cambridge: Cambridge University Press, 1986.

Ellul, Jacques. *The New Demons*. Translated by Edward Hopkin. New York: Seabury Press, 1975.

———. *The Technological Society*. Translated by John Wilkerson and introduced by Robert Merton. New York: Knopf, 1964.

Fitzmyer, Joseph A. "The Story of the Dishonest Manager (Luke 16:1–13)." *Theological Studies* 25 (1964): 23–42.

Fowl, Stephen E. "Believing Forms Seeing: Formation for Martyrdom in Philippians." In *Character and Scripture*, edited by William P. Brown, 317–30. Grand Rapids: Eerdmans, 2002.

———. *Engaging Scripture*. Oxford: Blackwell, 1998.

———. *Ephesians*. New Testament Library. Louisville: Westminster John Knox, 2012.

———. "Receiving the Kingdom as a Child: Children and Riches in Luke 18:15ff." *New Testament Studies* 39 (1993): 153–58.

———. "Learning to Be a Gentile: Christ's Transformation and Redemption of Our Past." In *Christology and Scripture: Interdisciplinary Perspectives*, edited by Andrew T. Lincoln and Angela Paddison, 22–40. Edinburgh: T&T Clark, 2007.

Garrett, Susan R. "'Lest the Light in You Be Darkness': Luke 11:33–36 and the Question of Commitment." *Journal of Biblical Literature* 110, no. 1 (1991): 93–105.

Goddard, Andrew. "Jacques Ellul on Idolatry." In *Idolatry,* edited by Stephen Barton, 228–45. London: T&T Clark, 2007.

Gorman, Michael J. *The Death of the Messiah and the Birth of the New Covenant.* Eugene, Ore.: Cascade Books, 2014.

Gray, Patrick. "Athenian Curiosity (Acts 17:21)." *Novum Testamentum* 47, no. 2 (2005): 109–16.

Green, Joel. *The Gospel of Luke.* New International Commentary on the New Testament. Grand Rapids: Eerdmans, 1997.

Gregory of Nyssa. *Commentary on the Song of Songs.* Translated by Casimir McCambley. Brookline, Mass.: Hellenic College Press, 1987.

———. *Life of Moses.* Translated and Introduced by Abraham Malherbe and Everett Ferguson. New York: Paulist Press, 1978.

Griffiths, Paul J. *Intellectual Appetite: A Theological Grammar.* Washington: Catholic University of America Press, 2009.

———. "The Vice of Curiosity." *Pro Ecclesia* 15, no. 1 (2006): 47–63.

Hahn, F. "Die Worte vom Licht Lk 11,33–36." In *Orientierung an Jesus: Zur Theologie der Synoptiker,* edited by P. Hoffmann, et al., 107–38. Freiburg: Herder and Herder, 1973.

Halbertal, Moshe, and Margalit, Avishai. *Idolatry.* Translated by Naomi Goldblum. Cambridge: Harvard University Press, 1992.

Hamilton, Jeffries M. "How to Read an Abhorrent Text: Deuteronomy 13 and the Nature of Authority." *Horizons in Biblical Theology* 20, no. 1 (1998): 12–32.

Hamm, Dennis. "Luke 19:8 Once Again: Does Zacchaeus Defend or Resolve?" *Journal of Biblical Literature* 107 (1988): 431–37.

Harak, Simon G., S.J. *Virtuous Passions.* New York: Paulist Press, 1993.

Harrison, Carol. "Taking Creation for the Creator: Use and Enjoyment in Augustine's Theological Aesthetics." In *Idolatry,* edited by Stephen Barton, 179–97. London: T&T Clark, 2007.

Hays, Richard B. *The Moral Vision of the New Testament.* San Francisco: HarperCollins, 1996.

Hens-Piazza, Gina. *1 & 2 Kings.* Abingdon Old Testament Commentaries. Nashville: Abingdon, 2006.

Hoehner, Harold W. *Ephesians.* Grand Rapids: Baker, 2002.

Horrell, David. "Idol-Food, Idolatry and Ethics in Paul." In *Idolatry,* edited by Stephen Barton, 120–40. London: T&T Clark, 2007.

Jennings, Willie James. *The Christian Imagination: Theology and the Origins of Race.* New Haven, Conn.: Yale University Press, 2011.

Jensen, Joseph, OSB. *Isaiah 1–39.* Old Testament Message. Wilmington, Ind.: Michael Glazier, 1984.

Johnson, Luke T. *The Gospel of Luke.* Sacra Pagina. Collegeville: Liturgical Press, 1991.

———. *Sharing Possessions: What Faith Demands.* 2nd ed. Grand Rapids: Eerdmans, 2011.

Kaiser, Otto. *Isaiah 13–39*. Old Testament Library. Translated by R. A. Wilson. Philadelphia: Westminster, 1974.

King, Martin Luther, Jr. "Letter from Birmingham City Jail." In *A Testament of Hope: The Essential Writings and Speeches of Martin Luther King, Jr.*, edited by James Melvin Washington. San Francisco: Harper & Row, 1986.

Laird, Martin. "Under Solomon's Tutelage: The Education of Desire in the Homilies on the Song of Songs." *Modern Theology* 18, no. 4 (2002): 507–25.

Lash, Nicholas. "What Authority Has Our Past?" In *Theology on the Way to Emmaus*. London: SCM Press, 1986.

Levenson, Jon. *Creation and the Persistence of Evil*. Princeton: Princeton University Press, 1994.

Lieu, Judith. *I, II & III John*. New Living Translation. Louisville: Westminster John Knox, 2008.

Lincoln, Andrew T. *Ephesians*. Waco: Word Books, 1990.

Link, Hans Georg. *The Roots of Our Common Faith*. Geneva: World Council of Churches, 1983.

Loader, J. A. "An Explanation of the Term *prosēlutos*." *Novum Testamentum* 15, no. 4 (1973): 270–77.

Lohfink, Gerhard. *Jesus and Community: The Social Dimensions of Christian Faith*. Philadelphia: Fortress, 1984.

Ludlow, Morwenna. *Universal Salvation: Eschatology in the Thought of Gregory of Nyssa and Karl Rahner*. Oxford: Oxford University Press, 2000.

MacDonald, Nathan. "Rescuing the Golden Calf: The Imaginative Potential of the Old Testament's Portrayal of Idolatry." In *Idolatry*, edited by Stephen Barton, 22–39. London: T&T Clark, 2007.

MacIntyre, Alasdair. *After Virtue*. 3rd ed. Notre Dame: University of Notre Dame Press, 2007.

Marion, Jean-Luc. *God Without Being*. Translated by Thomas Carlson. Chicago: University of Chicago Press, 1991.

Marshall, Paul. "Is Technology Out of Control?" *Crux* 20, no. 3 (1984): 3–9.

Martin, Dale B. *Biblical Truths: The Meaning of Scripture in the 21st Century*. New Haven, Conn.: Yale University Press, 2017.

———. "Heterosexism and the Interpretation of Romans 1:18–32." *Biblical Interpretation* 3, no. 3 (1995): 332–55.

McCarthy, David. *The Good Life: Genuine Christianity for the Middles Class*. Grand Rapids: Brazos, 2004.

Mitchell, A. C. "Zacchaeus Revisited: Luke 19:18 as Defense." *Biblica* 71 (1990): 153–76.

Moberly, R. W. L. *Old Testament Theology: Reading the Hebrew Bible as Christian Scripture*. Grand Rapids: Baker Academic, 2013.

Morgan, David. *Visual Piety: A History and Theory of Popular Religious Images*. Berkeley: University of California Press, 1998.

Neale, David A. *None but the Sinners*. Sheffield: JSOT Press, 1991.

Newhauser, Richard. "The Sin of Curiosity and the Cistercians." In *Erudition At God's Service: Studies in Medieval Cistercian History XI*, edited by John Sommerfeld, 71–97. Kalamazoo: Cistercian Publications, 1987.

Newton, Derek. "Deity and Diet: The Dilemma of Sacrificial Food in Corinth." Journal for the Study of the Old Testament Supplement Series 169. Sheffield: Sheffield Academic Press, 1998.

Origen. *Contra Celsum*. Translated by Henry Chadwick. Cambridge: Cambridge University Press, 1980.

Pieper, Josef. *Happiness and Contemplation*. South Bend, Ind.: St Augustine's Press, 1998.

Piketty, Thomas. *Capital in the Twenty-First Century*. Cambridge, Mass.: Bellknap Press of Harvard University, 2014.

Pope Francis. *Evangelii Gaudium*. Vatican City: Vatican Press, 2015.

Porter, Stanley E. "The Parable of the Unjust Steward (Luke 16.1–13): Irony is the Key." In *The Bible in Three Dimensions: Essays in Celebration of Forty Years of Biblical Studies in the University of Sheffield*, edited by D. J. A. Clines, Stephen E. Fowl, and Stanley E. Porter, 127–53. Sheffield: JSOT Press, 1990.

———. *Verbal Aspect in the Greek of the New Testament, with Reference to Tense and Mood*. 2nd ed. New York: Peter Lang, 1993.

Propp, William H. C. *Exodus 19–40*. The Anchor Bible. New York: Doubleday, 2006.

Radner, Ephraim. *The End of the Church: A Pneumatology of Christian Division in the West*. Grand Rapids: Eerdmans, 1998.

Reno, Russel R. "Review of *Intellectual Appetite: A Theological Grammar*." *First Things* (February 2010): 33–37.

Rosner, Brian. *Greed as Idolatry: The Origin and Meaning of a Pauline Metaphor*. Grand Rapids: Eerdmans, 2007.

Rowe, Kavin. *World Upside Down: Reading Acts in the Greco-Roman Age*. Oxford: Oxford University Press, 2009.

Schmemann, Alexander. *For the Life of the World*. Crestwood, N.Y.: St. Vladimir's Seminary Press, 2002.

Schnackenburg, Rudolf. *The Epistle to the Ephesians*. Translated by Helen Heron. Edinburgh: T&T Clark, 1991.

Schneider, Tammi. *Judges*. Berit Olam. Collegeville, Minn.: Michael Glazier, 2000.

Stubbs, David. *Numbers*. Brazos Theological Commentary. Grand Rapids: Baker, 2009.

Sumney, Jerry L. *Colossians*. Louisville: Westminster John Knox, 2008.

Thomas, John Christopher. *The Pentecostal Commentary on 1, 2, 3 John*. Cleveland: Pilgrim Press, 2004.

Thompson, Deanna A. *Deuteronomy*. Belief Commentary on the Bible. Louisville: Westminster John Knox, 2014.

Thompson, Marianne M. *Colossians and Philemon*. Grand Rapids: Eerdmans, 2005.

Tigay, Jeffrey H. *Deuteronomy: The Traditional Hebrew Text with the New JPS Translation.* Philadelphia: Jewish Publication Society, 1996.

Wadell, Paul. *Friendship and the Moral Life.* Notre Dame: University of Notre Dame Press, 1989.

Watts, John. *Isaiah 1–33.* Rev. ed. Word Biblical Commentary 24. Nashville: Thomas Nelson, 2005.

Weinfeld, Moše. *Deuteronomy 1–11.* The Anchor Bible 5. New Haven: Yale University Press, 1991.

Wells, Samuel. *God's Companions.* Oxford: Blackwell, 2006.

Wilson, R. McL. *Colossians and Philemon.* Edinburgh: T&T Clark, 2005.

Work, Telford. *Deuteronomy.* Grand Rapids: Brazos, 2009.

Wright, Christopher J. H. *The Mission of God.* Downers Grove, Ill.: InterVarsity Press, 2006.

Wong, G. C. I. "Isaiah's Opposition to Egypt in Isaiah XXXI 1–3." *Vetus Testamentum* 46, no. 3 (1996): 392–401.

Wyschogrod, Michael. "The One God of Abraham and the Unity of God in Jewish Philosophy." Paper delivered to the Society for Scriptural Reasoning. New Orleans, November 1996.

———. "The 'Shema Israel' in Judaism and the New Testament." In *The Roots of Our Common Faith,* edited by H.-G. Link. Faith and Order Paper 119. Geneva: WCC, 1983.

Yarbrough, Robert. *1–3 John.* Baker Exegetical Commentary on the New Testament. Grand Rapids: Baker, 2008.

SUBJECT INDEX

attention, to/away from God, 4, 8,
25–32, 43–46, 57, 65–66, 72, 110,
115, 142n41, 142n48

blindness, idolatry, 4, 9, 12, 28, 81,
84, 91, 115, 123, 126, 137n4

capitalism, 48, 49, 100, 119–21,
144n27
catechesis, 38–41, 47, 52,
107–8, 145n30
commandments, 13–14, 31, 32,
36, 42, 79, 117, 139n8, 143n1,
145n31, 162n12
communion, with God, 64–68,
70–75, 91, 127, 128, 135, 149n23,
150n33, 163n23
creation, 7, 8, 24, 58, 63–75, 98, 112,
124, 127, 134, 148n17, 148n18,
149n21, 149n23

deafness, idolatry, 4, 12, 28, 91, 123,
126, 137n4
desire, 13, 15, 17, 18, 25, 26, 35,
53, 57, 59, 63–73, 77, 90, 93,

106–10, 113–19, 127, 129,
130–35, 141n33, 149nn20, 24,
27, 150n37
distract/distraction, 26, 72, 85, 105,
118, 121, 125–28, 142n48

fabricate, idols or images, 2, 6, 14, 18,
23–30, 109, 125, 142n40, 142n45
forget, God, 24, 31, 32, 36–48, 51,
53, 54, 65, 125–27, 131
formation, 13, 23, 24, 67, 107, 108,
113, 118–21, 158n33

generosity, 48, 51, 52, 54, 69, 76, 78,
86, 125
gods, other, 14, 15, 26, 29, 31, 32,
34, 38, 40–46, 50, 55, 57, 80,
88, 106, 120, 121, 127, 143n3,
145n38, 148n15

icon, 25–26, 32, 124, 141n39
idolatry: of believers/people
of God, 5, 6, 8, 9, 11, 13, 26,
31, 125, 142n42; betrayal,
9–11, 19; folly, 7, 9–11, 19; of